D1308508

DeskJet Unlimited

Steve Cummings

PEACHPIT PRESS

DESKJET UNLIMITED
Steve Cummings

Peachpit Press, Inc.
1085 Keith Ave.
Berkeley, CA 94708
415/527-8555

0 9 8 7 6 5 4 3 2 1
Printed and bound in the United States of America
ISBN 0-938151-11-8

Introduction

If you own a Hewlett-Packard DeskJet, you possess one of the best personal-computer printers ever produced at an affordable price. *DeskJet Unlimited* will help you make the most of your investment. Whether you're looking for the simplest way to print attractive documents or for advanced details on DeskJet programming, whether you're interested in printing fancy illustrated newsletters or staid business correspondence, this book will show you how to get the job done.

Between these two covers you'll find a wealth of practical advice and how-to-do-it procedures on everything from basic maintenance through specific software programs to full-scale DeskJet programming. There's a great deal of material you won't find in the *Owner's Manual*. For example, I've included background details on how the DeskJet's ink cartridges work in Chapter 1, and I've devoted three full chapters to an extended discussion of what fonts are and how they should be used in Section II. For completeness, I've included most of the information from the DeskJet *Owner's Manual*, although the discussions of many important topics are considerably enlarged. In many places in the book, I've highlighted important concepts or procedures by printing them as supplementary tips, cautions, and notes. Whenever possible, I've pointed you toward other resources for further information.

One important point should be made clear at the outset: *DeskJet Unlimited* is primarily a book about using the DeskJet with MS-DOS computers, the 30 million or so IBM PC-compatibles now in use worldwide. Section III on application software is devoted exclusively to MS-DOS programs, and the utilities and special-purpose programs described in Chapters 4 and 18 through 20 are all DOS-based products. Nevertheless, if you're using the DeskJet with another computer or operating system, you'll still find much useful information in the first two sections on DeskJet basics and fonts, and in the extensive chapter on DeskJet programming in Section IV.

Chapter-by-chapter summary

Here's a summary of the contents of *DeskJet Unlimited*:

Section I, Fundamentals, introduces the DeskJet and how it works.

Chapter 1, Meet the DeskJet, provides an overview of the DeskJet's capabilities and its few limitations. You'll learn about the technology under your printer's hood, with special emphasis on the unique inkjet system designed specially for the DeskJet.

Chapter 2, DeskJet Hardware, focuses on the mechanical aspects of operating your printer: how to connect the DeskJet to your computer, how to use the function switches, how to operate the keypad buttons and lights, how to load paper, and how to perform basic maintenance.

Chapter 3, The Brain in the Machine, explains what's involved in getting the DeskJet to print what you want it to. You'll learn how your computer and the DeskJet communicate, and how the DeskJet's built-in computer translates the data it receives into printed text and graphics.

In Chapter 4, DeskJet Utilities, you'll see how a variety of inexpensive software programs that can make printing easier and more efficient by setting up the DeskJet for you, and by minimizing the time you spend waiting for your printer to finish.

Section II, Fonts, explores the rudiments of typography in theory and in practice with the DeskJet.

Chapter 5, Typographic Fundamentals, explains the differences between typefaces and fonts and offers definitions of many other basic typographic terms as well. You'll also learn tips on how to use type effectively to produce attractive documents that communicate well.

In Chapter 6, DeskJet Fonts, you'll get an overview of the kinds of fonts available for use with the DeskJet and how to access them in your documents. A short section is devoted to cartridge fonts.

Chapter 7, Using Soft Fonts, is devoted to a detailed exploration of the type of fonts offering the greatest variety and flexibility: soft fonts, the kind you can buy on floppy disks. You'll learn how to prepare your printer for soft fonts, how to install them on your computer's hard disk, and how to use them in your letters and reports. The chapter also covers a variety of font-oriented utilities that simplify soft font management and give you more font choices.

Section III, Application Software, contains a compendium of techniques for getting the most out of your DeskJet with your favorite programs.

Chapter 8, Working with Applications, outlines a general approach you can take with any program to ensure you're using the DeskJet to its top potential with that software.

Chapter 9, Controlling the DeskJet from DOS, shows you how to send printer commands and print plain text files directly from DOS.

Chapter 10, Word Processing, is devoted to the most popular PC application of all. DeskJet-specific techniques are detailed for top-sellers WordPerfect and Microsoft Word, and you'll also find information on many other popular word processors as well.

Chapter 11, Desktop Publishing, opens with an overview of desktop publishing and the DeskJet's capabilities in this area. I then discuss the most popular PC desktop publishing software from heavyweights Ventura Publisher and PageMaker to inexpensive but capable packages such as First Publisher.

Chapter 12, Graphics Software, describes the basic types of graphics programs (paint, draw, and illustration) and includes capsule studies of the top programs from each class.

In Chapter 13, Charting Software, you'll learn about the programs that let you communicate data visually via pie charts, bar graphs, scatter plots, and the like.

Chapter 14, Spreadsheets, describes the basic techniques you can use to control the DeskJet from any spreadsheet program. It then goes on to cover DeskJet-related specifics on 1-2-3, Quattro Pro, SuperCalc, and Excel, which together account for the vast majority of spreadsheet sales.

In Chapter 15, Database Software, you'll discover that although the DeskJet isn't the right printer for high-volume database printing, it can be ideal for the summary reports for which many people use their databases. dBase and Paradox receive specific attention here.

Chapter 16, Forms Software, shows you how to use the DeskJet to generate master copies of your own customized forms.

In Chapter 17, Microsoft Windows, you'll find an outline of Windows' capabilities and limitations when it comes to the DeskJet. I then run through the procedures for installing Windows for the DeskJet and for adding DeskJet support to an existing Windows system. The chapter closes with a discussion of SuperPrint, a software product that overcomes the printing limitations of Windows and speeds printing dramatically to boot.

Section IV, Special Topics, covers a variety of miscellaneous ways to use your DeskJet.

Chapter 18, Printing Envelopes, shows you how to load envelopes into your printer and how to print them conveniently from DOS or your word processor. An excellent envelope printing utility for the DeskJet is also profiled.

In Chapter 19, Printing Screenshots, you'll learn why and how to print out images captured from your PC's screen on the DeskJet. A variety of screen capture utilities are discussed, and there's a special section on capturing screens from Windows.

Chapter 20, Pretty in PostScript, introduces the special software that can turn your DeskJet into an excellent imitation of a true PostScript printer. While they do have a few limitations, these PostScript interpreter products work well and can save you a great deal of money if you need PostScript output.

Chapter 21, Printing with the Macintosh, shows you how to hook up your DeskJet to a Mac and print successfully. You wouldn't buy a DeskJet as a Macintosh printer, but if you have a DeskJet and want to use it with a Mac, this chapter has the instructions you'll need.

Chapter 22, DeskJet Programming, provides extensive coverage of all the commands you can issue from your computer to control the DeskJet. For each command, I've provided a quick reference summary as well as an extended explanation.

Chapter 23, Troubleshooting, offers advice on how to deal with just about anything that can go wrong with your printer.

Appendix A lists the DeskJet's specifications in larger type in than your Owner's Manual. Appendix B provides samples of many of the DeskJet's built-in character sets. Appendix C is an alphabetic reference to all the products mentioned in the book. Appendix D contains a brief list of sources for up-to-date information on the DeskJet. Completing the book is a comprehensive index. I've worked hard to make the index complete and consistent, so you should be able to find the topic you're interested in quickly.

The inevitable disclaimer

Although I've tried my best to make this book accurate, the number, variety, and complexity of the concepts and products I've covered make occasional errors almost unavoidable. Please be sure to test the procedures I recommend with sample data before relying on them for vital files or documents. Although I believe my judgements and recommendations regarding specific software products are fair and well-informed, you should use them to complement your own investigations. Keep in mind that most software is revised or upgraded every few months, so that some details that were up-to-date when I wrote the text will already be incorrect by the time the book is published.

Conventions

Tips, notes, and cautions are printed in italic type for emphasis. As in most computer books, keys you're to press are printed in boldface. Special keys that don't correspond to printed characters are indicated by ovals containing the abbreviations or symbols that appear on most keyboards, for example (ALT), (ESC), and (F2). The Enter or Return key is represented by the symbol (↵). When you're supposed to press two keys at the same time they are printed side by side, like this: (CTRL)C.

Any suggestions?

If there's anything you've learned about the DeskJet that you'd like to share with a wider audience, feel free to send me your tips and tricks in care of Peachpit. I'll see to it that they get into the second edition. Likewise, if there are any additional topics you'd like to see covered, or if you have any other suggestions about how to improve the book, please let me know.

Steve Cummings
December '89

Acknowledgements

These acknowledgements are brief, but my debt is great and my gratitude profound. Thanks first to my publisher, Ted Nace, for his generosity in proposing the book, his trust and help as the project took shape, and his patience during the delays before its completion. Thanks also to my editors, proofreaders, and parents, Selden and Celia Cummings. Both teachers, they found and helped me correct many glaring errors and stylistic lapses in my manuscript drafts; those that remain are my own fault. Thanks are due as well to Greg Wallace and Cathy Hiemstra at Hewlett-Packard who got me started with the DeskJet at the beginning and helped me get the facts straight at the end; to Skene Moody and Gary Elfring, who willingly provided their hard-earned DeskJet secrets; and to Bob Cowart for my career as a writer. Finally, deep and contrite obeisances to my wife Diana and my daughters Amy and Laura.

Production notes

DeskJet Unlimited was produced in my home office using PC-Write with Mouse on Fire for word processing, and Ventura Publisher for layout. Prinicipal fonts are Adobe's ITC Garamond Light, Avante Garde, and Sonata. Paperback Software's Keycap Fonts provides the keyboard symbols. I threw together an admittedly rough PostScript font of my own for a few stray symbols (such as the escape character, ←) with ZSoft's Publisher's Type Foundry. HiJaak, Hotshot Grab, GrafPlus, and Scrapbook+ were all used to capture the screen illustrations.

I used a Toshiba T1000 to write most of the text, a Mitsubishi MP286L laptop for testing DeskJet software and capturing the screenshots, and an Everex Step 386is with an Imtec full-screen monitor for layout and printing of the book itself. Final text pages were printed on a QMS PS810 laser printer. All the full-page sample DeskJet printouts (for example, the font sampler in Chapter 7 and the PostScript page in Chapter 20) were actually printed by a DeskJet Plus. The character set tables in Appendix B were also printed on the DeskJet. All pages were reduced photographically by 18 percent to the final 7 x 9" trim size. The book was printed conventionally.

Contents

SECTION I—Fundamentals

SECTION II—Fonts

Chapter 5: Understanding Typography

Chapter 6: DeskJet Fonts

SECTION III—Application Software

SECTION IV—Special Topics

Section V—Appendices

Fundamentals

1

Meet the DeskJet

∾

Before February 1988, the revolution in document quality begun by laser printers had yet to show up in most people's day-to-day letters and reports. Despite the laser printer's awesome ability to produce documents that look professionally typeset, laser machines were just too expensive for many personal computer users, and too big to fit on their desks.

All that changed with the arrival of Hewlett-Packard's DeskJet. The DeskJet is the first and only printer costing less than $1000 that can match the text clarity, font variety, and graphics detail of a laser printer—and it fits comfortably in almost any workspace. The advent of the DeskJet Plus in the

Spring of 1989 brought faster printing and still better text quality, making the DeskJet an even more compelling alternative to the laser printer hegemony.

The DeskJet's place in the printer landscape

HP built the DeskJet as a personal business printer for all those documents that have to look really sharp—business letters, short reports, occasional newsletters, anything for which appearance counts almost as much as content. In describing the DeskJet as a "personal" printer, I mean that you don't have to share it with other people—unlike a big office laser printer, the DeskJet can sit on your own desk, attached to your personal computer, available immediately whenever you need it. But this printer is clearly a tool for serious professionals. While its pricetag is modest in comparison with laser printers, the DeskJet is still not cheap enough for most computer hobbyists.

By design, the DeskJet has a combination of traits that make it nearly ideal for its intended role. Though it prints at the same resolution as a laser printer, the DeskJet is much smaller and lighter, considerably quieter, and much less costly, all of which make it easier for you or your boss to justify buying a DeskJet for your personal use.

Of course, the DeskJet isn't the printer for every job. For nuts-and-bolts business duties, especially when print volume is high, a fast, sturdy, conventional dot matrix printer is still the most economical and most productive printer you can buy. When you're printing in high volume but you need sharper-looking output than you get from a dot matrix, or if you want to get into desktop publishing in a big way, nothing short of an industrial strength laser printer will do—but the whole office may have to share it.

Inside the DeskJet: Inkjet technology

Key to many of the DeskJet's advantages is its inkjet technology. Like all inkjet printers, the DeskJet employs a tightly-packed array of tiny nozzles to transfer ink to the printed page. Each nozzle squirts its own precisely aimed jet of ink, and the DeskJet creates text and graphics by firing groups of nozzles corresponding to the intended pattern in perfectly timed bursts as the printhead moves sideways across the page.

Of course, there have been plenty of other inkjet printers, the most successful being HP's redoubtable ThinkJet. The DeskJet's real claim to fame is its sharp, high resolution output. With the tiniest ink nozzles going, the DeskJet competes dot-for-dot with the resolution of office laser printers like the LaserJet. Like most laser printers, the DeskJet lays down 300 evenly spaced dots per inch (dpi), both vertically and horizontally, or 90,000 dots per square inch. The dots are so small and they blend together so seamlessly that DeskJet text looks very nearly as clean as what you get from a typewriter or daisy wheel printer. When printing graphics, the DeskJet turns out the same 300-dpi resolution output, and the resulting images are as clear as you can get from any remotely affordable printer. By comparison with lasers, the DeskJet does a better job with solid black areas, since it deposits a uniformly dark swath of ink, while the blacks printed by lasers tend to be splotchy gray.

Actually, although the DeskJet's printhead can lay down no more than 300 dots along an inch of paper, it can be positioned with an accuracy of $\frac{1}{600}$" in the horizontal direction. Software that takes advantage of this precision can place the dots just where they should go to reduce the jaggedness of curved edges to an absolute minimum.

Because there's no pounding of a metal printhead on a platten, the DeskJet is much quieter than "impact" printers such as standard dot matrix models or the old-style "letter quality" machines (the kind with fixed, completely formed characters on a daisy wheel or ball). During each pass of the DeskJet's inkjet printhead, you hear a gentle rubbing sound, like a very quiet and unobstrusive sanding. In fact, the DeskJet is quieter overall than a laser printer, since there's no continuous fan noise, and nothing like the jet-taking-off whoosh you hear when a laser prints a page.

A quick heft will establish that the DeskJet is also much, much lighter and smaller than any laser printer, another reason it's more practical as a desktop companion for your PC. The DeskJet's inkjet print mechanism requires none of the relatively massive parts that make laser printer bulky, such as the drum and laser engine. The machine weighs a bit over 14 pounds—less than many comparably equipped 24-pin dot matrix printers.

Press hard, you're making five copies

The DeskJet shares one important limitation with all inkjet and laser printers: because the printhead doesn't forcibly strike the paper, the DeskJet can't make multiple-copy duplicates on carbon paper or carbonless forms. For filling out the occasional form, you'll have to scrounge up a typewriter or an impact dot-matrix printer, or make do with your own handwriting. If you have a lot of forms to fill out on a printer, you'd be better off with an impact printer.

Ink and ink cartridges

In spite of its advantages in lower weight and quieter operation, inkjet technology has had a checkered past. You may have heard about an alleged tendency for the ink nozzles to clog, and in fact, this was a frequent problem on early inkjet printers with touchy ink formulas. Since a clogged nozzle can't squirt ink, you'd see a horizontal defect running across every printed line at the level of the affected nozzle.

For the DeskJet design team, one of the major engineering challenges was to ensure that the ink delivery system would not clog as they increased resolution to an unheard-of 300 dpi. The solution they dreamed up was to put the entire printhead with its tiny ink nozzles into a disposable cartridge.

If you have a spare ink cartridge handy, turn it upside down and take a look at the bottom end, so that the green plastic fitting points toward the floor. On that protruding ridge that's now at the very top, you'll see a small, flat, gold-colored rectangle. Remarkably, the surface of that little wafer is the business end of the DeskJet. Drilled by the beam of a super-precise laser, two rows of nearly microscopic holes serve as the ink nozzles. There are 60 nozzles in all, but the DeskJet can only print a swath 50 dots high in one pass of the printhead. Why the extras? For one thing, some of the 50 printable dot positions are represented by a pair of nozzles, one for each direction. The remainder of the extra nozzles simply aren't used at all.

If you look closely, you'll see that the printhead wafer is connected to a multitude of tiny printed circuits that you can trace on that copper-colored ribbon, or flex circuit, over to the front side of the cartridge. There, the little

Anatomy of a Cartridge

The illustration below shows a disassembled print cartridge lying on its back. When installed in the DeskJet, the surface of the little printhead is oriented downward, parallel to the floor. If you lift the cover while your DeskJet is printing, you'll see that ink sprays downward onto the paper.

To squirt an ink droplet from one of the 50-odd nozzles on the printhead's surface, the DeskJet activates a firing chamber directly beneath the nozzle. The firing chamber consists of a tiny channel for ink within which an even tinier resistor is mounted. Current flowing through the resistor causes it to heat up, vaporizing the ink nearby to produce a vapor bubble. The vapor bubble is in contact with an adjacent droplet of still-liquid ink in the nozzle, and the bubble drives this droplet out of the nozzle and onto the paper. As soon as the droplet departs, a new column of ink is drawn up into the firing channel from a feed channel connecting the printhead to the main chamber of the ink cartridge.

As you can see in the illustration, the ink reservoir is a block of foam sponge that fills the main chamber. This arrangement ensures that the ink remains uniformly distributed and completely liquid.

Whenever the cartridge isn't in use, the DeskJet parks it on top of a *service station* at the far right of the carriage on which the printhead travels. The service station is designed to keep the nozzles from drying out, to protect them from paper dust, and to remove any ink plugs that may have formed. All this is described in more detail in Chapter 2 in the section, "The DeskJet's Service Station."

traces end at round metal contacts which electronically mate the cartridge to the DeskJet proper, allowing the DeskJet to control the firing of each ink nozzle.

Inside the cartridge, ink is stored in a spongy foam material that keeps it evenly distributed no matter how much is left. As the ink nozzles fire, ink is sucked up from the foam into tiny channels leading to the printhead.

As if inventing the mechanical and electronic technologies in the cartridge itself wasn't hard enough, Hewlett-Packard had to come up with an ink to match the cartridge design while delivering excellent print quality. The ink had to print dark, solid blacks, it had to be non-toxic, it had to flow freely without spattering, it had to adhere well without running or spreading on a huge variety of ordinary papers, and it had to keep doing all these things when exposed to extremes of humidity and temperature. Formulating the ink proved to be almost as much of a challenge as was the cartridge design; in fact, the cartridge design had to change to reflect the ink formula, and vice versa.

The ink formula that HP eventually settled on satisfies all these requirements. It virtually never clogs the printhead. It dries almost instantly on contact with the paper to a rich black, and it looks great on just about any kind of paper you can feed into the machine. While earlier inkjet printers required special papers, you'll get excellent quality from standard bonds and xerographic papers. The ink is water-based, which means that it will smear if you let it get wet. In fact, you can smudge the ink if you touch it as the page is coming out of the machine—my daughter taught me that. Although large solid black areas look great, all that water-based ink tends to saturate the paper, making it tend to wrinkle a bit.

Other DeskJet technology

OK, enough about the inkjet angle—the DeskJet offers several other important benefits in addition to the ones that stem from its printing technology. For many people, probably the most attractive of these is the DeskJet's facility with fonts.

We'll cover fonts in detail in Section II. For now, it's worth noting that the DeskJet has only one built-in typeface: typewriter-style Courier, printable in various sizes and styles. Without buying additional fonts, you can print text in several different Courier fonts, the range of choices depending on whether you have an original model DeskJet or a DeskJet Plus. You can also choose from a generous variety of different characters, ranging from ordinary letters and numerals to foreign language characters to legal and mathematical symbols.

And you're certainly not limited to the built-in, or *internal* fonts. The DeskJet accepts fonts of your choice both on cartridges or floppy disks. With a potentially limitless selection of typefaces, the DeskJet can serve capably for light-duty desktop publishing.

Not a speed demon

As far as speed is concerned, the DeskJet suffers by comparison to laser printers and fast standard dot matrix models, but it's plenty fast enough for its intended role in knocking out letters and short reports. In my time trials, an "average" full page of 10-point letter-quality Courier text took about 50 seconds to print. That gives the DeskJet an actual "throughput" speed of about 70 characters per second (HP rates the letter quality mode at 120 cps, but manufacturers' ratings never take paper handling time into account). The Laser Jet Series II, by contrast, can print plain text at nearly its rated speed of 8 pages per minute, or around 8 seconds per page.

Paper handling

Which brings us to paper handling, another area where the DeskJet shines. The single-sheet paper bin holds about 100 sheets of plain bond or letterhead, and the bin is built into the front of the unit where it's a snap to load. There's also a convenient, built-in, one-at-a-time envelope feeder—you just push the envelope into the guides, press a couple of buttons, and go. The feeding mechanism works smoothly and maintains good alignment, and paper jams are exceedingly rare.

The next time you print a page, take a look at the way those little "flippers" along either side of the output area help push the paper out. This fascinating mechanism is completely unique in the printer kingdom. It's there to ensure that paper covered with drying ink falls smoothly and reliably into the output tray.

The DeskJet does commit one paper-handling gaffe: pages come out face up, so they stack in reverse order. There's also a limitation necessitated by the time it takes the ink to dry: the printer can't be commanded to move the paper in the reverse direction except in tiny increments. Otherwise, the ink would smear. And in case you've wondered, there's no provision whatsoever for pinfeed paper.

Miscellany

A keypad with eight buttons and several indicator lights lets you control several important functions such as paper feeding and font selection directly from the DeskJet's front panel. However, your software will often override the settings on the front panel.

The DeskJet also sports a modest (16K) buffer, a place where incoming data can be parked while it waits to be printed. The buffer could have been larger, perhaps, but it's roomy enough to accept the equivalent of about four or five full pages of single-spaced text in one nearly instantaneous dump. That way, as soon as the last page of your document is sent to the buffer, you can go back to work, while the DeskJet whirs along and finishes printing.

All in the family....

A final DeskJet advantage is that the machine understands most of the same printer commands used by Hewlett-Packard's LaserJet family of laser printers. Because the printer commands available are numerous and quite powerful, they've collectively earned the right to be called a programming language, which HP calls its Printer Command Language (PCL for short). Here's a list of all of HP's PCL laser printers:

- LaserJet (original model)

- LaserJet Plus

- LaserJet 500 Plus

- LaserJet Series II

- LaserJet 2000

- LaserJet IID

- LaserJet IIP

In addition, a number of other HP printers understand portions of the PCL language. The list includes the ThinkJet, the QuietJet, and the PaintJet, all popular inkjet printers.

For most users, the big benefit of this common command language is that you can generally use the DeskJet with most any program, even if the software isn't specifically designed to work with the DeskJet—just install your software as if you had a LaserJet and you should be in business, although you may sacrifice a few DeskJet features (we'll cover the ins and outs of software compatibility in section III).

For programmers, the command language compatibility of HP's printers means that the same program can be made to work with the entire HP line with little or no modification. Chapter 22 contains an introduction to PCL programming on the DeskJet and DeskJet Plus.

The DeskJet versus the DeskJet Plus

While the DeskJet and DeskJet Plus both print text and graphics at 300 dpi, the newer DeskJet Plus has several advantages. Here's the list of features that distinguish the DeskJet Plus from the original DeskJet:

- The Plus comes with three built-in *landscape* fonts for printing wide documents "sideways" (in landscape mode, the printed page is oriented so that it is wider than it is tall, as contrasted with the ordinary *portrait* mode—just look at the picture below). In the original DeskJet, you could only print in landscape mode with a special font cartridge.

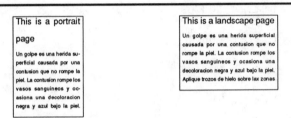

Figure 1-1: Portrait and landscape pages

- On the Plus, fonts can be larger, up to 30 points high. Fonts for the original model are limited a maximum of 24 points but are usually no taller than 18 points.

- The Plus comes with built-in Courier italics, while the original requires an optional font cartridge to print italics.

- The Plus lets you install up to twice as much memory for soft fonts in the form of optional RAM cartridges (512K on the Plus versus 256K on the original).

- Text quality of the most commonly used optional fonts, Helv and TmsRmn, is improved on the Plus.

- The Plus prints text "up to" twice as fast, graphics up to five times faster, according to Hewlett-Packard. The Plus' paper feeding speed is about double what that of the original model.

One big change is primarily responsible for the improved speed: as its internal thinking machine, the original DeskJet used a relatively primitive 4 megahertz (MHz) Z80 microprocessor, while the DeskJet Plus uses a faster and more capable 8 MHz Z180 chip.

Put together, the improvements in the Plus are substantial. If by chance you're reading this book before buying, be sure you pass over those ads for the original model and get the Plus, unless you're getting one heck of a good deal.

2

DeskJet Hardware

℘

Before you start sending orders to the DeskJet from your computer, you need a working familiarity with the nuts and bolts of the printer itself. Your DeskJet *Owner's Manual* has the instructions you need for unpacking and setting up your printer the first time. There are plenty of diagrams to get you oriented, along with a basic discussion of the panel controls and the DeskJet's minimal maintenance requirements.

This chapter covers some of same ground but adds details the manual leaves out. You'll get background information and practical tips on how to best connect the DeskJet to your computer, on how to use the printer's function switches, and on how the paper feeding system works. You'll also find expanded coverage of the DeskJet's keypad controls, and on maintenance topics, including a section on the pros and cons of refilling DeskJet ink cartridges yourself.

Making connections

To move the information you want to print from your computer to the DeskJet, you need a cable to connect the two, and a place to plug it in on either end. The DeskJet comes with both serial and parallel ports (connectors) built-in as standard equipment. That's fortunate, since almost every computer you'll ever come across will have at least one of these types of ports as well.

With so many computers as potential cable-mates, it can be tough to figure out how to hook things up properly. First, you have to connect the right port on your computer to the right port on the printer, using the right cable. In addition, you may need to change the positions of some of the tiny function switches (known generically as *DIP switches*) at the bottom front of the DeskJet.

As you know, this book concentrates on using the DeskJet with IBM-compatible microcomputers, including PCs, XTs, ATs, PS/2s and all the myriad workalikes and clones. If you have one of these machines, you can skip to down the section "PC to DeskJet" below.

♪ *Note for Macintosh users: The Mac is conspicuously absent from the* Owner's Manual's *extensive coverage of various makes and models of computers. HP is now marketing a Mac-compatible version of the DeskJet called the DeskWriter. However, it's certainly possible to connect a Mac to an ordinary DeskJet, a procedure described fully in Chapter 21.*

If your computer isn't IBM PC-compatible, you'll still be able to get excellent results with the DeskJet, but it may take more work to make the right connections. Fortunately, the DeskJet *Owner's Manual* has a lengthy section detailing the cabling requirements and function (DIP) switch settings for many computer makes and models, along with other necessary setup procedures. If your computer or a similar model isn't listed in the manual, you can call the Hewlett-Packard technical support line at 208-323-2551 for help. You can also try various function switch settings and cable connections as long as you make sure you're connecting serial to serial or parallel to parallel. If you're connecting via a serial cable, you'll find the necessary instructions in the "Data Communications" section of your DeskJet *Owner's Manual* and the corresponding section of your computer's manual.

PC to DeskJet

The one big choice you have to make when connecting your PC- or PS/2-compatible computer to the DeskJet is whether to join the two machines through their serial ports or their parallel ports. Since both methods work, how do you decide? It's easy: use the parallel method.

In a parallel connection, 8 chunks of printer data travel from the computer to the printer simultaneously, an 8 abreast arrangement, if you will. In contrast, a serial hookup can only send one chunk at a time in electronic single-file. So parallel connections are inherently quicker.

What's more, the "language" of serial communications isn't tightly standardized, so you must be careful to make several special software settings correctly. Otherwise, printer and computer may not be talking the same jive, and your printer may not print. It's not really that hard to make the necessary adjustments, but the potential for error is definitely greatest with a serial hookup.

Is there ever a reason to use a serial connection between a PC- or PS/2-type computer and a DeskJet? Not unless your parallel port goes dead and you need to keep printing before you can get it fixed. Use parallel.

Understanding function switch settings

At the bottom front of the DeskJet, tucked away inside a little recess, lie two sets of tiny switches that have a big impact on how your printer works. If you stand the DeskJet on its hind end and look closely at the switches, you'll see that each set comprises a single component, a little plastic block in which the switches are mounted. Miniature switches packaged together in this way are referred to rather loosely as DIP switches, and you'll find them on many computer products, including most video and memory cards and probably your computer's main circuitboard itself.

HP prefers to call the DeskJet's DIP switches "function switches," which describes their role better. The function switches control several important printer "defaults," the settings that are automatically in effect each time you turn on the DeskJet (you can override many of the defaults with software commands). Among the default settings you can determine with the function switches are the paper or envelope size, the graphics resolution, parameters for serial communication with your computer, the set of characters you can print, and more.

The problems with DIP switches are pretty obvious—they're small and therefore hard to change, and they don't come with a written key to tell you which setting does what. More expensive printers like the LaserJet Series II have done away with DIP switches, replacing them with a sophisticated front panel control that lets you change default settings and gives you a readout in English to tell you what you're doing. In the DeskJet, you're stuck with the DIP switches, but you'll probably need to change them only rarely, if at all.

As it's shipped from the factory, the DeskJet's function switches are set appropriately for most people with IBM-compatible computers. In the Appendix of the DeskJet *Owner's Manual*, you'll find a diagram showing the function switches and how to set them properly to get the default options you want.

Using the Keypad Control Panel

All of the DeskJet's operating controls are located on a simple 8-key keypad on the front right of the printer. We'll cover their use when appropriate in later sections, but we'll touch on them briefly here for quick reference.

It's important to know that you can access most of the functions available from the keypad via software commands from your computer. In fact, your

Figure 2.1: *The DeskJet's keypad*

application programs may override the settings you choose manually with the keypad. However, three keys—UP, DOWN, and PRIME—perform functions that cannot be controlled by software.

Keys and Lights

The keypad's eight buttons are divided into two rows, front and back. Between the two rows is a display with several indicator lights, most of which are associated with a particular button.

The four buttons up front are the ones you'll probably use most often, and they're larger. From left to right, the keys in the front row work like this:

The FF (form feed) key ejects the paper currently in the paper path. If there's nothing in the paper path, a page is loaded when you press the FF key.

The FONT button steps you through the fonts currently available, one at a time, allowing you to select the font you want to use for printing. If you've installed a font cartridge in either or both slots, the cartridge fonts become part of the round-robin sequence you step through with the FONT key. On the other hand, you can only select downloadable soft fonts through commands from your computer (see Section II for complete information on fonts).

The active font is indicated by one or more lights above and to the right of the FONT key. If the light closest to the FONT key, the one labelled with a small rectangle of red lines, is glowing, the selected font will print at half size (as you'll learn in Chapter 6, most DeskJet fonts can be used at full size or half size).

On the DeskJet Plus, the light next to the little image of a horizontally-oriented page indicates that the current font is a landscape font, and the page will print sideways. If the landscape light isn't on, an ordinary portrait font is selected. (The terms *portrait* and *landscape* were introduced in Chapter 1 and are discussed in more detail with reference to fonts in Chapter 6.)

The MODE button simply switches the DeskJet back and forth between its best "letter-quality" mode and a faster draft mode, as indicated by the nearby light.

❈ *Tip:*   *Use the MODE button to switch quickly between draft mode, which saves time and ink, and the default "letter-quality" mode, for finished copies.*

The ON LINE button switches the DeskJet back and forth between two modes: an on-line, "ready to print" mode, and an off-line mode which halts printing temporarily, allowing you to load more paper or select a different font.

The ON LINE indicator light glows when the DeskJet is online and ready, and is off when the printer is offline. The light blinks when the DeskJet runs out of paper during a print job. If this happens, be sure not to turn the printer off, and don't press the RESET button. Instead, just reload the paper tray, and then press the ON LINE button.

If both the ON LINE and BUSY lights are flashing, you have a paper jam. Consult the troubleshooting section in Chapter 23 for how to proceed, but don't press the RESET button if you don't want to lose data waiting to be printed (data may still be lost, however).

The four remaining keys serve less frequently needed functions. They're smaller so you won't press them accidentally, since two of them, RESET and PRIME, will cause problems with a print out. Starting from the left, the back row keys work as follows:

The button at the far left is the UP key and is labelled with a double arrowhead pointing towards the front of the printer. UP advances the paper a tiny distance each time you press it.

The next key to the right is the DOWN key, and is labelled with a double arrowhead pointing toward the rear. It moves the paper back into the paper path a little at a time.

Pressing both the UP and DOWN keys at once loads an envelope into the paper path. You must first place the envelope into position for printing as described in Chapter 18.

Moving to the right, the PRIME key comes next. Its function is to redistribute ink into the printhead's ink channels when clogs occur, ensuring that a smooth, even coating of ink reaches the paper.

⌒ *Caution: Pressing PRIME uses a small but measureable amount of ink—don't do it unless there's a real problem with print quality. Also, don't press PRIME while a print job is in progress, since the DeskJet will lose track of where it's printing on the paper.*

The RESET key is located to the far right. Pressing RESET completely restarts the DeskJet, ejects the sheet of paper currently in the paper path, if any, clears the printer's buffer of print data, and reactivates the default font. "Permanent" downloaded fonts remain intact, but "temporary" fonts are also cleared (see the discussion of permanent versus temporary downloaded fonts in Chapter 7).

Finally, there's the BUSY light, which has no associated key. The BUSY light glows steadily when the DeskJet is receiving data from your computer, and turns off as soon as the data flow stops. It blinks when the DeskJet has received data in landscape orientation but hasn't yet printed the page. While the BUSY light is on, the FF, FONT, and MODE buttons don't do anything.

Again, both the ON LINE and BUSY lights flash when there's a paper jam. Consult the troubleshooting section in Chapter 23 for how to proceed, but don't press the RESET button if you want to retain the data waiting to be printed (you may still lose data, however).

Paper feeding

The DeskJet's main paper feeding mechanism is simple and essentially foolproof. You just slide out the paper tray extender, push in a stack of paper with its right side flush against the right side of the tray, and slide the paper tray extender back in. I'll discuss the procedure for loading envelopes in Chapter 18.

✂ *Tip:* *The DeskJet prints on the side of the paper that's on the bottom in the input tray. If you want to print on both sides of a sheet, place the printed side face up in the paper tray when you're feeding the page in again. Contrariwise, if you want to print the same side twice, put the page in the paper tray face down for the second pass. The edge of the paper that enters the printer first becomes the top of the printed page.*

The Printable Area and the Unprintable Region

For technical reasons, the DeskJet cannot print all the way out to the very edges of a piece of paper. The maximum area on which you actually can print is referred to as the *printable area.* On ordinary 8½"x11" letter-size paper, the printable area measures 8" across and 10⅓". It is bounded by an *unprintable region* consisting of a ⅙" margin at the top of the page, a ½" margin at the bottom, and ¼" margins along the left and right edges of the paper. When you print in landscape orientation, so that text runs across the long edge of the page, the printable area is now 10⅓" wide by 8" tall, and the unprintable margins become ¼" at the top and bottom, ½" on the left, and ⅙" on the right. Although you can set larger margins than those that define the printable area, you cannot set make them any smaller.

Care and feeding

Besides being less expensive than a laser printer at the time of purchase, the DeskJet is less costly to maintain. The only item you'll need to replace occasionally is the print cartridge. According to HP itself, the DeskJet requires absolutely no scheduled maintenance.

The DeskJet's Service Station

Whenever the DeskJet isn't actively printing, it pulls the cartridge into the service station, a device at the far right of the carriage on which the print cartridge travels.

As the cartridge is parked on the service station, ramps raise a rubber cap so that it contacts the printhead. The cap covers the printhead tightly, sealing out dust, and sealing in moisture so the ink in the nozzles doesn't dry out. To remove paper dust that has accumulated during printing, the service station also has a soft rubber wiper that brushes against the printhead as it moves into or out of the parked position. The wiper scrapes the dust into the thin slots on either side of the printhead. When you throw away the cartridge, the dust gets dumped too.

Original service station

In summer 1989, HP introduced a new service station design. Some DeskJet owners had found their ink cartridges running low much too quickly, a problem that was traced to the service station's pump mechanism. In the original design, a flexible tube attached to the underside of the cap maintains high humidity in the cap and is part of a pump system used to clear clogged nozzles. When you press the PRIME button on the keypad, a few droplets of ink are sucked out and drained onto an absorbent pad below. In the new design, the tube and pump have been eliminated. Pressing PRIME agitates the printhead back and forth against the wipers and causes it to spray a small amount of ink into the cap. The results are the same—cleared nozzles—but less ink is wasted. DeskJets with the old service station (those whose serial number prefix is less than 2937) can be upgraded at no charge to the new unit. Order a do-it-yourself kit, part number 02276-677801, by calling HP's Repair Center at 503/757-2002. You can also send your printer to the Center if you prefer.

Ink—Priming the pump

Once in a while, however, you may have to intervene to restore print quality. If print is faded or if dots or lines are missing, and assuming you haven't simply run out of ink, the cure is simple—just press the PRIME button on the keypad. As described in the sidebar on the DeskJet's service station on the opposite page, the unit will go through a special sequence to remove clogs from the printhead, restoring the print to its full intensity.

When the ink runs out

Of course, ink in the print cartridge doesn't last forever. HP estimates officially that a cartridge will last 525,000 letter-quality characters of the sizes typically used for body text. That translates very roughly into about 250 single-spaced pages or 500 double-spaced pages. You should get twice that many pages in draft mode. New cartridges carry a $19.95 list price and are available direct from Hewlett-Packard (call 800/538-8787) or from local dealers. Some mail-order houses also carry them, but usually not at tremendous discounts. Cartridges are easy to replace—just snap them in according to the procedure illustrated in the *Owner's Manual.*

Unfortunately, there's no "fuel gauge" to let you know when your current cartridge is running low. The only way you'll know you're running out of ink is when the print starts to fade, and pressing PRIME doesn't restore it.

Refilling ink cartridges

HP advises against it, and please don't think I'm recommending the practice, but it is possible to refill the DeskJet's ink cartridges with ordinary "washable" fountain pen ink at considerable savings. In researching this book, I've talked to many people who have extensive experience with reloading their cartridges, and who claim that it works just fine and causes no apparent adverse effects.

Before you decide to start refilling your own cartridges, however, you'd be well advised to consider the potential problems that might result. Given that each cartridge has its own self-contained printhead, you can't really hurt anything as far as the cartridge itself is concerned—if the printhead should clog for good, you'd just have to buy another cartridge. However, HP is concerned that you could damage other parts of the DeskJet as well. Repeated spraying of a foreign ink into the service station cap or tube could gum up the works and cause a malfunction over time. Your warranty certainly won't cover any problems that stem from ink cartridge refilling and if you make a serious mistake (using a very wrong kind of ink, for example) you might void your warranty altogether.

Of course, the big benefit of reloading your cartridges is lower cost. A 2-ounce bottle of fountain pen ink will only set you back about $2, and you can use it for several cartridge refills. Another plus is that reloading lets you switch colors. At the moment, HP sells only black cartridges.

Aside from the potential for long term ill effects, the major immediate disadvantage is lower print quality, depending on the type of paper you use. As you'll recall from the first chapter, HP spent a tremendous amount of time and money developing an ink that would produce high-quality output on just about any type of paper and that was as non-toxic as possible. According to my sources, fountain pen ink causes slightly more spattering than the regular cartridge ink, but it works well otherwise on common grades of copier paper, as well as the more expensive "laser" papers.

If you want to try your luck at reloading a cartridge, you'll need a bottle of ink and a 20 cubic centimeter syringe with a 1½" 21 gauge needle. Since it's illegal to own medical needles and syringes in many states, you may wish to procure the type used in chemistry, which have blunt needles, or use a glue injection device. As far as the ink itself is concerned, my consultants recommend Shaeffer's Skrip and Mount Blanc in dark colors as good ink choices. You can use equivalent inks from other manufacturers, but be sure the one you choose is a washable type.

Start by putting on gloves and old clothes, since the procedure can get messy. Before you put the needle on the syringe, draw up about 15 cc's of ink. Screw on the needle and remove its cap. Taking care to avoid sticking yourself, stab the needle through the little hole on the top of the cartridge wall and into the spongy material that holds the ink, so that the tip of the needle is in the center of the cartridge. Inject the ink, withdraw the needle, and put it in a safe place if you plan to reuse it (recap the needle very carefully).

After a reload, press the PRIME button to distribute the new ink properly. If you've switched colors, you'll notice the color of your printouts gradually change from the old color to the new one, as the remaining ink from last time moves out of the ink channels.

You can repeat the reloading process as often as you dare, though my advisers recommend an upper limit of three times—the frequent injections eventually cause cavities to form within the spongy innards of the cartridge. To keep track of your reloads, it's a good idea to mark the cartridge each time.

Keeping your DeskJet clean

⌒\ *Caution: Use water only, not other cleaning fluids, to remove excess ink from the DeskJet. Remember, the DeskJet's ink is water-based.*

HP does advise you to keep the innards of the machine clean. Paper dust tends to build up in the vicinity of the print carriage and could conceivably gum up the works. All you have to do is blow out the dust occasionally. Any ink sticking to the metal platen, the carriage guide, and the paper rollers should be removed with a soft moist cloth. Use a cloth moistened with water only—avoid any type of cleaning fluid.

3

The Brain in the Machine

～

Once you've set up your printer and connected it physically to your computer, the DeskJet is ready to take your orders. You can now tell it what to print and how to print it. This chapter will give you a little background about how PC-to-DeskJet communications work, and how the DeskJet translates the messages it receives into printed pages. While the discussion is a little technical, it will help you to understand some of the quirks in the way your printer works—for instance, why some pages take longer to print than others, and why the DeskJet works better with some programs than with others. With that understanding as a foundation, you'll learn in later chapters how to produce the best possible printed documents in any situation.

Down the wire

As in all computer-based communications, a constant flow of minute, precisely timed voltage fluctuations serves as the language with which your computer commands the DeskJet. At this most basic level, the presence of a tiny voltage on a data wire is understood as a "1," while no voltage means a "0." With only two possible values, 1 or 0, a single *bit* of data doesn't convey much information. But string together a long sequence of 1s and 0s, and you have a code that can carry complex messages between your computer and the DeskJet.

In any such interchange, your computer dominates the conversation, issuing a series of instructions for the DeskJet to follow. Your PC can send two main types of data to the DeskJet over the cable that connects them: codes representing the text and graphics that the DeskJet is actually supposed to print, and commands that control other operations of the printer.

Occasionally, though, the printer sends a brief message back the opposite way, to let the computer know how the printing chores are going. For example, the printer might signal that it's out of paper or that it can't respond to further instructions for some other reason.

Understanding print data

We'll start this discussion of computer-DeskJet communications by looking at the coded information that represents the actual text and graphics to be printed. These codes are the *print data*.

The DeskJet creates everything it prints out of individual tiny dots of ink. At the level of the printhead, one dot is just like the next, whether it's part of the letter *A* or part of a picture of an eagle in flight. However, there's a considerable difference between the data your computer sends to the DeskJet to print text and the data it sends to print graphics. Thus, there are two subtypes of print data: text print data and graphics print data.

Text print data

When you first turn on your DeskJet, it powers up in text mode. In text mode, the computer communicates the characters it wants the DeskJet to print in a standardized coding system known as ASCII (for "American Standard Code for Information Exchange"). In the ASCII code, each *byte*, or series of eight successive bits (1s and 0s), represents one text character.

If you have any knowledge of binary (base 2) arithmetic, you'll realize that a series of 1s and 0s is just a way to represent a numeric value. To make the binary ASCII codes easier for humans to read, they're usually expressed in ordinary decimal numbers instead of binary notation. A capital *A*, for instance, is character 65 in the ASCII code. To get the DeskJet to print that *A*, your computer must send the value 65 as a byte to the printer.

Now let's look at things from the DeskJet's perspective. Its ultimate mission is to turn on and off just the right ink nozzles at just the right times to create a pattern of dots that you'll recognize as the letter *A*. From this point of view, that ASCII code 65 doesn't help, because it doesn't say anything about which nozzles to turn on, or when the nozzles should start spraying. What the DeskJet needs is electronic intelligence of its own—a behind-the-scenes computer, if you will—that can translate incoming ASCII codes into the sequence of electronic impulses necessary to fire the ink nozzles in the correct pattern. Because the DeskJet has these built-in smarts, when your software requests a letter *A*, it's like signing up for a package tour to Europe—all the little details are handled for you.

Exactly what that letter *A* looks like when it actually gets printed depends on which font is active when the DeskJet receives your command to print it. The active font can be set with the DeskJet's keypad, or through software control, a topic we'll introduce a page or two hence.

The ASCII coding system is almost universal throughout the computer universe, and it's certainly not specific to the DeskJet. Each of the most common letters, numerals, and punctuation marks has a standard numeric value in the ASCII code that almost all printers understand. Expressed in the printer's binary tongue, the possible character codes range from 00000000 to 11111111 (remember, there are eight bits in a byte). In decimal numbers, that's 0 to 255, meaning that the ASCII system can code for a total of 256 different characters.

Of these 256 available codes, the ASCII system actually defines only 128. That accounts for all the numeric digits, all the upper and lower case versions of the 26 letters, and a good supply of miscellaneous punctuation marks. In addition, certain ASCII standard codes don't represent printable characters at all, but rather signify commands that your computer or printer should follow. But more on that shortly. At any rate, another 128 character codes are undefined in the standard ASCII code. These are frequently used for special characters, such as foreign language characters and mathematical symbols, depending on the font you're using.

Graphics print data

The DeskJet functions very differently when called upon when printing graphics than it does when printing text. Whereas a single ASCII character code sent by your computer can call forth hundreds of ink dots en masse, the computer must individually control the placement of each and every dot in a graphics image by a corresponding bit of graphics data. Images represented in this way are referred to as *bitmapped graphics,* or simply bitmaps, meaning that each bit of data is "mapped" to a particular location on the image.

Remembering that eight bits make a byte, it follows that each byte of graphics data can only produce eight dots in a picture. Compare that to the hundreds of dots one ASCII code byte can print in text mode, and you can see why you must send far more data to print a bitmapped image than to fill an equivalent area with text. To "paint" a one square-inch area with a high-resolution graphic, you need 90,000 bits, since the DeskJet can print 300 dots per inch both vertically and horizontally. Dividing by eight, that's about 11,000 bytes. To cover that same square inch with standard-sized text, say 12-point, would cost you only about 85 bytes.

The major implication of this vast disparity is that graphics printing is considerably slower than text mode, simply because it requires such a large volume of data. The DeskJet Plus, which is considerably faster than the original model, can print a full page of graphics in about 1½ minutes. Printing a page of text takes only 50 seconds.

The DeskJet does have two built-in functions to speed up graphics printing by compressing data so that fewer bytes need to be sent. In most cases, this helps a little, but not a lot. If you're just interested in filling space as fast as possible, another way to speed things up is to program the DeskJet to use a lower resolution graphics mode (Chapter 22 on programming has the necessary instructions). If you reduce the resolution from 300 dots-per-inch maximum, the DeskJet prints more than one dot for each data bit, so the effective image is larger. Unfortunately, the picture also loses sharpness and clarity.

Object graphics: Not available

As an alternative to bitmaps, computer-generated images can also be stored as *object graphics*, also known as *vector graphics*. Although the DeskJet is not capable of interpreting of object graphics, many software programs and some printers are. As a DeskJet owner, understanding object graphics will help you buy and use the right graphics software for your needs.

In the object graphics technique, an image is built up from a composite of separate various shapes, or "objects," such as lines, circles, rectangles, and polygons. The key point is that each of these individual objects is described as a mathematical formula, rather than as a collection of dots. A straight line object, for example, might be defined as starting at a certain point and extending a given distance for a particular length.

In a dot printer that can handle object-type graphics commands, the objects eventually get translated into a dot pattern, of course. The process is similar to the way a single character code gets converted into a printed character when the DeskJet prints text. However, even the proud LaserJet has only very rudimentary object graphics capabilities, and few programs bother with them. You have to move up to a PostScript printer to get a machine that can really make use of object graphics.

Printers such as the DeskJet that don't understand the language of object graphics can still print images stored by your software in object format. The only trick here is that the software itself must translate the objects into bitmapped form, and then send these bitmaps to the DeskJet.

Compared to bitmapped graphics, one of the big advantages of the object variety is that they require far less data. Our hypothetical straight line object might only require a couple of bytes for each part of the line's description (its point of origin, angle of deflection, and length), as compared to hundreds or perhaps thousands of bytes to create an identical bitmapped line. Another point is that a line object always requires the same amount of data, no matter how long it is.

Likewise, all you need to know to draw a circle is the position of its center and its radius—after all, circumference = πr^2, right? Squiggly lines and more complex shapes take fancier formulae, but still occupy less data than the equivalent dot-by-dot bitmap. Overall, an object-type graphics file takes up much less memory in your computer, and much less space when it's stored on disk. For a more extensive look at the pros and cons of the two types of graphics, see Chapter 12.

Controlling the DeskJet: a primer on printer commands

In day-to-day use, a printer spends the vast majority of its time actually printing the data you send it—you send a numeric code (a byte of data), the printer interprets it, and out comes the corresponding pattern from the ink nozzles. A few special codes provoke a different response from the printer, however. With these codes, you can command the printer to do something such as change fonts, move the paper, switch from text to graphics mode or vice versa, or even reset itself altogether. In the DeskJet's case, some of the software that can be sent from the computer duplicate functions on the printer's keypad, but there are many functions that can only be controlled through the commands

The varieties of printer command languages

Although all printers respond to commands in the same general way, each printer recognizes a different set of specific commands. It's as if each printer speaks and understands its own language. If you send the command that activates a new DeskJet font to an Epson printer, the Epson will do something else—or just sit there and scratch its printhead. That's why you have to tell your application software which printer you're using before you can print successfully—it's the only way for the program to know that it should be sending its printer commands in the DeskJet language, instead of Epson, NEC or some other tongue.

In an ideal world, once you told the program you're using a DeskJet, you wouldn't have to worry about printer commands at all. Instead, your application software would take care of the dirty work for you. Say you're using your word processor to write a letter, and you want to emphasize your demand that Al's Great Guys stereo store return your money right <u>now!</u> To print the underline, you should only have to hit the keys that activate your word processor's underlining feature. When it prints your letter, the program would send the underlining command to the DeskJet, without any further intervention on your part.

Printer drivers

For this ideal scenario to work in real life, your program must have a key piece of software called a *printer driver*. A printer driver is a software module tailored to your particular printer that merges into your application program. The driver serves much like an interpreter, translating the program's own codes for, say, underlining, into the corresponding command in the printer's native tongue.

Alas, the world remains imperfect. Many software programs come with advanced DeskJet drivers, and speak the DeskJet language fluently, controlling all of the printer's more advanced features handily. On the other hand, some programs have limited drivers, and can speak only a kind of pidgin DeskJet-ese. Others lack a DeskJet driver altogether, and at best will only let you print plain, unformatted characters in a single font.

If you run up against one of these backward programs, you'll have to take matters into your own hands or go without the print features you want to use. Chapter 8 contains an overview of how to get the DeskJet to work best with your each application program, and an introduction to using DeskJet commands on your own. In Chapter 4, you'll learn about add-on utilities that can translate between your program and the DeskJet.

DeskJet printer commands

No matter what software or utilities you own, there may be times when it helps to know a little about the DeskJet's commands and how to use them. For now, we'll just set the stage—when you're ready for the details, see Chapters 8 and 22.

Here's the basic scoop: DeskJet printer commands are simply ordinary bytes of data, numbers just like the ones that code for a particular ASCII character or a bunch of dots in a graphic. However, the DeskJet is primed to recognize a few special code values that signify the beginning of a command, instead of data to be printed. If you know these special numbers, you have the passwords that give you access to total control of the DeskJet.

Back in our discussion of ASCII character codes earlier in this chapter, I pointed out that some of the standard ASCII codes don't code for text characters, but rather for printer commands instead. DeskJet commands all begin with one of these unprintable ASCII codes, also known as *control codes*.

In some cases, a single control code constitutes an entire command—the DeskJet receives that one byte, takes an immediate action, and goes right back to printing. For example, if you send the code value of 12 (the *form feed* control code) to your printer, the DeskJet responds by ejecting the current page. One control code, however, works differently. When you send the code for the *escape character*, the DeskJet pauses and waits for further instructions, in the form of one or more additional bytes. These additional bytes are not themselves control codes; they would ordinarily represent printable text characters. But when preceded by the escape character, these ordinary codes take on special meaning to the DeskJet.

In case you're interested, the code for the escape character is 27 (in decimal notation). A command beginning with the escape character is called an *escape sequence*. Escape sequences are much more powerful than one-byte control codes. They are the keys to controlling a multitude of DeskJet print options, allowing you to select a particular font, change margin settings, load an envelope into the printer, or switch to graphics mode, and much more.

Let's look at an example of a typical escape sequence. To turn on underlining, you would send the following sequence to your printer, expressed in decimal numbers: **27 38 1ØØ 49 68**.

To make escape sequences (somewhat) easier to read in print, they're usually written out in the ASCII characters represented by those numbers. Since the escape "character" isn't really a character, it's represented by the abbreviation ^Es_c. Written in this format, the sequence we just examined would look like this: ^Es_c**&d1D**.

You're probably thinking that escape sequences look like gibberish, and I agree with you. Again, we'll wade through some of the muck in Chapter 8 and get in chin-deep in Chapter 22.

4

DeskJet Utilities

Batman wouldn't be anywhere today without his utility belt, and DeskJet owners need utility software just as much. Utility programs take the drudgery out of many of the miscellaneous printing challenges that inevitably crop up. In this chapter, we'll look at two main kinds of DeskJet utilities: print spoolers, that speed up your printing sessions, and setup utilities, that let you set up margins, change fonts, and otherwise control your printer almost effortlessly.

Although the utilities profiled in this chapter are distributed through conventional commercial channels, you should be aware that an excellent source of printer utilities is shareware and freeware. There's a vast quantity of try-be-fore-you-buy software available at user group meetings, on electronic bulletin boards, and from a number of mail-order purveyors. It costs little or nothing to test a shareware program, and if you decide to keep it the registration fees are usually modest. Currently there isn't much in the way of DeskJet-specific shareware, but you should be able to adapt programs written for the LaserJet family.

✄ *Tip:*   *The best shareware supplier is the Public Software Library, which lists a number of print spoolers and setup utilities in its exhaustive catalog. Call 713/665-7017 for information or a copy of their monthly magazine and catalog.*

Speedup utilities

The DeskJet is reasonably speedy as desktop printers go, but you'll still spend many minutes drumming your fingers as you wait for long documents to print. Do yourself a favor and get a *print spooler* as soon as you can. Print spoolers are software utilities that can drastically cut how much time you wait on your printer. They don't actually reduce the time it takes the printer to pop out the last page of a document, but spoolers do allow you go back to work with your computer long before the print job is finished.

Here's the problem that print spoolers address: your software can send output to the printer much faster than the printer can digest it. The printer needs time to process the data and commands it receives, and even more time to do the actual printing. Software is almost always much faster, and it usually spends most of its time during a print session just waiting to send more data to the printer. In the DeskJet's case, the printer has a small (16K) buffer to which your software can transfer data almost instantaneously. But as soon as that buffer fills up things slow way down. You'll wait right along with your software—until the printer has accepted all of the software's output, you'll be unable to use your computer.

Print spoolers attack the problem by commandeering your software's printer output, diverting the codes and commands to a storage area in memory or on disk. Since the transfer doesn't have to wait for the printer, it can occur at top speed. As soon as all the printer output has reached this temporary parking place you get control of your computer again, and you can go on working on your letter, spreadsheet, or what have you. Meanwhile, the spooler takes over the chore of spoonfeeding the data to your printer. It does this behind the scenes as you work, so you can print and work at the same time.

The Cadillac of print spoolers is LaserTorq, featured in the profile just ahead, but any print spooler that works is better than none. If funds are short and you have time to experiment you can give shareware a try. Another option is the print spooler in PC-Kwik's Power Pak, a collection of excellent speedup utilities that can streamline your whole system. In addition to the spooler, the Power Pak tool kit includes a disk caching utility for faster disk performance, the best keyboard speedup program I've tried, and a screen speedup program as well. The entire package retails for about $80, less than LaserTorq alone.

Profile: LaserTorq

$99/LaserTools Corp.
3025 Buena Vista Way
Berkeley, CA 94708
415/843-2234

Despite LaserTorq's name, this print spooling utility is one of a DeskJet owner's best friends. Most importantly, LaserTorq is fast. The program is designed so that it springs into action as soon as the printer signals it's ready for more data, and only then. By contrast, most other spoolers simply attempt to send the next chunk of data at predetermined intervals, which often means they wait too long.

Figure 4-1: The LaserTorq window, popped up over Quicken

LaserTorq is convenient, too. You can pop up a little window that tells you how much memory you've set aside for temporary spooler storage and how much of your print job has been completed so far. Commands available on the window's menu allow you to empty the spooler buffer, stopping your print job, to eject the current page from the printer, and to suspend printing temporarily. While printing is suspended, LaserTorq continues to divert printer data from your software to the buffer. This way, you can stop printing to take a phone call or attend to other business, then pick up where you left off later without losing anything.

As far as I know, LaserTorq is the only print spooler that has been adapted specifically for the DeskJet. Since it knows how to translate ordinary graphics printer data into DeskJet compressed graphics data LaserTorq can actually speed up graphics printing by as much as a factor of four. Of course, if your software has already compressed its graphics output this feature has no effect—but very little software does this. (Chapter 22 includes a section explaining the DeskJet's graphics compression modes.)

Setup Utilities

Although it's wise to have a rudimentary acquaintance with the DeskJet printer commands introduced in the previous chapter, there's an alternative to mucking around with escape sequences and control codes when your application program doesn't know how to send the right printer commands for you. Several software *setup utilities* let you pick the action you want the DeskJet to perform from simple menus. Instead of typing a row of alphanumeric soup when you want to, say, change to a new font, all you have to do is find the font on the utility's menu and press a key. The utility takes over, generating the correct command for the font change, and automatically sending it to the DeskJet.

In more detail, the functions you can carry out via setup utilities include:

- **Controlling basic printer operations.** Setup utilities often let you load or eject a page, advance the paper, and reset the printer to its default settings, without having to reach over to the keypad.

- **Choosing page settings.** Page settings refer to the characteristics of a printed page: the margins, the length of the paper, the number of lines per page, the orientation (portrait or landscape) and so on. If your application program won't let you set margins, for instance, you can use a setup utility to do the job.

- **Managing fonts.** You probably bought your DeskJet largely because of its ability to print sharp text in many attractive fonts. Woe to you if your application software won't let you select fonts. Since some programs override the choices you make from the keypad, you may be stuck with the DeskJet's built-in fonts, all of which are variants of boring, typewriter-style Courier, even if you've installed a font cartridge.

  A setup utility can make the font change for you, often from within the application program. You won't have to manually key in your font choices or convey your typographic desires via those complicated escape codes. The right utility will download your soft fonts for you and let you switch to any internal, cartridge or downloaded font whenever you like. In fact, some utilities concentrate entirely on font management. Fonts and font management utilities are covered in Section II.

- **Emulating other printers.** If your word processor or other application doesn't speak the DeskJet's language, a utility that translates commands intended for another printer into DeskJet format can make a good solution. With one of these *emulation* utilities, you can set up your application program for a different printer that the program does know how to control, such as a LaserJet or an Epson. When your program starts to print, the emulation utility intercepts commands meant for the LaserJet or Epson, and converts them into corresponding codes that the DeskJet understands. The result is instant DeskJet compatibility. And since emulation utilities do their translations "on the fly," during the actual printing process, they're able to change fonts, margins, and other settings within a document, not just between documents, as with some setup utilities.

  DeskJet utilities in emulation category include LaserControl, which emulates Diablo, NEC, Qume, Epson, and IBM Graphics printers; DwLaser, which emulates the IBM Quietwriter II (but only in the Displaywrite word processor); and LaserTwin, which offers the most important emulation of all, that of the LaserJet. Somewhere in this list, you'll find a printer that your software knows how to work with. LaserControl and LaserTwin are profiled later in this chapter, while DwLaser is discussed in Chapter 10 on word processing.

Utilities in residence

The typical setup utility works as a memory resident program (or TSR, for terminate-and-stay-resident, if you prefer). Like all TSRs, these utilities load into memory and stay there behind the scenes, while you go on to start your word processor, spreadsheet, or what have you. Just before printing, and without leaving your main program, you can press a special hotkey to pop up the utility screen. At this point, you can set new margins, change fonts, or issue other commands, all with a few quick keystrokes. When you're finished, you go right back to your work, exactly where you left it.

The ability to access a setup utility from within your application program can be extremely convenient, but all TSRs carry a few potential drawbacks. They occupy memory, of course, and can reduce the amount of memory available for your documents and other files. In fact, DeskJet setup utilities tend to be fairly large programs, and if your main application program is particularly memory-hungry you may not even be able to run it after you've loaded a setup utility. Conflicts between two or more TSRs can also complicate your life. The ideal solution is a setup utility that lets you choose to run it either as a TSR or as a standalone program.

Access: Setup utilities

Fontastic/$120

Koch Software
11 W College Dr. Bldg G
Arlington Heights, IL 60004
312/398-5440

Printer Genius/$89.00

Nor Software, Inc.
P.O. Box 1747
New York, NY 10156
212/213-9118

Picking a setup utility

So far, the DeskJet hasn't attracted as much attention from software developers as has its LaserJet cousins, and there aren't many setup utilities from which to choose. The short list includes Fontastic, Printer Genius, LaserControl, LaserTwin, and the utilities that specialize in font management covered in Chapter 7.

Profile: LaserControl

$150/Insight Development Corp.
2200 Powell St., Suite 500
Emeryville, CA 94608
415/652-4115

LaserControl has a dual mission: to help you set up your printer the way you want it to work, and to emulate other printers when your software doesn't know how to print with a DeskJet.

You can run LaserControl either as a pop-up memory resident utility or as a standalone program. Either way, an easy-to-follow set of menus lets you control DeskJet settings such as font and type style (bold or italics), lines per page, margins, graphics resolution, and so forth. There's also a handy command for ejecting finished pages that are still sitting in the printer, so you don't have to press the FF button.

With LaserControl, the whole setup process can be automatic, so that you don't even have to look at the menus. You can have LaserControl store a file with all your preferred DeskJet settings. At the beginning of a work session, you just tell LaserControl to send the file to your printer by typing **LC** followed by the name of the file on the DOS command line—the DeskJet is instantly ready to go.

LaserControl also lets you DeskJet emulate other popular printers, so that you can use the DeskJet with software that doesn't normally work with it. If a program knows the proper commands for a Diablo 630, an NEC 3550, 5510, or 7710, a Qume Sprint V, an Epson FX-80, or an IBM Graphics printer, it can now work with the DeskJet as well. Obviously, LaserControl can't make your program aware of features such as 300-dpi graphics that are unique to the DeskJet, but at least you'll be able to use the features that are available on the printer you're emulating.

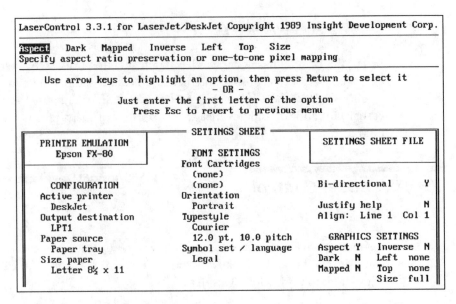

Figure 4-2: Laser Control's main screen. The current menu bar allows you to choose options for graphics printing.

In addition to its setup features and emulating capabilities, LaserControl knows how to get the DeskJet to print justified text (text that aligns perfectly with both margins) using proportionally spaced fonts like TmsRmn and Helv, even when the application doesn't have this capability. One well-known program in this category is WordStar 3.3, though later versions of WordStar can justify unaided. LaserControl also lets you print the screen you're currently displaying in text or CGA graphics mode (see Chapter 19 for more on screen snapshots).

Profile: LaserTwin

$179/ **Metro Software, Inc.**
2509 N. Campbell Ave., Suite 214
Tucson, AZ 85719
800/621-1137

LaserTwin could be the only utility software you need to buy for your DeskJet. By getting your modest DeskJet printer to emulate the more powerful LaserJet Series II, LaserTwin gives you superb control over the DeskJet from within the vast majority of contemporary programs. Even if your software is completely ignorant of the DeskJet, you can get great results as long as the program knows how to command the LaserJet. You can, for instance, print any font or any graphics in "sideways" landscape orientation, even though the DeskJet doesn't normally permit this. What's more, you can use any LaserJet downloadable font in a DeskJet document, as long as your application program supports downloadable LaserJet fonts.

The list of programs that benefit from LaserTwin includes all the PC word processors known to humanity, Ventura Publisher, Windows programs like PageMaker and Excel, 1-2-3, and a number of forms preparation products that don't work at all with the DeskJet. If you're skeptical of what LaserTwin can do, get a copy of the promotional brochure—the sample printouts from Ventura, TeX, and AutoCAD are pretty convincing.

To use LaserTwin, you start by setting up your application software to print to a LaserJet, not the DeskJet. As a TSR, LaserTwin works by intercepting the output destined for that imaginary LaserJet. For each page worth of printer output generated by the program, LaserTwin assembles all the text and graphics data, the printer commands, and the fonts into a high-resolution

```
           LaserTwin
   (c) Metro Software Inc. 1989
       All Rights Reserved

 Version ....... 2.04 USA 1304
 Printer .......... HP DeskJet
 LaserTwin memory used .... 26K
 Memory remaining ........ 384K

At the DOS prompt type:
>LT A       - Make driver Active.  Printer becomes HP Series II.
>LT I       - Make driver inactive.  Printer returns to normal mode.
>LT U       - Unload driver from memory.
>LT R       - Reset printer, delete all temporary fonts and macros.
>LT F       - Form feed, print current page.
>LT M       - Print in draft mode (higher speed).
>LT E       - Print in highest quality mode.
>LT J       - Print in normal image size mode.
>LT K       - Print in reduced image size mode.
>LT P       - Print in continuous paper mode.
>LT Q       - Print in cut sheet paper mode.
>LT X#      - Turn spooling on (# - 2=high, 1=medium or 0=low priority)
>LT Y#      - Turn spooling off (# - 0=clear or 1=suspend)
>LT S       - Display current status of program.
```

Figure 4-3: *This is the screen of options you get from LaserTwin*

graphics image of the final page. It then sends out this "bitmap" page image in the form your DeskJet will understand.

This process is functionally identical to what happens when you send a page of printer data to a real LaserJet. The only difference is that the LaserJet has a powerful computer off its own, which carries out the page-composition process inside the LaserJet, rather than in your computer. But the LaserJet must still assemble internally a bitmap for each page it prints.

As you can guess, creating the page images and sending them to the DeskJet can take LaserTwin some time, even if you have a fast computer. That's why the utility comes with a print spooler of its own. The printer output from your program and the resulting page images are stored temporarily on your hard disk (which is required). While you go back to work in your program LaserTwin operates behind the scenes to finish composing the pages, and to send them to the DeskJet as fast as the printer can accept them.

LaserTwin comes with a set of downloadable fonts that match the built-in ones on the LaserJet Series II. An optional font pack supplies all the fonts on the LaserJet cartridges available from HP.

Besides the improvement in printer control LaserTwin can give you, another advantage for some people is that you can use identical software setups for both the LaserJet and the DeskJet. If your company uses both printers, just install all your software for the LaserJet, pile on the LaserJet fonts, and run LaserTwin when you want to print to a DeskJet.

Drawbacks? Since LaserTwin prints everything in graphics mode, pages of text roll out more slowly than they would if you used the DeskJet's text mode. Also, because it's not a true setup utility, LaserTwin won't help in those situations where the program you're using puts limits on which fonts or formatting commands you can use. If you want the most from a program like this, you may still want want a separate setup utility such as LaserControl or Printer Genius.

Fonts

5

Understanding Typography

Now that you have a printer that can turn out typeset-quality documents right from your desktop, the challenge lies in knowing how to make it live up to its typographic potential. To point you in the right direction, this chapter introduces the rudiments of typography.

Like any craft, typography has its collection of special terms, and you'll be introduced to most of the important ones here. You'll learn the difference between a typeface and a font, and the significance of mysterious terms like *serifs, kerning,* and *leading.* You'll also find some practical tips on topics such as how to choose the right font, and how to use type effectively to make your documents look really sharp.

Type fundamentals

Before you bought your DeskJet or heard anything about fonts or desktop publishing, you may not have paid much attention to the differences between one printed character and the next. Of course, it's obvious when you think about it that every character has its own design. Compare these three sets of symbols carefully:

AQ AQ AQ

I guess you can see that all three specimens consist of the letters *A* and *Q*. But what makes each character design distinct from its counterparts? For one thing, their proportions—width compared to height—are a little different. Other differences you may notice are the relative heights of the smaller lowercase letters, the thickness of the *strokes*—the lines that make up the characters—and how the thickness, or *stroke weight* varies. To get even more detailed, notice that the lines in each *A* simply trace different paths, and that the tail of each *Q* joins the main part of the character at different angles and at different places.

One other aspect of character design is worth pointing out. The *A* on the left has little lines or bars extending out from the main parts of the character, while the *A* on the right is just straight lines, and doesn't have these bars. The term for these little lines is *serifs*. A character without them is a *sans serif* character (sans means "without" in French).

By the way, the imaginary horizontal line upon which the characters rest is called the *baseline*. While the bottoms of rounded characters such as *o* sometimes extend below the baseline slightly, *gs*, *ps*, and a few other lowercase characters have long downward strokes called *descenders*. Similarly, the upward strokes of letters such as *h* and *l* are known as ascenders. Ascenders usually end at the same height as the tops of uppercase letters, but in some cases are taller.

Typefaces

The term *typeface* designates a complete set of characters, all sharing a similar design. A single typeface encompasses as many letters, numbers, punctuation marks, and miscellaneous symbols as the typeface designer wishes to create. When you consider all the variations of letters used in all the European languages, all the symbols used in mathematics and scientific notation, and the tremendous range of special punctuation marks, you can see why some exhaustively complete typefaces include several hundred characters.

Typeface designers strive to impart a consistent appearance to all the characters in the "face," so that they look like they belong together. In a given typeface, the various characters will have similar proportions, their strokes will be roughly comparable in width, and the strokes will vary in width in a similar fashion.

Typefaces are often broadly classified as serif or sans serif since the characters in a typeface all usually either have serifs or don't have serifs. Among serif typefaces, the appearance of the serifs is an important distinguishing design element. In some fancy typefaces, serifs aren't enough, and the designer adds ornate flourishes and curlicues.

Another way to classify typeface designs is based on relative width of the characters in the face. *Monospaced* typeface designs, such as Courier and Letter Gothic, consist of characters which are all the same width. Monospaced typefaces were originally created for typewriters, where each metal bar had to be the same size. With a combination of large serifs and extra white space, a skinny little *i* fills up just as much room on a line as a wide *w*.

♪ **Note:** *Hewlett-Packard refers to monospaced typefaces as fixed pitch faces. The two terms are synonymous.*

In *proportionally spaced* typefaces, the width of each character varies according to the taste of the designer. Proportionally spaced faces generally look classier and more professional than the monospaced variety. They're easier to read, and they let you fit more characters on a page since there's no wasted space around the *i*s, *l*s, and *t*s. Numerals in a proportionally spaced typeface are usually monospaced, in order to make columns of numbers line up.

Here are examples of monospaced and proportionally spaced typefaces:

```
This text is printed in
the monospaced Courier
typeface. Notice how
each character lines up
with the one above it.
That's because they're
all of equal width.
Courier is a popular
typewriter typeface.
It's the only one built
into the DeskJet.
```

This text is printed in proportionally spaced Helvetica. In this typeface, nothing lines up from line to line, since each letter has a different width. Helvetica is said to be the world's most frequently used typeface. HP's Helv is one of many imitations of Helvetica available for the DeskJet.

Still another typeface classification system revolves around a face's intended function. *Text* or *body* faces are for long blocks of text, and are designed for easy reading. *Display* faces are meant to arrest the reader's attention, and are used in larger sizes to make headlines, titles, and other snippets of text stand out. *Decorative* or *novelty* faces are so flashy and strongly stylized that they may distract attention from your message, but they're fun to use and can set a special mood. Then there are *symbol* faces for non-text purposes. Here are some examples:

Benguiat is a Display Typeface.

This is a novelty typeface called Savage. It's not available for the DeskJet.

Here are characters from a musical symbol typeface:

Finally, *typeface families* are collections of two or more typefaces of very similar design, but different in some aspects. Along with the regular version of a typeface, a typeface family may contain italics, boldface, compressed (squished horizontally) or expanded (stretched) versions. Other characteristics, such as the character proportions, the presence and type of serifs, and so on—remain roughly the same.

Confusingly, the members of a typeface family are often referred to as *type styles*, suggesting that they represent variations on a single basic typeface. In the DeskJet's case, that's partly true, because the printer can render any font in boldface (more on this in Chapter 6). But to print in italics, the DeskJet needs a separate italics font.

Understanding typeface names

Typeface designs can't be copyrighted, but their names can. That's why so many typefaces that look the same are marketed under different names. Font vendors who don't want to pay to license the "real," original version of a face can easily create their own faithful imitation. All they have to do is more or less trace the outlines of the original typeface's characters and give the result a new name. Though the vendor can't sell the "new" typeface as the original, he or she is free to describe the imitator as "similar to" Times Roman, Helvetica, or whatever the original face is legally called. Even HP has taken this approach with its TmsRmn and its Helv. SWFTE's versions of the same typefaces are Roman and Helvette.

Fonts

Finally, we arrive at the term that's the darling of desktop publishers, *font*. In everyday speech and in most magazine articles on DTP, the terms font and typeface are used interchangeably, which is fine for most purposes. But there is a difference that's often important when you're shopping for type.

Defined accurately, a typeface is the design for a set of characters, while a font is that design turned into a specific subset of characters, or *character set*, at a specific size (the way typographers measure font size will be described shortly). In the poem below, you can see examples of several different fonts. They look a lot alike because they're all based on the same typeface, but each font is a different size:

Here is one font.

Here is another.

Based on Times Roman,

All four are like brothers.

We'll get to the character set part of the font definition in a moment. For most people, the practical reason to get the terms typeface and font straight is this: when you buy a font for the DeskJet, you're getting the ability to print at only one size. In other words, you must buy a different font for each size at which you want to print. True, you may find several fonts, all of the same typeface, in a commercial font package. That means you'll be able to print at several different sizes—but not necessarily at any size you please.

Character sets

A character set is a particular collection of character symbols selected from all those available in a typeface. The reason a character set rarely contains all the characters in a typeface is simple: the ASCII code system used by your PC and the DeskJet can only accommodate 256 characters at a time, while many complete typefaces include more than 256 characters.

All nineteen of the DeskJet's built-in character sets are shown in Appendix B; some optional fonts offer additional character sets besides. A quick scan of the Appendix will show you that most character sets start with all the ordinary letters, numbers, and punctuation marks, and then add special characters suited to a specific purpose: foreign languages, mathematics and engineering, or character-based graphics (see Chapter 6 for a discussion of character graphics). On the other hand, some character sets (and the typefaces from which they're drawn) consist entirely of special symbols such as math symbols, character graphics, little pictures, bar codes, or musical symbols.

A character set that tries to offer something for everybody is the one used for screen displays in the IBM PC and thousands of workalike computers. This set is reproduced in the DeskJet's internal fonts, and is known as the PC-8 set in DeskJet parlance. Most users find the selection of characters adequate, though there are the critics who say that in trying to please everyone, the PC-8 character set satisfies no one. For everyday business use, the PC-8 character set does have a few glaring omissions—the trademark, registered trademark, and copyright symbols (these can be found in the DeskJet's Legal character set, by the way).

✄ *Tip:* *Use the DeskJet's Legal character set to print the trademark (™), registered trademark (®), and copyright (©) symbols.*

Type size is expressed with two separate terms, point size and pitch. *Point size* refers to how high the characters are, measured from the top of the highest ascender to the bottom of the descenders. A *point* is a typographer's unit of measurement very nearly equal to ¹⁄₇₂nd of an inch. That means there are about 72 points to an inch. Just for completeness, 12 points make a *pica*, and you can therefore tap out 6 lines of pica type within a vertical inch on that old typewriter.

Pitch is a the number of characters that will fit side-by-side in an inch, measured horizontally across a line of text. Another way to look at pitch is as a measurement of the width of individual characters—the larger the pitch, the more characters fit in on a line of text, so the skinnier they have to be. A pitch value only makes sense when you're referring to monospaced type—in proportionally spaced typefaces, the number of characters per inch depends on which characters you're talking about.

There are still more typographic terms you'll run across frequently, many of which pertain to the way text is spaced and positioned in your document. We'll get to the most important of these concepts in a bit, but we'll linger on the topic of fonts for a little longer first.

Choosing and using fonts

You bought the DeskJet to make your documents look better, and a lot of the improvement will come from your printer's ability to print text in a variety of high-quality fonts. But to get the results you're expecting, you need to know how to select the right fonts for a given document, and how to use them effectively.

How to pick the right font

Just like wine connoisseurs, dyed-in-the-wool typographers can go on forever discussing the subtle strengths and weaknesses of each specimen of their stock-in-trade. In the typographer's case, the subject is fonts, which are unabashedly described with jargon such as "even color," or "warm and friendly, not overbearing."

For most people, though, choosing a font doesn't have to be a full-time preoccupation. Heed a few basic guidelines, and you can't go wrong.

Fonts for body text:

For text passages of any length, your main priority in choosing a font is to find one that's easy to read. Here are some of the font characteristics that influence readability:

1. Simplicity. The font's typeface design should not call attention to itself.

2. Size. A font that's too small is obviously hard to read, but overly large fonts can also require too much effort from your reader. In most situations, you should use a font in the range of 9 to 14 points. If you have to go smaller to cram a lot of copy into a small area, use a typeface whose lowercase letters are tall, as measured by the height of a lower case x (this distance is thus referred to as the *x-height*). By contrast, a smaller x-height is better when you're filling a vertically long column, as in a newsletter or newspaper.

3. Weight. Use a font based on a typeface of medium stroke weight. If it's too light, it won't stand out from the background. If it's too heavy, the extra thickness tends to obscure the empty areas within the characters (the *counterforms*), which help the reader recognize the character.

4. Uniformity. The stroke thickness of the font's typeface should be fairly uniform. If not, the thin strokes will verge on invisibility, the heavy strokes will obscure character definition, and the contrast between them will cause a scintillating effect that further reduces readability.

5. Slant. Use upright fonts instead of italics (slanted) ones for long stretches of text. Italics slow the reader down, but they're good for emphasizing a word or phrase.

6. Serif versus sans serif. Both types of typefaces can be equally legible, depending on other characteristics, but custom may make your reader prefer one or the other. In the U.S., serif typefaces have long predominated.

Typefaces well-suited to body text are legion. Some of the perennial favorites include Times Roman (TmsRmn or Dutch), Helvetica (Helv or Swiss), and Palatino. This book is set in ITC Garamond.

Fonts for display text:

For headings, emphasized quotations, or other brief passages, you're freer to use more stylized display typefaces for their inherent visual appeal. Readers attracted by the look of the type will be willing to make a little more effort to get the message, as long as the text is short. On the other hand, it's perfectly acceptable to stick with a simple typeface for display text, and just use a larger-sized font. In many books, for example, headings are set in good old Helvetica.

Beyond these very general guidelines, the choice of typeface is a matter of personal taste. If you feel uncomfortable with that responsibility, take the easy way out: buy HP's TmsRmn and Helv in a smattering of sizes, or their equivalents from another vendor, and leave it at that (we'll cover the forms in which you can buy fonts in Chapter 6).

Designing with type

It's not enough just to pick your font. You also have to decide how you're going to use it in your document. Among the design issues you need to consider are how to mix fonts, how to create emphasis, and how to space and position your text for best readability and optimal overall appearance. While matters of art and taste can hardly be codified, there are some simple rules that will help you avoid the most glaring errors.

Mixing fonts:

1. Limit the number of typeface families in a document. Just because the DeskJet gives you the ability to mix fonts freely in a single document doesn't mean you should do so. What's great about having a variety of fonts to pick from is that you can choose the one or two that best suit the tone and meaning of your document— not that you can fill your document with a distracting melange of different faces. Like ornate individual typefaces, frequent typeface changes attract attention to the type itself, distracting the reader from the meaning of your text.

For most documents, one or two typeface families should suffice. For example, a common practice is to use a serif face for the body of your text, and a sans serif face for the headings. When in doubt, go with the smaller number of typefaces.

2. Use typefaces that contrast significantly when you want to indicate the differences in function between various sections of text. The right reason to use multiple typefaces is to highlight the difference between, say, headlines and the body of the text, or between a general discussion and a supporting collection of dense facts and figures. But when you do decide that a typeface change is in order, make sure the typefaces you juxtapose are significantly different. Again, a good starting point is to use a serif face for one function, a sans serif face for the other.

3. Use even point size multiples. Again, the "point" in varying type size is to emphasize the differences between different portions of your text. You want the reader to notice the size contrasts, at least on the subconscious level. Don't make it hard to distinguish them—no two fonts in the same document should be closer than two points apart. For example, you might select a 12 point font for your main ideas, and a 10 point font for explanatory material the reader might want to skip.

⌒ *Caution:* *When you want to emphasize a point, stay away from underlining, and above all don't use all capital letters. Both reduce readability significantly.*

4. Use italics instead of underlining to emphasize important phrases. Typists adopted underlining to indicate emphasis primarily because typewriters can't produce italics or boldface, but underlining tends to make text look cluttered

and crowded. The DeskJet can print both italics and boldface, so you don't need to underline unless you really want to for some special reason.

Even more important, AVOID USING ALL CAPITAL LETTERS TO CREATE EMPHASIS. MORE THAN ANY OTHER FACTOR, ALL-UPPERCASE TEXT REDUCES THE READABILITY OF YOUR COPY. (Seen enough?) The uniform height of the letters makes it very hard for the eye to distinguish individual characters. What's more, all-uppercase passages take up considerably more space than ordinary text.

Spacing and positioning text:

1. The vertical distance between lines (the *leading* or *linespacing*) is one of the most important factors in creating a readable block of text. Most word processors and desktop publishing programs put in too little leading for you, with the result that the text is overly dense and hard to read.

Leading is measured in points, measured from the baseline of one line to the next. You'll often see it written with the typeface's point size—a 12 point face with 14 points of leading is expressed as 12/14, for example.

Although the optimal amount of leading varies from document to document and from typeface to typeface, a good place to start is is with leading of at least 120% of the typeface's point size. For 9- to 11-point type, use 1 to 3 additional points of leading; add 2 to 4 points of leading to 12 point type; and so on. Add more leading for long lines of text, for bold or sans serif faces, and for faces that have strongly contrasting stroke weights.

2. When a block of text is *justified*, the horizontal boundaries of all the lines in the block are aligned with one another. The most common "unjustified" alternative is *ragged right*, in which the lines are flush on the left, but vary in length on the right.

Ragged right text is easier to read, because the spaces between letters and words are even, and because the varying line lengths serve as reference points when the eye looks for the beginning of the next line. Still, try not to make the text *too* ragged on the right, or your reader will get distracted by the striking shape of the column.

Justified text gives your document a formal "published" appearance. Almost all word processors can automatically justify your text for you, but they don't all do an equally good job of it. Justification is achieved by several methods: you can hyphenate words, you can increase the space between the words (the *wordspacing*) and between the individual letters (the *letterspacing*). You must use these techniques carefully, though, since too many hyphens create clutter, and too much space separates breaks up the flow of the text, making it harder to read. If you use justification, you'll have to look at your document closely after it's printed to make sure these problems aren't severe.

3. Whether or not you justify, wordspacing and letterspacing are important for optimum readability.

When words are too far apart, the eye has to hurdle the gaps and reading slows down. The wordspacing should be smaller than the leading, or the eye will move down the lines instead of across. To fit a given amount of text into a defined space, adjust the wordspacing, not the letterspacing, whenever possible.

Letterspacing should above all be even, to allow the eye to "glide" over the words without jerky movements. You may want to adjust the letterspacing to create an effect that's not too light or too dark. In general, you can space letters more closely in brief passages—headlines and the like—than in the main body of your text. The process of evenly adjusting the letterspacing for a group of characters at the same time is known as *tracking*.

Kerning is used to tighten or loosen the space between two adjacent characters. It's a common practice because the ordinary spacing alloted to some characters becomes too large when the characters are paired with certain others. For example, consider the capital *T* and the adjacent *h* in the word "The." The typeface is designed so that when you print the *T*, enough room is left so a tall character like the *h* won't touch it. The space alloted to the *T* doesn't change if you erase the *h* and substitute a short *o*, but the space is now too big, since the *o* can nestle in under the bar at the top of the *T*.

Kerning corrects this problem. It's especially useful for type you print in large point sizes of type, where the extra spaces become more noticeable. Some word processors let you kern manually, and the major desktop publishing programs will do it for you automatically as well.

4. The length of each line is another factor that influences readability. For long passages, choose a combination of line length and font size so that each line contains about 55 to 70 characters, or about 9 to 12 words.

Where to turn for more advice

These days, it's easy to find people who want to give you tips on typography and document design. For starters, try *Looking Good in Print*, and *WordPerfect 5: Desktop Publishing in Style*. Both are available from Peachpit.

6

DeskJet Fonts

∾

In concept, a DeskJet font is a particular set of characters in a particular typeface that you can print at a specific size. In practical terms, however, a font is something built into the printer, or something you buy on a disk or as a cartridge. This chapter introduces you to the way your printer handles fonts in general and to each of the forms of DeskJet fonts in particular. Later in the chapter, you'll find sections on cartridge fonts and two special font-related topics, graphics fonts and character graphics. Chapter 7 is devoted to soft fonts, the kind you buy on disks.

How the DeskJet handles fonts

In the printer, a font is stored as a big collection of data representing the dots that must be printed to construct each character. The DeskJet keeps all this font data in its equivalent of a table, in which the set of dots for each character is referenced by that character's unique code number.

Although the DeskJet can store many fonts simultaneously, only one of them can be active for printing at a time. When you ask the DeskJet to print a particular character, it looks up that character's dot data in the active font table. The data tells it which dots to print, and out comes the character you wanted.

To print text in another font, you must first *select* the new font (we'll see how that's done in a moment). In response, the printer shifts its attention to the data table for the new font. When the next printable ASCII code comes along, the DeskJet takes its instructions for printing the character from the new font table, and the letter or number you so on the page reflect the change.

DeskJet font capabilities and limitations

Although the DeskJet is the first printer for under $1000 to offer 300-dpi text printing in a wide array of fonts, it does have its limitations when it comes to font selection. This section summarizes what you can and can't do with DeskJet fonts.

Font size

The DeskJet is capable of printing a relatively limited range of font sizes. You'll hear various opinions about the maximum possible point size of DeskJet fonts, but all of them are based on the same basic facts: Your printer can cover an area of only 50 dots high in a single pass of the printhead. Since a dot is 1/300", this means you can print no more than 1/6" inch, or 12 points, on one pass. To allow for larger fonts, the original DeskJet can print characters using two passes of the printhead, for a total height of 100 dots (24 points). The DeskJet Plus can do even better, as it can make as many as four printhead passes to print a character. Unfortunately, however, DeskJet fonts can't usually be 200 dots (48 points) tall—another limitation gets in the way. On both models of the printer, a single character can be no *wider* than 127 dots. Except for novelty fonts whose characters are very tall and skinny, this width limitation restricts the size of DeskJet Plus fonts to about 30 points.

�֍ *Tip:* *If the top and bottom portions of tall characters are out of alignment, you can cure the problem by setting the DeskJet to print unidirectionally. Normally, to save time, the DeskJet prints continuously as the printhead moves in both directions across the page. However, some DeskJets are unable to maintain precise alignment between the left-to-right and right-to-left passes of the printhead, a defect that shows up when printing characters larger than 50 dots high. In the unidirectional print mode, the printhead goes all the way back to the extreme left side of the carriage at the beginning of each pass, ensuring proper alignment. To switch to unidirectional mode, use a setup utility or send the escape sequence ESC&k0W.*

One way to make larger fonts suitable for headlines is to remove all the lowercase letters. As you'll recall from Chapter 5, a font's overall point size is measured from the top of the tallest ascender to the bottom of the lowest descender. Since uppercase letters have no descenders, an all-uppercase font can be enlarged to fill the space that would normally be taken up by the descenders of the lowercase letters. This method works best for the original DeskJet, permitting fonts up to 30 points tall (see Chapter 7 for sources of these and other soft fonts). While the same technique could theoretically be used to make 60-point DeskJet Plus fonts, the width restriction means that many of the characters would be too narrow.

✖ *Tip:* *You can print text characters as graphics to get around the size limitations on DeskJet fonts. For details, see the section "Graphics fonts" at the end of this chapter.*

Font options: half-size, boldface, and draft mode

In Chapter 5, you learned that a regular Courier font and boldface Courier are two different fonts, technically speaking, and likewise, that while 12-point TmsRmn and 24-point TmsRmn look very similar, they too exist independently. Now it's time to learn the DeskJet's exceptions to the rules.

Built into the DeskJet are software routines that can transform any font in a variety of ways. For example, most DeskJet fonts can be scaled by the printer to half its labelled size. If you have a 12-point Helv on board, you can print it at both 12 and 6 points by sending the correct command to the DeskJet. The same holds true for boldface fonts. In this case, the printer simply makes each character one or two dots wider when you request the boldface version of the font.

The drawback of these automatic modifications is that they're mechanically applied to every character without a human designer's for each individual character. As a result, the resulting type doesn't look as crisp as you get from a font originally designed for the smaller size or for bold printing. If you want the best possible text quality from your printer, you'll need to buy, load, and select genuine bold fonts, rather than relying on the DeskJet's automatic bolding feature.

✂ *Tip: If you've installed a font that permits automatic boldface and a separate genuine boldface font of the same typeface and size, the command for boldface printing will turn on the automatic bolding feature instead of selecting the real bold font. Print quality will suffer as a result, and characters may not be spaced properly. There's no way to solve this problem short of redefining the information in the fonts themselves so that the automatic bolding feature is turned off. This is a technically demanding job, but your font vendor may be able to assist you.*

You can view the DeskJet's draft mode as another one of these automatic font transformations. In draft mode, some of the dots in each character are omitted. The resulting type is gray rather than solid black but still very sharp, and ink consumption is reduced substantially.

Although the DeskJet can theoretically print any font at half size, in boldface, or in draft mode, you can only use these automatic modifications on fonts that permit them. Each font contains separate settings that turn the half-size, boldface, and draft mode options on or off. If the font allows automatic bold printing, it will also include a setting telling the DeskJet whether to add one or two dots to create the bold effect.

Italics

The DeskJet does not have an automatic italicizing feature. To print text in italics with the DeskJet, you need a separate italics font, period.

Landscape fonts

Although the DeskJet can print text in its "sideways" landscape orientation, you're extremely limited in your selection of fonts for this mode. Your only options are font cartridges K and L, and the DeskJet Plus's built-in landscape Courier fonts (cartridge K has the basic landscape Courier fonts available on the DeskJet Plus, while cartridge L supplies several landscape versions of Courier and Letter Gothic). The printer does not accept landscape soft fonts. Both Courier and Letter Gothic are monospaced typefaces, and it's not possible to print proportionally spaced text in landscape mode.

✂ Tip: *To print in landscape mode with an original model DeskJet, you must install landscape cartridge HP22707K or HP22707L. Do not use the K cartridge in the DeskJet Plus, since the printer already has these fonts built in.*

To understand these limitations, it helps to know how the printer manages sideways printing. There aren't really any separate landscape fonts. Instead, the DeskJet just rotates the characters of a regular monospaced font counter-clockwise by 90°. However, rotating the individual characters is the easy part. The real trick is to print them in the correct places on the page.

Remember that the DeskJet printhead always moves from side to side across the page it's printing, never up and down, and that you always feed paper lengthwise into the printer. In landscape mode, the part of the paper printed first—what would be the top in portrait mode—becomes the right side of the page. Obviously, it follows that the last part of the page to exit the printer is its left side. In other words, the first character you would read, the one at the top left margin, gets printed on the very last pass of the printhead. Clearly, the DeskJet cannot print the characters in the order in which they are received from your software. Instead, the printer must store a page worth of text in its buffer before it can begin to print a landscape page. Then, for the first pass of the printhead, it sifts through the buffer to find and print one character from each line in the text, the one that belongs at the right margin of the page (of course, a given line may not have a character at the right margin). For the next pass, it picks out the character from each line that belongs in the next column to the left, and so on.

To figure out which character belongs where on the page, the DeskJet relies on the simple assumption that each character occupies an equal amount of space horizontally, along a line of text. There's not enough RAM in the DeskJet's buffer to store and manipulate spacing specifications for each character on an entire page, nor is the printer programmed to make the necessary calculations. This explains why landscape fonts must be the monospaced kind.

⌢ *Caution:* *In landscape mode, printing starts only after the DeskJet has received a full page of data or a form feed command (explained in Chapters 8 and 22), or after you've pressed the FF button on the keypad. This is because the DeskJet must know where the data for the page ends in order to figure out where to place the landscape characters. If you send less than a full page of data to the printer without a form feed command, the BUSY light will blink to indicate that the data has been received, but printing won't begin until you press the FF key.*

♪ *Note:* *By the way, although the DeskJet technically can't print graphics in its own landscape mode, many software programs are able to achieve the same results. The trick is to rotate the graphic into the sideways orientation within your computer, then send the resulting image to the DeskJet in portrait mode. The printout looks the same as if the DeskJet had its own landscape mode.*

Types of DeskJet fonts

Though all DeskJet fonts work the same way, they're supplied in three different forms:

Internal fonts: every DeskJet has a limited complement of fonts permanently hardwired into the printer. The DeskJet Plus has several additional internal fonts not available on the original DeskJet.

Cartridge fonts: the DeskJet has two slots just behind the keypad controls on the right, intended for optional font cartridges sold by HP. Each cartridge permanently stores font data for one or more fonts. Once you've placed a font cartridge into a slot, you can select the cartridge fonts from the keypad or via software commands, just as if they were built into the printer. You'll find more information on using cartridge fonts later in this chapter.

Soft fonts: another way to add fonts to your DeskJet is to buy them in the form of files recorded on floppy disks. To use these *soft fonts*, you must download the font files from your computer to the printer, where they're stored in the memory of special RAM cartridges you must first install. Once you've downloaded a soft font, you can select it via software commands, but not via the keypad. Although a bit less convenient than cartridge fonts, soft fonts are usually a better buy. You'll find a complete discussion of the pros and cons of soft fonts along with instructions for using them in Chapter 7.

Actually, there's one more type of font: the kind generated entirely in graphics mode. We'll cover graphics fonts in the last section of this chapter.

Selecting the font of your wont

The simplest way to select the font you want to print with is via the FONT button on the DeskJet's keypad. Just press the button repeatedly until the desired font you've activated the desired font. When you've selected the right font, its indicator light glows.

Often, however, you'll want to change fonts by way of software, rather than with the keypad. For one thing, any soft fonts you've downloaded to your DeskJet are inaccessible with the FONT button, and you can only select them via printer commands from the computer. Nor is the FONT button effective when you want to switch fonts within a document—there's no way you could hit it at the right time. In this case, you have to manually place the commands for changing fonts at the right locations in your document, or let your software program send the commands for you. In some cases, you may find it simply more convenient to select fonts with software, so you don't have to reach over and press the FONT button.

An introduction to font selection commands

When you select a font from the keypad, you're setting all its attributes— typeface, point size, pitch, and so forth—at once. To select a font via printer commands, however, you or your software must set each of these attributes independently using separate escape sequences. For example, to specify the typeface of the font you want to activate, you must send the DeskJet an escape sequence calling for that typeface by its code number (every typeface has one). You'd send another escape sequence to specify the font's size, and still another to indicate italics or boldface.

♪ **Note:** *Actually, as you'll learn in Chapter 7, there is a way to select a font with a single command in some circumstances, but it's not as reliable as specifying each font attribute separately.*

Even though each font attribute can theoretically be controlled independently through printer commands, don't get the idea that you can break the rule about a font having a fixed point size and pitch. While there are separate commands for each font attribute, you can only select the attributes that are available in the specific fonts you've installed. If you order up a nonexistent point size, for instance, the DeskJet will simply substitute the font closest in size to your request.

Obviously, having an application program or a setup utility issue the commands to select your desired font for you is far more convenient that doing it yourself. But in the event that you need to select fonts on your own via printer commands, you'll find complete instructions in Chapter 22.

Using font cartridges

Font cartridges are without question the most convenient format for adding optional fonts to your DeskJet. They're a no fuss, no muss solution—just plug in a cartridge and you're instantly ready to print using any of the cartridge fonts.

To date, you can only buy font cartridges from HP. Third-party font suppliers don't make them (they sell soft fonts instead).

Font cartridge anatomy

Inside a font cartridge, the font data is stored in permanent form on ROM (read-only memory) chips. At the bottom of the cartridge is an electronic connector that goes into a mating slot in the printer, and lets the DeskJet communicate with the ROM fonts.

The label from a typical cartridge is pictured below in Figure 6-1. Just under the HP logo, the label lists the cartridge number. This number is simply HP's own catalog number for the cartridge, but I guess it's a better name than something like "SX-900 Plus." Under the part number in tiny print is a short message indicating the character sets available for the fonts in the cartridge.

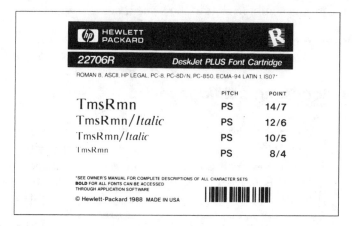

Figure 6-1: *A DeskJet font cartridge label*

Most of the cartridge label is devoted to a list of the fonts contained in the cartridge. The name of each font is printed as a sample of what the font looks like at actual size. Then comes a column for pitch (note that most monospaced fonts can be printed at either of two pitches). The pitch column reads PS for proportionally spaced fonts, since these fonts don't have a set pitch value. Finally, there's a column for the font's point size. Again, many fonts can be printed at full- or half-size, and you'll see both sizes on the label if that's the case.

Installing font cartridges

⌒ **Caution:** *Never install or remove a font cartridge when the DeskJet is turned on.*

Remember one critical point about installing and removing font cartridges: don't do it when the power is on. Otherwise, there's not much that can wrong with a font cartridge. Once the slot cover is off, you just pop the cartridge in the slot, connector side down, like toast in a toaster—you can't even plug it in backwards. For me, the hardest part of the installation is taking off the little plastic piece that covers the slot. You can't do it with your fingers— use a small flatblade screwdriver, a rounded dinner knife, or the tip of a pen instead. You can install a single font cartridge in either slot, and you can put cartridges in both slots at the same time.

⌢ *Caution: There is one combination of font cartridges that won't work: don't install a landscape cartridge and the Epson emulation cartridge at the same time.*

Accessing cartridge fonts

Since there's a direct electronic connection between a font cartridge and the DeskJet, cartridge fonts act just as if they were part of the original equipment of your printer. You can select a font on any installed cartridge by pressing the FONT button on the keypad repeatedly until the indicator light next to the font's abbreviation on the top of the cartridge glows.

If you're trying to select the half-size version of the desired font, keep pressing the FONT button until both the font's indicator light and the indicator closest to the FONT button (the one marked with a series of several red lines) are glowing. If you're selecting a landscape font, press the FONT key until both the font's indicator and the indicator for landscape mode glow. You can also access cartridge fonts using printer commands as detailed in Chapter 22.

Graphics fonts

As you know, the DeskJet puts rather serious limits on how large a normal font can be—roughly 18 points with the original model, and 30 points in the DeskJet Plus. Unfortunately, even 30 points is too small for attention-grabbing headlines. But there is another way to add large letters to your document: as graphics.

Most people think of graphics as recognizable pictures of something, but there's nothing to stop you from creating a graphic in the shape of a letter. And just like any other DeskJet graphic, a graphical letter can be any size you like, up to a full page. Check out some of the examples in Figure 6-2.

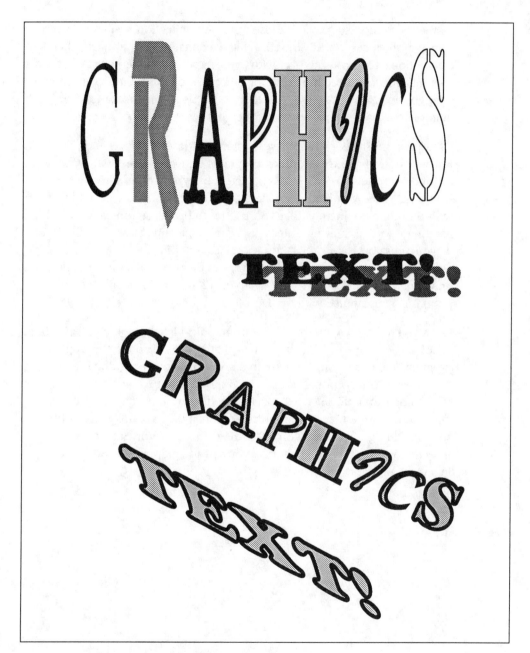

Figure 6-2: *Text created as graphics in Corel Draw*

As the illustration suggests, size isn't the only limitation you can overcome using graphics-based text. Since the character images are graphics rather than conventional text, you can play with their shapes and patterns to your heart's content. You can stretch, shrink, or otherwise distort them, rotate them or arrange them along a curve, fill them with stripes or polkadots, or stack multiple copies of them on top of one another.

Of course, most people aren't very interested in designing letters yourself. But you don't have to. Graphics programs typically come with a range of typefaces and let you enter the characters by typing them directly from the keyboard. Once you have the letters on your screen, you can modify them with the same commands that you use to edit other graphics. If you think you might want to buy a graphics program for creating classy headlines, one of your best bets is Corel Draw. Corel Draw comes with a host of great typefaces that print well on the DeskJet, and it's an excellent general purpose drawing program as well (see Chapter 12 for more details on graphics programs you can use with the DeskJet).

Once you're happy with the way your graphical letters look, you save them on disk (be sure to use a file format that can be read by the application program you'll be using to assemble and print your final document). The easiest way to incorporate graphics with ordinary text is to use a desktop publishing program, since it's specifically designed for that job. But it's also possible to merge text and graphics with many conventional word processors, including Microsoft Word, WordPerfect, and WordStar. And with the Inset utility described in Chapter 10, you can add graphics to your documents in almost any word processor.

7

Using Soft Fonts

Once you get hooked on the idea of using fonts creatively, you won't be satisfied by the limited selection of fonts available built into the DeskJet and on the cartridges sold by HP. For the variety you want, you'll need to turn to soft fonts.

Just in case you missed the definition earlier in the book, soft fonts are fonts supplied on floppy disks. To install them in your DeskJet, you transfer or *download* these files to the printer, much as you do when you print ordinary text or graphics files. Once they reach the DeskJet, soft fonts are stored in the memory provided by special RAM cartridges you must add to the printer first.

Why use soft fonts?

Soft fonts can claim three major advantages over fonts that come on cartridges: variety, flexibility, and lower cost.

If you look only at the HP catalog, you wouldn't know that a large variety of typefaces are available in soft fonts for the DeskJet, far more than you can get on cartridges. At this writing, HP sells only three soft font packages, representing various sizes of just three very conventional typeface families. Turn to the third-party font suppliers, though, and you'll find a much larger range of soft font offerings encompassing many different typeface designs, from ordinary text faces to ornate decorative faces. What's more, it's possible to convert any of the huge number of LaserJet soft fonts to DeskJet format. Though font quality suffers slightly in the conversion process, this opens up a vast cornucopia of typeface possibilities (more on LaserJet to DeskJet font conversions later in this chapter).

Even if you don't covet infinite typeface variety, you'll enjoy greater flexibility with soft fonts. You can mix fonts from one package with those from any other, even from another font supplier. By contrast, the particular set of fonts on a cartridge is permanently fixed. Let's say you have a DeskJet Plus and you want to print a newsletter using 30 point TmsRmn for the headlines, 10 point Helv for the captions, and 12 point TmsRmn for your body text, a common set of font choices. Unfortunately, there's no combination of two font cartridges that offers all three fonts. Buy HP's TmsRmn/Helv soft font package, however, and you can download just the fonts you need from all those in the assortment.

From most suppliers, soft fonts also cost much less per font than do cartridge fonts. Many font vendors sell soft font sets with several different typefaces represented in each set. Font packages that generate soft fonts from master outlines (see the section on font generators later in this chapter) give you the ability to create as many different size fonts as you like, within the range allowed by the DeskJet—and all for one price.

The bad news

For all their good points, soft fonts also have some drawbacks compared to cartridge fonts. For one thing, they take up lots of room on disk, room that you might want to use for programs and files instead. Another difficulty is that you have to customize printer drivers for your soft fonts, a process that tends to be complicated and time-consuming. Finally, soft fonts must be downloaded to your printer, which also takes time. You'll learn how to minimize these problems later in the chapter.

Getting started with soft fonts

In order to use soft fonts, you'll have to take care of several preliminaries. First, you'll need to purchase additional memory for your DeskJet in the form of RAM cartridges. Next, you'll probably want to install the soft fonts you use most often on your hard disk, if you have one. Finally, you'll need to plan and implement a strategy for downloading the fonts to your printer.

Adding RAM cartridges: a must for soft fonts

⌒ **Caution:** *You must add at least one RAM cartridge to use soft fonts in your DeskJet. DO NOT install or remove RAM cartridges while the DeskJet is on.*

Before you can even begin to work with soft fonts, you must bolster your DeskJet's memory capacity. As it comes from the factory, the DeskJet can't accommodate even a single soft font. To use soft fonts, you must install at least one optional RAM cartridge in the machine. RAM cartridges are available in 128K and 256K models, but the latter work only with the DeskJet Plus. You can mix or match the two kinds of RAM cartridges in the PLUS.

The RAM cartridges install in the same slots used for font cartridges, located just behind the main keypad controls on the printer's right side. To install a RAM cartridge, remove the plastic panel covering one of the slots with a small flatblade screwdriver. Then insert the RAM cartridge so that the connector on the bottom of the cartridge plugs into its counterpart at the bottom of the cartridge slot.

Sources of soft fonts

At the moment, DeskJet soft fonts are a bit scarce. HP offers only three soft font packages, and two of these work only in the DeskJet Plus. One advantage of HP's soft fonts is that they're supported by the printer drivers of some applications—I doubt you can find even a single printer driver with built-in support third-party soft fonts. Conveniently, HP supplies a font downloading utility with its soft font packages.

At this writing, probably the most popular DeskJet soft fonts are the ones marketed by Elfring Soft Fonts. An sample of Elfring's 30-point uppercase-only Roman is included in the soft font sampler in Figure 7-1. You can buy a set of fonts covering a variety of sizes from a single typeface, or pick from several collections organized by function: one for headlines, one for spreadsheets, and one for symbols. Elfring also sells an excellent font management utility called TSR Download, profiled later in this chapter, and a utility for selecting DeskJet font options such as automatic boldface and half-sized printing.

An alternative way to obtain DeskJet soft fonts is to purchase a font generating package. Instead of supplying separate, ready-to-use font files for each font, font generators give you master typefaces which you can turn into as many sizes of specific fonts as you want. Font generators are discussed later in the chapter.

Finally, there's one other source of DeskJet fonts: the vast catalog of LaserJet fonts. Two inexpensive utilities covered later in this chapter can convert almost any LaserJet font to DeskJet format. Hundreds upon hundreds of LaserJet fonts are available from suppliers too numerous to list. In fact, you can obtain many LaserJet fonts for free from user groups and electronic bulletin boards such as CompuServe.

Understanding font filenames

It's very easy to accumulate so many soft fonts that you lose track of which is which. After all, you need a separate font file for each unique combination of typeface, point size, and style (regular or italic). DOS allows only 11

ELFRING'S 30-POINT ROMAN FONT

Elfring's 24-point Helv

Here is a Garamond-like LaserJet font converted to DeskJet format.

Here is 18-point Abbey from SWFTE. It's another LaserJet conversion.

SWFTE's version of 18-pt. Cooper Black. Yet another LaserJet conversion.

This is MoreFont's 26-pt. Opera, outlined.

26-pt. Showtime with a fountain fill. Also from MoreFonts.

Figure 7-1: *A DeskJet soft font sampler, printed on a DeskJet. The page has been reduced by 18 percent.*

characters total in a filename, not enough space for a full description of all the font's characteristics.

Making the best of a bad situation, HP has ordained a coding scheme for naming DeskJet (and LaserJet) soft fonts. True, font names that follow this convention still look like gibberish. However, once you know the code you can learn a lot about a font from its name, and it will be much easier to find the font you want in a crowded directory on you hard disk.

⌒ *Caution: Unfortunately, many soft font suppliers don't follow HP's font naming convention. If you use such fonts you'll just have to learn whatever naming system the vendor dreamed up, or rename the files to conform to the HP code.*

Here's the pattern for soft font filenames in HP's coded system:

AABBBCDD.EEF

and two examples:

TR12ØMPN.DJP

CO145XØ8.DJP

The first two characters in the name, *AA* in the pattern, are an abbreviation for the font's typeface. In the examples, **TR** stands for Times Roman, and **BW** for Broadway.

The next three characters, represented by *BBB* in the pattern, give the font's size, in half-point increments. You have to imagine the decimal point between the second and third characters in this group. In the first example, the characters **12Ø** indicate that the font is 12.0 points high. In the second example, **145** means the font is 14.5 points high.

The sixth character, *C* in the pattern, stands for the font's style, weight, or both. **M** in the first example indicates an ordinary medium weight, upright font, while **X** in the second example signifies a bold-italic font. Here are the style and weight designations you'll see most often:

M	Medium
R	Regular
B	Bold

I   Italic

L   Light

X   Bold italic

(M and R are roughly synonymous)

The seventh and eighth characters in the name, represented by *DD* in the pattern, tell you what sort of character spacing the font employs. The letters **PN** in the first example indicate that this is a proportionally spaced font. If you find numbers instead of letters in this position in the name, as in the second example, they mean that you're dealing with a fixed space font. In the example, **Ø8** indicates this is a 8 pitch font.

Now we come to the font name's extension, starting after the period in the name. The first two letters of the extension, *EE* in the pattern, tell you what character set the font contains. Common character set abbreviations include:

DJ   Fonts that include all the standard DeskJet character sets

IB   IBM PC screen set, same as PC-8

LG   Legal

M#   Math, # is the number of the specific math set from 0 to 9

R8   Roman-8

SF   Various older LaserJet soft font sets

US   US ASCII

The final character refers to the font's orientation, portrait or landscape. That's *P* for portrait, *L* for landscape. Since DeskJet soft fonts always have the portrait orientation, the last letter in any font's filename extension should always be **P**. (Landscape soft fonts are available for the LaserJet, however.)

Mastering soft font challenges

Soft font users face three major challenges: soft fonts require lots of disk storage space, they need custom software drivers, and you have to download them to the DeskJet. Let's look at each of these requirements and consider strategies for coping with them.

Soft fonts and disk space

As you'll remember from Chapter 6, DeskJet fonts are bitmapped fonts, meaning that they specify the location of each and every dot in each and every character. With all the bits the font needs to represent all those dots, a font takes up a lot of room in the DeskJet's memory. The actual amount of memory consumed by a font depends on its size (since larger characters have more dots than smaller ones), the typeface design, and the number of characters in the character set. The range is usually between about 6K for 6 point fonts through about 15K for 12 point fonts to 45K or so for the 30 point fonts you can print on the DeskJet Plus.

Each soft font takes up a little more space on disk as it does in the DeskJet's RAM. When you consider that you need a separate soft font file for every point size, it's easy to see how you can wind up devoting several megabytes on your hard disk to a modest soft font collection.

✂ *Tip: One way to cut disk space requirements dramatically is to use one of the font generating packages mentioned earlier. MoreFonts and Glyphix create and download the specific font you request from small master typeface files as you print. The outlines are stored on disk, but not the fonts generated from them, which saves you lots of disk space. More on font generators later in this chapter.*

Managing your soft font files

Because soft font files are large, it's most convenient to store them on a hard disk, where they'll be accessible without having to shuffle and swap floppy disks. Downloading from a hard disk goes much faster, too. Assuming you do have a hard disk, the best way to keep track of your DeskJet soft fonts is to create a special directory for them. Making a new directory called **FONTS** is simple:

1. Switch to the root directory of you hard disk. If your hard disk is drive C, type

   c:⏎), then cd \⏎).

2. Now type the command **md \fonts⏎)**. The disk will chatter as DOS creates the directory you've specified.

Once the directory is ready, copy all the font files you use regularly there, where it'll be easy to find them when you need them. You may want to store soft fonts you use only occasionally on floppy disks, so they don't consume space on your hard disk that you could use instead for additional programs or documents.

Soft fonts and printer drivers

You may as well face the fact that it can be difficult or impossible to mix your soft fonts freely in a given document. The problem is that the DeskJet drivers in most programs are only set up to handle a limited number of soft fonts.

As you'll recall from Chapter 3, a printer driver is a supplementary software module that you must install into your main application program to get the program to work with your printer. The driver functions much like an interpreter, translating the commands a program uses for functions such as font or margin changes into the corresponding codes in the printer's native tongue.

As far as fonts are concerned, the driver detects the places in your document where you've switched from one font to another, and issues the corresponding font selection commands to the DeskJet when it's time to print that part of the file. A really good driver will even download the new font if it hasn't already been sent to the printer. In addition, the driver supplies the program with spacing information for each character in the font. The program uses this spacing information, called a *width table*, to format the text properly, so that the characters are positioned properly within the margins you've set up.

In the days before laser printers, computer printers had very few fonts, and a program could get by with one simple driver for each printer (still, that made for a tremendous number of drivers). With jillions of optional fonts in the picture, though, things get even more complicated. Since each typeface has a different numeric code and each font has a different width table, two DeskJets with two different sets of optional fonts are almost like two separate printers. Depending on your software, you may need a completely different driver for each set of optional fonts you install.

When you're talking about hundreds of fonts from many different suppliers, it's clearly impossible for anyone to write a DeskJet driver that will work with every available soft font. The DeskJet drivers that come with most application programs can only access the cartridge and soft fonts sold by HP, and often only a limited selection of these. That means that to get your program to print using your particular collection of soft fonts, you're going to have to come up with a custom driver somehow.

Many word processing programs, including WordPerfect and Microsoft, allow you to create your own drivers tailored to your soft fonts. Unfortunately, the process is difficult, time consuming, and fraught with the possibility for error. If you own one of these top-selling programs, your font vendor may let you off the hook by providing you with a special utility that creates custom soft font drivers for you. If you use a less popular program, though, you'll probably have to develop your own driver, assuming the program permits you to do so. Consult the program's publisher or ask your font supplier for help.

Downloading soft fonts

The remaining challenge with soft fonts is that you have to download them, a process that's a little tricky and can certainly be time consuming. These days, many application programs download your soft fonts for you, once you install the correct driver. If your program is capable of doing the downloading, all you have to do is tell it where you've stored the fonts you've used in your document (in other words, in which disk drive and directory they're located). When you give the print command, the program downloads the fonts called for without any further effort on your part. Microsoft Word and WordPerfect can both download soft fonts automatically.

Unfortunately, there are plenty of other programs that can't download soft fonts. What's more, it often makes sense to do your own downloading, even if your software can take care of the job. One reason is that the downloading process takes time. If you use a particular set of downloaded fonts for most of your documents, you can download all the fonts in the set when you first turn on the DeskJet each day. That way, your software just has to switch from one font to the next, rather than going through the whole downloading process again each time you select a new font. (Remember this, though: even if you never change the soft fonts you use during a given day, turning off the DeskJet clears the printer's memory, wiping out any soft fonts you've downloaded.)

If you don't rely on your application program to do your font downloading for you, you have two alternatives: you can do it yourself with DOS commands, or you can enlist the help of a font management utility. I heartily recommend the downloading utilities—they make the job almost painless. Still, I'll cover both methods in a moment, after some background on how the DeskJet keeps track of the downloaded fonts.

Soft font ID numbers

The DeskJet requires that every downloaded font be assigned a unique identification number during the downloading process. This ID number isn't permanently matched to that particular font. Instead, it's assigned arbitrarily at the time the font is downloaded either by you, if you're downloading from DOS, or by whatever software does the downloading for you. The ID number can be anything from 0 to 32767. Once the font has its ID number, an application program or utility can select it by that number with an escape sequence (or you can do the selecting yourself, as described in Chapter 22).

Though you can use the same ID number for different soft fonts if you like, only one font with a given number can be resident in the DeskJet at any one time. If you assign an ID number that's already in use to a new font, the previously downloaded font will no longer be accessible.

Permanent versus temporary soft fonts

Another choice that must be made at downloading time is whether the font will be assigned to permanent or temporary status. "Permanent" fonts remain intact when the printer receives a "soft reset" command, which many programs send every time they start or finish a printing job. You can still erase a permanent font from the DeskJet's memory, but to do so you must send a specific command to erase one or all of the current soft fonts.

To make the font you're downloading permanent, an appropriate escape sequence must be sent to the DeskJet immediately after the font itself has been downloaded. If you don't issue this escape sequence, the font you've downloaded will automatically be considered "temporary," and the DeskJet will erase the font from memory when it receives the soft reset command.

Either way, of course, all your soft fonts will vanish from the DeskJet's memory when you turn the printer off.

Managing DeskJet font memory

Even if you install the maximum amount of soft font RAM possible, 512K for a DeskJet Plus, you may have much less useable font memory than you think. This problem is especially noticeable with larger soft fonts—often you'll be unable to install a few large fonts whose total memory requirements are far less than what's apparently available.

The explanation lies in the design of the DeskJet's font memory circuits, which can only be accessed in 64K blocks. Although a large font can spill over from one block to the next, the character data you're actually using cannot cross a 64K boundary. That means that some large fonts simply won't fit in the DeskJet.

In addition, the DeskJet puts the font being downloaded into the largest free memory space still available, even when that's an inefficient decision. For example, if you have a 256K RAM cartridge you have four separate 64K blocks of memory available for font storage. If you download four 30K fonts, the DeskJet stores each one in its own 64K block, leaving 34K available in each block. So, although there's theoretically 136K left free in the cartridge, you can't download any additional font that's larger than 34K.

✄ *Tip: To fit the maximum possible number of fonts into the useable memory space, download your soft fonts in decreasing order according to their memory requirements. The best way to maximize the number of fonts you can download into your RAM cartridges is to download the largest soft fonts first, then the next largest, and so on. Let's see how this would have worked with the fonts in the example above. If you had started by downloading your largest font, say a 60K font, and had then downloaded a 40K font, you would still have had enough room for four 30K fonts—two would have fit in each of the two remaining 64K blocks of RAM.*

Downloading soft fonts from DOS

In essence, downloading a font file to the DeskJet using DOS commands is as simple as copying a file from one disk drive to another. Unfortunately, the process of downloading fonts from DOS is complicated by several factors. For one thing, you have to assign a font ID number to each font you download, and then keep track of these numbers yourself. For another, you must send an escape sequence to the printer before you download the font itself. Once the font is transferred, you must send another escape sequence to assign either permanent or temporary status to the font.

The major problem here is that on the DOS command line, you can't type the escape character, the one that begins every escape sequence (the escape character is ASCII code 27 in decimal notation and is represented by the symbol ← on your screen). The easiest way to get around this problem involves creating a batch file containing the escape character. Chapter 9 has all the details on controlling the DeskJet from DOS using this method, but I've summarized the instructions you'll need for soft font downloading here.

Before you begin, make sure you know the full filename of the font you want to download, as listed in the disk directory, and that you know the path (the disk and directory) where the font file is stored. For the rest of these instructions, I'll assume that your font is named TR120RPN.DJP and that it's parked on hard disk C: in the FONTS directory. The complete path and filename would then be *C:\FONTS\TR120RPN.DJP.*

The first step is to create the special file ESCAPE containing the escape character. Chapter 9 has the instructions in the section "The ESCAPE solution." Then, with the DeskJet powered up, connected, and online, you're ready to do the download. First, you must send the initial escape sequence that tells the DeskJet to expect a soft font download. Here's how:

1. Switch to the disk and directory where your fonts are stored by typing **c:**⏎, then **cd \fonts**⏎.

2. At the DOS prompt, type

   copy escape+con lpt1⏎

When you press ⏎, the cursor will drop down to the next line on your screen.

3. Now type

*c7D

This escape sequence tells the DeskJet to assign a temporary ID number to the font you're about to download, in this case 7. You can use any number you like between 0 and 32767 as long as it's not in use already by another font (don't type a comma for numbers larger than 999). Make note of the number you assign, because you'll need it to select the font for printing.

4. Press (F6) followed by ⏎ to send the escape sequence to the DeskJet.

Now download the font itself. On the DOS command line, type

copy c:\fonts\tr12Ørpn.djp lpt1 ⏎

This is the same COPY command you use to copy a file from one disk to another—the difference is that you've specified the printer port as the destination for the copy. As soon as you press ⏎ to start the download the disk will chatter as DOS sends the font file to the DeskJet. When the download is complete, you'll see the message:

1 File(s) copied

If you want the font you've just downloaded to remain "permanently" in the DeskJet's memory until you specifically erase it, or turn the printer off, you must finish the download by sending an escape sequence. If you just want to use the font once and don't mind if it gets erased, the DeskJet will automatically assign the font to temporary status. See the section "Permanent vs temporary soft fonts" earlier in this chapter for more on how permanent and temporary fonts work.

You'll need the ESCAPE file again to make the font permanent. Here are the steps:

1. On the command line, type

copy escape+con lpt1⏎

Just as before, the cursor drops down to the next line.

2. Type

*c5F

3. Press ⒡⒡ then ⏎ to send the command to the DeskJet. You've just protected the downloaded font against accidental erasure.

Downloading multiple fonts

You can download as many fonts as the DeskJet's RAM cartridge memory will hold—just repeat the above steps for each font in turn.

If you have specific sets of soft fonts that you use frequently, you can automate the downloading process for each set with a batch file. Again, Chapter 9 gives details on how to create batch files for controlling the DeskJet. As with all batch files, your font downloading batch file should be named with the .BAT extension. For example, you might call it FONTSET1.BAT.

For each font you want the file to download, enter the following three lines in your file:

echo ←*c#D >lpt1

copy /b *fontname* **lpt1**

echo ←*c5F >lpt1

In place of the word *fontname* above, type in the font's complete path and filename. Substitute a number between 0 and 32767 (don't use commas) for the # symbol in the first line as the font's temporary ID, using a different number for each font you download.

⌒\ **Caution:** *It's critical to use the ECHO command instead of COPY on the first and third lines. COPY would read those *'s in the escape sequences as DOS wildcards, and would try to copy files on your disk whose names end in c# D and c5F. Also, be sure to enter the > before lpt1 on the first and third lines, but not on the second line.*

For example, suppose you want to create a batch file to automatically download two fonts stored in your DJFONTS directory. If the fonts are named named CEN18RB0.DJP and PAS16RB0.DJP, your batch file should contain these lines:

```
echo ←*c10D >lpt1
copy /b \djfonts\cen18rb0.djp lpt1
echo ←*c5F >lpt1
echo ←*c11D >lpt1
copy /b \djfonts\pas16rb0.djp lpt1
echo ←*c5F >lpt1
```

Notice that I've arbitrarily assigned the temporary font ID numbers 10 and 11 with the first echo command for each font. You could use any other numbers instead, as long they don't conflict with those already in use by fonts you've previously downloaded.

To download the font set using your new batch file, all you have to do is type the name of the batch file at the DOS prompt, and press ⏎. In our example, you'd type **FONTSET1**⏎.

Downloading with font utilities

Now that you have some background on how the DeskJet handles your soft fonts in its memory, it's time to get practical. How do you actually download the fonts? The easiest and most reliable way is with the help of a good font management utility. Downloading with a font utility is as simple as finding the desired font on a menu and pressing a key. In addition, font utilities often have lots of extra features for helping you keep track of your fonts, and for making the downloading process seem faster.

In choosing a font management utility, you can opt for one which concentrates entirely on the font-related functions, or you can rely instead on one of the general purpose setup utilities that also has font management capabilities (these were described in Chapter 4). Either way, an ideal font utility should above all be easy to use—otherwise, you might as well do the downloading yourself with the DOS commands described in the next section. Specifically, look for these characteristics:

You should be able to control all the utility functions using simple, easy-to-follow menus.

The utility should automatically list the names of all the DeskJet soft fonts on your disk(s) for you, so that you can choose the fonts to download simply by picking their names from the list. If you have to type in the font names yourself, you'll waste time keeping written records of the names and doing the typing, and it's easy to make mistakes.

The utility should enable you to download sets of routinely used fonts all at once directly from the DOS prompt, without having to specify each font one by one from the menu. Typically, a program with this feature creates a separate file containing the names of the fonts you want in your set. When you give the command to download your font set, the utility then reads the file to see which fonts it should download.

At your option, you should be able to operate the downloading either as a standalone program (so you can reserve as much computer memory as possible for your application program) or as a pop-up memory resident (TSR) utility (so you can download fonts without leaving your application).

The two best font utilities for the DeskJet are BackLoader and TSR Download, each of which rates a profile here. In addition to these two programs, many downloading utilities for the LaserJet will work adequately, including some available as shareware.

Using your soft fonts

Downloading your soft fonts to the DeskJet is only half the battle. The other major hurdle you'll face is selecting the soft font you want to use, so that you can print your text in that font. Whenever possible, use your application program to select the font you'll be printing with. If your program lacks a driver for your soft fonts, your next best bet is to use a font management utility. If all else fails, you'll have to select them yourself from within your application or via DOS commands. Use the general approach for sending commands to the DeskJet outlined in Chapter 8, and see Chapter 22 for the details on using the font selection commands.

Profile: BackLoader 2

$89 /Roxxolid Corporation
3345 Vincent Road
Pleasant Hill, CA 94523
800/336-7699

The supreme DeskJet font management utility is BackLoader, now in release 2. BackLoader makes using soft fonts so much quicker and easier that you should consider buying it even if all your application programs can download soft fonts for you.

Like most DeskJet utilities, BackLoader is a memory resident program, and you can pop it up whenever you need it. But where other font utilities do their downloading when you ask them to—which seems to make sense—BackLoader takes a different tack. It starts by downloading all your most frequently used fonts to the DeskJet, so they'll be there when called for. Then, as you print each document, BackLoader monitors the printer output from your program. When it detects a font selection command, BackLoader checks its list of all the fonts currently installed in the DeskJet. If the font is already available in the printer, BackLoader just passes the font command on. On the other hand, if the font isn't yet installed, BackLoader downloads it on the spot. If there's no more room in the DeskJet's memory for another font, BackLoader removes the fonts you've used least recently until the new font will fit.

All this assumes that your application program knows enough about the DeskJet to send the right font selection commands in the first place—in other words, that the program has a driver that allows it to work with your soft fonts. But even if your program doesn't know Courier from Cooper Black, you can still change fonts to your heart's content with BackLoader.

This very powerful feature relies on simple "tags" you define as abbreviations for your fonts. For instance, you might define the tag ~6 as an abbreviation for a 10 point Times Roman italic font, and ~7 for 10 point regular Times Roman. To use the italic font in a document, you would type **~6** just before the word you want printed in italics, and **~7** after it. When BackLoader detects the tag in your printer output, it downloads the corresponding font, if necessary, and then selects it. The tag technique allows you to vary fonts in almost any kind of printed document, whether it's a spreadsheet, an accounting report, or a database. Of course, since the application program doesn't know what you're up to, it can't control the spacing of individual letters, and you may not get properly aligned columns and margins if you vary fonts within a block of text or a table.

BackLoader also lets you use the same method to insert any printer command in any document. Once you've defined the control code or escape sequence, you just enter an easy-to-remember (and easy-to-type) abbreviation in the file, and BackLoader will see to it that the DeskJet gets your orders.

Such outstanding service is impressive enough, but it's only half of the story. When BackLoader downloads a font, it doesn't take complete control of your PC. Instead, it works in the background, sending a small chunk of the font data out every few fractions of a second. Where this comes in handy is when BackLoader is downloading that set of frequently used fonts at the beginning of a session, or if you choose to manually download a font. Instead of staring at your screen for a minute or two as you wait for the download to finish, you'll be returned to your work moments after it gets started. As you work, BackLoader will continue to send the fonts to the DeskJet, but you'll hardly notice the interruptions.

BackLoader 2 even makes the process of cataloging your soft fonts automatic. Since it can search your entire hard disk for font files, you don't have to keep your fonts in one directory, if that's your preference. You do have to tell it which cartridge fonts you've installed, if any.

Profile: TSR Download

$35/Elfring Soft Fonts
P.O. Box 61
Wasco, IL 60183
312/377-3520

Another excellent font management utility for the DeskJet, and a real bargain, is Elfring Soft Fonts' TSR Download. Mr. Elfring is the purveyor of one of the best collections of DeskJet soft fonts available, and sells similar products for the LaserJet family.

TSR Download doesn't have quite as many features as BackLoader, but it covers the crucial bases, and it's considerably less expensive. Only $35 gets you a copy of the program, and for just $40 more you can add a full set of DeskJet fonts, Elfring's imitations of Times Roman and Helvetica in sizes from 8 to 30 points. The 30-point fonts contain only numerals, punctuation marks, and uppercase letters, so they work on the original DeskJet as well as the DeskJet Plus.

As its name indicates, TSR Download is a pop-up memory resident utility, but it can also be run as an ordinary non-resident program if you prefer. When you pop up the memory resident version, it displays a list of the filenames of up to 100 soft fonts in the current font directory. When you highlight a particular filename, you'll see a brief description of the font in understandable English.

To download one or more fonts, you start by marking them on the list. While you're making your selections, TSR Download displays a running total of their memory requirements in the DeskJet along with the memory consumed by any fonts that have already been downloaded. When you're ready to download, you hit the **d** key to send the marked fonts off to the printer. Once you've downloaded your fonts, you can select any of them as your default font. The program also lets you remove fonts from the DeskJet's memory when they're no longer needed.

As an alternative to pop-up downloading, you can use TSR Download's font list to create files containing the names of your favorite sets of soft fonts. To download one of these sets, you supply its filename when you run TSR Download. The program will transfer the fonts to the printer and then quit, without becoming memory resident.

An accompanying program, FONTCAT, prints a complete listing of all your soft fonts, showing each font's name, typeface, point size, and so on. Another plus with TSR Download is that its manual includes a succinct primer on soft fonts. And though it's primarily intended for managing fonts, TSR Download lets you control other important aspects of DeskJet setup as well. You can eject a page, reset the printer, switch from portrait to landscape mode and back, and choose the number of lines per inch.

Font generators

Ordinary soft fonts may be more flexible than the cartridge variety, but they still limit you to printing at fixed point sizes. To overcome this limitation, several companies market font generators, which build fonts according to your specifications.

The DeskJet soft fonts sold by HP and many other suppliers are distributed in separate ready-to-download files for each point size. In a TmsRmn soft font collection, for example, there'll be one file for the 12 point font, another for the 14 point font, and so on. You must download the specific font file for each point size you want to print, and you can't print in 13-point TmsRmn at all, because there's no file for a 13-point font in the set.

By contrast, a font generator package doesn't come with any size-specific font files. Instead, it consists of a program that converts a *master outline* of the typeface you select into a downloadable font at whatever point size you wish to generate. With a font generator, you can build a complete library of fonts at every point size the DeskJet can print, for each master typeface you own.

Font generation programs face a significant challenge in maintaining the quality of the generated fonts across the entire range of point sizes that are possible. To make a large character, for example, you can't just double the number of dots in a small character, because smooth curves would take on a jagged, stairstep appearance. Instead, you have to add more dots to fill in the rough edges. Likewise, you can't start with a large character and shrink it down—if you'll try, the result will have too many dots, and will be smudged-looking and maybe even unreadable.

To avoid these problems, a font generation program has to use complex software routines to convert the master outline to a font that's optimized for a particular size. There's a lot of room for alternative solutions to this challenge, and as you'd expect, some font generators do the job better than others.

Before the fact vs on the fly

Ignoring differences in quality the fonts they generate, there are two broad categories of font generators. The approach taken by Fontware, the leading font generation product for LaserJets, and by MoreFonts, is to generate the fonts in advance, and then store them on disk for downloading when you need them. Once you've generated a font with Fontware, the resulting file is just like the ones you buy from HP.

Another way to skin the same carrot is to generate the fonts only when you need them, during the printing process itself. In this system, used by Glyphix, the font generator also takes care of downloading the newly generated fonts for you. This way, you only have to store the font generator program and the master outline on your hard disk, not finished font files totalling many megabytes. Of course, there's a disadvantage in generating fonts on the fly—it takes longer than downloading prefab fonts.

Fontware

Bitstream's Fontware is the best known and most widely used font generating product for LaserJets and their ilk, and the line of Bitstream typefaces is extensive and of high quality. Unfortunately, the WordPerfect 5.0 version of Fontware is the only one that generates DeskJet fonts at this writing. In addition, the quality of Fontware's DeskJet fonts isn't as high as that of its excellent LaserJet offerings. Still, since the Fontware starter kit is free to registered WordPerfect users it can't hurt to give it a try. Fontware generates its fonts before you print, rather than on the fly. That means you must make room for both the bulky Fontware program and all the fonts you generate on your hard disk.

Profile: *MoreFonts*

$99.95/MicroLogic Software, Inc.
6400 Hollis St., Suite 9
Emeryville, CA 94608
800/888-9078

MoreFonts, a font generator from MicroLogic Software, is one of the best values in DeskJet fonts. For one low $99.95 price, MoreFonts comes standard with 14 typefaces that you can turn into fonts in any point size the DeskJet can print: up to 23 points for the original DeskJet, and 45 points for the DeskJet Plus via limited character sets. But MoreFonts doesn't stop there: font downloading, screen fonts for applications that display in graphics mode, and special font effects are all part of the package.

The typefaces supplied with MoreFonts cover a lot of typographic territory. The core of the set is two complete typeface families, creditable imitations of the ever-popular Times Roman and Helvetica. The members of each family include Italic, Bold, Bold Italic, and regular faces. Five display faces, including MoreFonts' versions of Broadway, Cooper Black, Coronet, University, and Bodoni, are provided for eye-catching headlines and titles. There's also a version of Letter Gothic, a monospaced sans-serif typeface whose narrow characters often make it a better choice for reports than Courier.

What's more, your fonts aren't limited to plain all-black characters. During font generation, any of the available typefaces can be gussied up with a variety of special effects. For example, you can select from eight patterns for the interiors of the characters—the parts that are normally solid black—in-

Figure 7-2: MoreFonts lets you view the special effects you're adding before you actually generate the font.

cluding stripes, a wood grain effect, "starry night," and so forth. In addition, you can add shadow effects ("drop shadows") or outlines of varying thickness. If you have a graphics monitor, you can see sample characters to get a good idea of how your custom font will look in print. Figure 7-2 shows an example of a MoreFonts screen showing a gaudily dressed-up rendition of the MoreFonts Showtime typeface (the Broadway imitation).

Once you've chosen the size, character set, and any special effects you want for your new font, you can print out a sample at the touch of a key. MoreFonts will make the necessary printer drivers for WordPerfect, Word, XyWrite, First Publisher, so you can go right to work with these programs without worrying about the messy details of width tables and so on. After installing a MoreFonts font in WordPerfect, for example, you just select the new font's name from WordPerfect's list of available soft fonts to make it available for your documents. Unfortunately, MoreFonts doesn't work with Windows—while the utility does a great job of installing LaserJet fonts for Windows, the DeskJet driver for Windows doesn't support soft fonts from any source.

MoreFonts is as easy to use as it is powerful. You control the whole program from an intelligently designed drop-down menu system using either the keyboard or the mouse. With thorough context sensitive help always available, you can dispense with the manual once you've installed the program. Although you have to generate each font you want to use ahead of time and store it on disk, the program itself and the stock typeface outlines require a reasonable 700K, far less than the Bitstream system.

Profile: Glyphix

$99.95/SWFTE International
P.O. Box 219
Rockland, DE 19732
800/237-9383; 302/658-1123

Glyphix, a popular and inexpensive font generator for LaserJet printers, had just been upgraded to work with the DeskJet at the time this book went to press. Though slightly behind MoreFonts in getting to market, Glyphix offers much the same list of features. You can create fonts in any size that suits you from a variety of master typefaces, either ahead of time as soft font files, or on the fly at print time. Glyphix gives you special effects too. You can choose reversed type, various shades, stripes, and shadows for any font you generate.

Glyphix goes MoreFonts one better in letting you break the DeskJet's 30 point font size limit. When you want to print text in a font larger than 30 points, Glyphix translates the characters into graphics and sends the resulting data to your printer. The result is just as good as if you'd used a built-in DeskJet font.

If you're a Microsoft Word or WordPerfect user, you'll appreciate the trouble SWFTE has gone to in tailoring special drivers for your word processor. The Word and WordPerfect drivers let you make full use of all your Glyphix fonts, including special effects, from these programs. In addition, they give Glyphix the same sort of DeskJet memory management capabilities as BackLoader. With Word or WordPerfect, Glyphix knows which fonts have already been downloaded, and automatically downloads only the ones you need when your document calls for them. Likewise, it deletes rarely used fonts to make room for new ones when necessary. Unfortunately, all these features work only with Glyphix fonts, so you're on your own if you want to mix them with fonts from other vendors.

Converting LaserJet fonts to DeskJet format

LaserJet owners can choose from literally hundreds of different soft fonts, but so far DeskJet users are stuck with relatively few. You can stake a claim in the LaserJet typographic gold mine with one of two utilities that convert LaserJet fonts to a format the DeskJet can understand. This solution isn't perfect, but it's more than good enough for most people.

The reason you can't use LaserJet fonts on a DeskJet isn't because HP set out to deprive you. Instead, the design team recognized that LaserJet-format fonts wouldn't have produced optimum text quality on the DeskJet because of inherent technical differences between the two printers. For one thing, the LaserJet reads font bitmaps horizontally, while the DeskJet reads them vertically. More important, a dot printed by the LaserJet is slightly oblong, while one printed by the DeskJet is closer to being perfectly round, meaning that the same dot pattern would result in slightly different character appearance on the two printers. HP therefore decided to create a new font format that would give the highest possible text quality on the DeskJet.

The big question is whether you would have noticed the difference between that "highest possible" quality and the second-best quality you can get from LaserJet fonts. For most people, the answer is probably "no." Although close scrutiny will reveal that the converted fonts have more of the jaggies than true DeskJet fonts do, the characters are still quite sharp. Besides, having hundreds of fonts to choose from, many of them free for the asking, should make up for the loss of quality.

A couple of obvious limitations confront any font conversion utility for the DeskJet. One is size—you can't convert fonts that are larger than the DeskJet can print. Another is the fact that the DeskJet doesn't accept downloaded landscape fonts, so LaserJet landscape fonts won't work either.

✂ *Tip:* *To use LaserJet fonts without these limitations, turn to the LaserTwin emulation utility profiled back in Chapter 4. Rather than converting the fonts to DeskJet format, LaserTwin uses them to build its own graphic image of the page, including text, just as a real LaserJet would. It then sends this page in graphics mode out to the DeskJet. This way, you can print LaserJet fonts of any size or orientation.*

JETDESK

JETDESK's approach is to convert LaserJet fonts to DeskJet format as you download them. All you do is type the name of the program on the DOS command line, followed by the name of the LaserJet font file you want to download. JETDESK reads the file, translates it to DeskJet format, and downloads it, and you can then select it with whatever means you normally use. You can convert multiple files at once by specifying them with DOS wild cards, but JETDESK will only work with fonts that are 18 points or smaller.

Profile: LJ2DESK

$42/S.H. Moody & Associates
1810 Fair Oaks Ave.
South Pasadena, CA 91030

LJ2DESK is a more complete solution to the challenges of LaserJet-to-DeskJet font conversion. In addition to the conversion program proper, the package comes with several great utilities that make it much easier to choose the fonts you want to convert and to use them once they're in DeskJet format. If you use soft fonts from any source, whether or not you're interested in converting LaserJet fonts, you should add LJ2DESK to your utility collection.

In contrast to JETDESK, LJ2DESK carries out the conversion process ahead of time, creating permanent DeskJet font files you can store on your disk. This saves you time in the long run, since you don't need to wait for the conversion every time you download.

To save memory and downloading time, you can pick out particular characters from those in the original LaserJet font, omitting the ones you don't plan to use. During the conversion you can make adjustments in the positioning of each character relative to the baseline, and in the font's x-height, the height of a lowercase *x*. LJ2DESK can convert up to 100 fonts in a single pass. All the fonts prepared by LJ2DESK are formatted so that you can print them on the DeskJet at half size, in boldface, or both.

Several other utilities come with LJ2DESK. Before you convert the font, you can use FONTVIEW to display the original font's characters one by one on

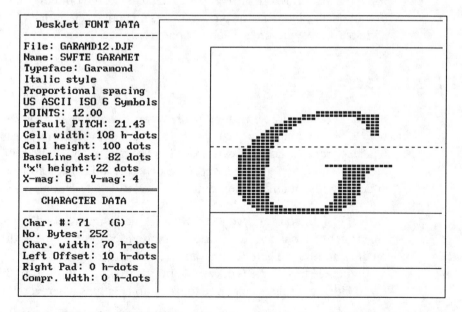

Figure 7-3: The FONTVIEW utility lets you examine any DeskJet or LaserJet font.

a graphics monitor. That way, you can decide which characters you want to convert, or whether you want to convert the font at all. When FONTVIEW is finished, it displays the complete escape sequence you'd need to send to select that font. You can also view DeskJet fonts with FONTVIEW, as shown in the illustration in Figure 7-3.

Then there's the FONTWID utility. FONTWID is a necessity for using the converted fonts with your word processor or desktop publishing program, but it should be in your library even if you don't ever plan to use a LaserJet font. FONTWID reads any LaserJet or DeskJet font file and constructs a width table containing all the information you must supply to your word processor when you create a custom driver for the new font. Without the width table, the word processor won't be able to space the characters properly, and will botch formatting chores such as letterspacing, centering, and justification. If you ever have trouble finding width table information for any DeskJet font, turn to FONTWID.

Rounding out the LJ2DESK package is a font downloading utility and a simple batch file that prints out the complete character set of your new font. Utilities that automatically create the proper drivers for your soft fonts for WordPerfect and Microsoft Word are available separately.

Font effects

If you're looking for something really distinctive in the way of a typeface, why not create your own? Actually, I'm not suggesting that you design a new typeface from scratch, but what you might want to try is doctoring up an ordinary typeface with a few special touches. A judiciously applied special effect or two can turn a humdrum typeface into a one-of-a-kind standout.

With the right software, you can replace the normally solid black of the characters with shades, lines, or even random patterns, you can draw bold outlines around the letterforms, and you can add shadow effects or patterns around the letters. Some typographic purists frown on this sort of thing, but if you like the results, you're free to use your creations wherever you see fit.

Owners of LaserJets and PostScript printers have far more options in choosing software for font special effects. So far, only the MoreFonts and Glyphix font generators described earlier in this chapter let you perform such trickery, and only on their own fonts. For the LaserJet, the best font effects program available is called, well, Font Effects. Font Effects isn't available for the DeskJet, but you can convert LaserJet fonts modified with the program to DeskJet format using the LJ2DESK utility.

When you use MoreFonts, Glyphix, or Font Effects to create special effects, the resulting characters comprise real fonts that you print in the DeskJet's standard text mode. Another route to special font effects is through graphics mode. Graphics programs such as Corel Draw and Artline not only let you add patterns, outlines, and shadows to the characters you type, but they also let you change the outlines of the characters themselves. In this case, though, you have to enter all the text you want to print with the effects into your graphics program—you can't print a word processor file in the modified font.

Access: Font utilities

Font Effects/$95
SoftCraft, Inc.
16 N. Carroll St. #500
Madison, WI 53703
608/257-3300

JETDESK/$19.95
Koch Software Industries, Inc.
11 West College Drive, Bldg G
Arlington Heights, IL 60004
312/398-5440

Application Software

8

Working With Applications

∽

With this chapter, we begin a long section devoted to helping you get the most from your DeskJet with your application programs, so that your printed documents will look as classy as possible no matter what programs you use.

In this preliminary chapter, you'll learn fundamentals that will help you achieve harmony between the DeskJet and almost any program. Major topics we'll cover include how and why to choose the best DeskJet driver available for your software, and, when drivers fail you, the various methods for sending printer command from within an application program.

The remaining chapters of the section cover ways to get the most from you DeskJet using DOS and the most popular application programs ranging from word processing to spreadsheets and databases to graphics and desktop publishing.

Choosing a DeskJet driver

Without exception, the safest, smoothest route to excellent results with the DeskJet is to use a program comes with a good DeskJet driver of its own.

You'll recall that printer drivers are special software modules specific to your particular printer that "dock" into your main application program. A driver serves as the interpreter between your program and the printer, translating what the program wants to print into commands the printer can understand. A well-written DeskJet driver will let you access both text and graphics modes, mix internal, cartridge and soft fonts in the same document, control spacing of your text and resolution of your graphics, and tap the improvements available in the DeskJet Plus.

Given the rapidly growing popularity of the DeskJet, it shouldn't be long before all the major applications supply decent DeskJet and DeskJet Plus drivers. At the moment, though, that utopia is still some distance in the future. Many programs still don't provide DeskJet drivers at all. Many others have inadequate drivers, or their drivers don't support the new features of the DeskJet Plus. A small toolbag of utilities (covered in Chapters 4 and 7) and software tricks (introduced in this chapter) will get you through these tight spots.

How to get the DeskJet to work with any program

In the chapters to come on specific applications, I'll let you know whenever the program under discussion includes a DeskJet driver, and tell you how to use it for best results. We'll also cover any limitations the driver may have, and how to circumvent them. If a driver is lacking altogether, I'll offer workarounds tailored to that program that will get you as close to as possible to printing paradise.

For now, though, let's look at the approach that the head-scratching DeskJet owner should take when confronting the generic application program. Here are the steps to follow:

1. Consult your software owner's manual to see if the program comes with a printer driver designed for the DeskJet. If you own a DeskJet Plus, try to find instructions that pertain specifically to that model—otherwise, you may give up some of the features of your improved printer.

In addition to reading the main manual, be sure you also look for any supplementary instructions, and for a README file on the program disk, that may contain further printer advice. Software vendors are always playing catchup to make sure that their programs can work with with popular new printers. Even if there's no mention whatsoever of the DeskJet in your software documentation, a DeskJet driver may have been created since the manual was printed.

If the program does come with specific support for the DeskJet, read the description of what DeskJet features you can and can't use. Often, you'll face limitations such as being only able to print with certain fonts. If the driver supports every feature of your DeskJet model, you're home free. If you find some limitations, skip to step 4.

2. If you don't find specific DeskJet instructions listed anywhere, call the software publisher, and ask if they've come up with a DeskJet driver yet. If so, the publisher will send it to you for free or for a nominal fee. (On second though, even if the program does have a DeskJet driver, call the vendor anyway—they may have a newer, better version of the driver to send you.) If the publisher confirms that there's no DeskJet driver, it's on to step 3.

3. If your software just doesn't supply a DeskJet-specific printer driver, your next best bet is to install a LaserJet driver instead. These days, the LaserJet is as much a standard as any other printer make or model, and every program worth its salt comes with a LaserJet driver. Since the DeskJet understands most of the same commands that control the LaserJet, you can substitute a LaserJet driver for the missing DeskJet one with good to excellent results.

Using a LaserJet driver, you'll certainly be able to print text, but the characters may not be spaced properly. Graphics files may print just fine, or not at all, depending on the program in which they were created. Test the system, take note of any problems you find, and skip to step 4.

✂ *Tip:* *To get reliably superior printouts using a LaserJet driver, use the LaserTwin utility profiled in Chapter 4. LaserTwin is a LaserJet emulation utility that lets your DeskJet print any page an LaserJet can handle.*

4. If the DeskJet or LaserJet driver you've adopted won't let you achieve the printed results you want, or if you're using some stoneage program that doesn't even support the LaserJet, you have two choices. First, consider using a utility such as BackLoader (Chapter 7), which lets you place DeskJet commands in any document, or LaserControl (Chapter 4), an emulation utility that makes the DeskJet emulate a number of common printers, one of which the software probably does recognize. If you don't want to use a utility, go on to step 5.

5. If all else fails, you'll have to send the necessary commands yourself. If your program permits, you can add the printer commands within your document, a process discussed in the remainder of this chapter. If not, you must send the commands via DOS, as described in Chapter 9.

Doing it your way

The rest of this chapter is devoted to an introduction to DeskJet commands (control codes and escape sequences) and how to use them in conjunction with application programs to get the printouts you want. First, you'll learn about the various ways you can send printer commands from different applications. Then we'll look at some of the most important escape sequences.

♪ *Note:* *Chapter 22 on DeskJet programming describes all of the commands individually and in detail. Even if you don't plan to write your own drivers or standalone programs for the DeskJet, you may want to read Chapter 22 once you're familiar with the basic commands.*

Escape sequences

Back in Chapter 3 you met your first escape sequence, the one used to turn on underlining. It's time for a closer look at the underlining command and what each of the characters in that escape sequence do. Here it is again, printed first in the format usually used for escape sequences: **ᴱsᴄ&d1D** and then in decimal notation: **27 38 100 49 68**. Reading from left to right, there's a one-to-one correspondence between the two printed versions of our sequence. **ᴱsᴄ** represents the escape character, code 27. The ampersand is code, 38, the lowercase *d* code 100, and so on.

Unfortunately, as you can see immediately, the code numbers HP chose for the escape sequences don't translate into printed characters all that well—the notation looks dense and inscrutable. And besides being hard to read overall, HP's code uses some letters and numbers that look too much alike. For example, many escape sequences use the lower case letter l (that's "el," as in "lois lane" or "lex luthor"). Of course, a lower case "l" looks much like the numeral "1" (one), a number that also appears frequently in escape sequences.

It's a perfect setup for making horrendous mistakes in entering these codes. The stopgap solution HP came up with was to print the "els" in cursive. But in HP publications, you're on your own when it comes to distinguishing upper case "O"s (ohs) from "0"s (zeros). In this book, however, I'll use Ø (a zero with a slash through it) to represent zero, and an ordinary O for capital *O*.

Even without the mistaken identity problems, DeskJet escape sequences are simply unattractive jumbles, with nothing mnemonic about them. Upper and lower case letters, numbers, and miscellaneous punctuation marks seem to appear randomly. Actually, there is a trace of a pattern in the coding system, which you can read about in Chapter 22. The practical point is this: be sure you concentrate on your typing while you enter escape sequences, and proofread very carefully.

Printer commands for the sorcerer's apprentice

The available DeskJet commands are so numerous and powerful that they can be considered a special-purpose programming language. But for most everyday text printing chores, a handful of printer commands will suffice.

Being able to change fonts, margins, and type style *within* a document is the most important reason for learning how to use printer commands. If you want to italicize one word in a line, and then underline another in that same line, like this:

Joyce's *Ulysses* is a thick book.

you must find a way to send four commands to the printer within the stream of characters on that line. One escape sequence must come just before the italicized *Ulysses* to turn on the italic font, and another immediately after to restore the ordinary font. You then have to bracket the underlined thick with a second on/off pair of escape sequences.

So, what you need is a way to place or *embed* printer commands directly into a document at the point in the file where they are to take effect. However, if the reason for embedding commands in a file makes sense, the method is not so obvious. The problem is that you can't just type in the necessary codes from your keyboard. Even though you have keys labelled (ESC) and (CTRL), pressing these keys won't do the trick—application programs use them for their own commands, as you well know.

Unfortunately, there's no standard system for sending commands to the DeskJet (or any printer, for that matter) that will work in all application programs. Yes, the computer eventually has to deliver the right codes to the printer cable, but how you tell it to do that varies significantly from program to program. And a good many programs make no provision for printer commands at all. As always, the best way to find out how your software works is to consult the owner's manual. If the program permits you to send printer commands to your DeskJet, there should be a reference in the index to "printer commands" or "escape sequences." Meanwhile, though, the following discussion should prepare you for what you'll find in the manual.

♪ ***Note:*** *If your program does not permit you to embed printer commands in your files, you can still control many printer features from DOS. See Chapter 9 for details.*

Some programs have a special mode just for the purpose of embedding printer codes. You give a particular command that signals the program to interpret the next keystrokes you type as printer codes, instead of acting on the keys as it normally would. When you're finished entering the printer codes, you press another special keystroke to return to normal program operation. In WordPerfect 5.0, for example, you type the keystroke sequence (SHIFT)(F8) **4 6 2 1** to activate the Printer Commands feature, then type in the printer codes themselves. When you're through typing printer commands, you press (F7) to return to your document.

Programs that use this system may let you enter the printer commands themselves in several different ways. In some cases, you simply type the associated keys. For example, in the text editor Brief, you press the (ESC) key to embed the numeric value of the escape code in your file (in Brief, as in most other programs that use this system, you see the escape character ← on your screen). On the other hand, other programs including WordPerfect require you to type in some or all of the code numbers digit by digit, as discussed in the next few paragraphs.

In programs that don't have a special mode for entering printer commands, you may be able to embed the necessary codes typing them directly into your file preceded by a particular character such as the backslash (\). When the program detects this special character, it knows to send the characters that follow directly to the printer. You still can't type "unprintable" characters such as escape or the control codes, so you have to enter them as numerals.

Lotus 1-2-3 Release 2.2 and earlier and many other spreadsheets and databases work this way. In 1-2-3, the escape sequence for turning underlining on would be embedded in a spreadsheet file as **\Ø27&d1D.**

The numerals **Ø27** represent the numeric value of the ASCII code for the escape code. When 1-2-3 reads this value as it prints the file, it send will a code 27 as single byte to your DeskJet, not separate bytes for the codes for "Ø", "2," and "7." Since the rest of the entries in the sequence are ordinary keyboard characters, you can enter by typing them directly.

Some programs require you to enter the entire sequence of printer code values in numeric form, even the codes for characters you'd be able to type directly on the keyboard. In a program of this type, you'd have to type in the escape sequence for underlining shown above as \Ø27\Ø38\1ØØ\Ø49\Ø68.

Using common printer commands

Now that you know how to embed printer commands in your documents, the question remaining is which commands to use. Here's a quick introduction to the escape sequences and control codes you'll need most often. Again, these and all the other escape sequences and control codes are covered in detail in Chapter 22.

Underlining

The DeskJet offers several different underlining options, all of which are detailed in Chapter 22. To cut down on the confusion, only the escape sequences for the standard type of underlining are listed here. To underline a word or phrase, you embed a pair of escape sequences in your text, one immediately before the passage to be underlined to turn underlining on, and one immediately after the passage to stop the underlining.

      ^{E}s$_c$&dØD   Turn underlining on

      ^{E}s$_c$&d@   Turn underlining off

Here's an example of underlined text, followed by the file that produced it showing the embedded escape sequences.

The rain in Spain falls <u>mainly</u> on the plain.

The rain in Spain falls ^{E}s$_c$&dØDmainly^{E}s$_c$&d@ on the plain.

Printing bold text

As you'll recall from Chapter 6 almost any DeskJet font can be printed in boldface. Here are the escape sequences that turn boldface type on and off:

        ^Es_c**(s3B**   Begin boldface printing

        ^Es_c**(sØB**   End boldface, return to ordinary text

To print the line

> A motion to adjourn is **always** in order.

your file should read

> A motion to adjourn is ^Es_c(s3BalwaysE_{sc}(sØB in order.

Printing italic text

The DeskJet understands two escape sequences related to italics: one to switch from ordinary straight up-and-down characters to slanty, italicized text, the other to switch back to regular characters.

⌢ *Caution: You can only switch to italics with the simple command you're about to learn if you have an italics font installed in your printer that's otherwise identical to the font you're currently using (same typeface, point size, character set, and so forth). Note especially that the original DeskJet's internal font set does not include an italic version of Courier, a deficit that was corrected in the DeskJet Plus.*

To print a word, a phrase, or an entire page in italics, surround the passage with these codes:

        ^Es_c**(s1S**   Enable italics

        ^Es_c**(sØS**   Italics off

For example, to print the second verse of Genesis as rendered in the King James Bible,

> And the earth was without form, and void;
> and darkness *was* upon the face of the deep.

your file should look like this:

And the earth was without form, and void;
and darkness ^{E}s$_C$(s1Swas^{E}s$_C$(sØS upon the face of the deep.

Printing super- and subscripted text

To print one or more characters above or below the normal text baseline, embed the following escape sequences around the characters to be super- or subscripted:

^{E}s$_C$(**s1U**   Turn on superscripting

^{E}s$_C$(**s-1U**   Turn on subscripting

^{E}s$_C$(**sØU**   Turn off super- or subscripting

So, to print

$$E = MC^2$$

your file should look like this:

E = MC^{E}s$_C$(s1U2^{E}s$_C$(sØU

Setting margins

With the proper escape sequences, you can reset the margins as often as you like within a single document.

^{E}s$_C$&a#**L**   Left margin

^{E}s$_C$&a#**M**   Right margin

Margins are measured in columns, so replace the # in the above sequences with the numeric value of your desired margin, in columns. The size of a column depends on the current print pitch. You can use Table 8-1 to figure out the column number for the margin you want.

Pitch	Column for Desired Margin		
	.5"	1"	2"
5	2	5	10
10	5	10	20
16.67	8	16	33
20	10	20	40

Table 8-1: *Column settings for various margins, to be used in escape sequences*

For fractional margins greater than an inch, add the column numbers for the component measurements. For a 1½" margin at 10 pitch, for example, you'd send the escape sequence E_{s_c}&a15L (15 = 5+10).

Changing page orientation

In portrait mode, the long edge of the paper runs vertically, and you have lots of lines but not so many columns. In landscape mode, the long edge is oriented horizontally, so you can fit long lines, though not as many on a single page.

The DeskJet is capable of printing in either orientation, although in the landscape orientation only a very few fonts are available, and you can't print graphics at all. The DeskJet Plus has a couple of built-in landscape fonts, but you need a landscape font cartridge for the original DeskJet. If you do have landscape fonts installed in your printer, selecting landscape mode automatically selects the one that's most like the font you were using in portrait mode, so you don't have to specifically select a font unless you want to.

To switch from portrait to landscape or vice versa within a document, here are the escape sequences you'll need (the l's are lowercase "el"s):

E_{s_c}&l1O   Select landscape orientation

E_{s_c}&lØO   Select portrait orientation

Creating a page break

If you want a new section or chapter in your document to start at the top of the page, you'll need to send a command that makes the DeskJet eject the current and page and start in again with the next one. The command in question is the form feed, or Ctrl-L, a one-byte control code with the ASCII value of **12**.

Selecting print quality

As you'll recall, the DeskJet can print text using a razor sharp, letter quality mode, or in a faster but somewhat less impressive-looking draft mode. In most cases, it's easier just to lean over and hit the MODE button on the keypad. But if you do want to change modes via software, the necessary escape sequences are:

^{E}s$_C$(s2Q   Letter quality mode

^{E}s$_C$(s1Q   Draft mode

Choosing fonts

Chapter 6 introduced you to the techniques for selecting fonts via printer commands, but the details are complicated. Although I'll leave the full disussion of font selection commands for Chapter 22, the italics and boldface commands given above qualify as commands in that category.

9

Controlling the DeskJet from DOS

~

Although there are quicker, easier, more elegant ways to get the DeskJet to do your bidding, sometimes your best bet is to control the printer directly from DOS. Two situations in which it's handy to communicate with the DeskJet from DOS immediately come to mind. Here's the first: you'd like to print a short DOS text file directly from the DOS prompt, without going through the bother of loading the file into your word processor first. Unless you want to reformat the file, you don't gain anything by printing a DOS text file from your word processor, and you lose time as you wait for the word processor to get itself started and then to import the file.

The second scenario involves sending printer commands to the DeskJet. Let's say that to print a particular document to your liking, you need to switch to another font or set new margins before you start printing. The problem is that you're using WERDS.EXE, a backwards application program that doesn't have a DeskJet driver, and doesn't allow you to embed your own escape sequences directly in the file.

A better-than-nothing solution is to send the DeskJet setup commands from DOS, and then run your application and print the document. You'll have to be content with the same font, margins, and other settings for the entire document, but at least you aren't stuck with the printer settings in effect before you started.

Printing DOS text files

Plain DOS text files are everywhere. Good examples are the READ.ME files that software companies often place on program disks, and the files you download from an electronic bulletin board (such as CompuServe) or e-mail (electronic mail, such as MCI Mail) system.

A plain text file is the kind that looks like it's supposed to— not full of strange characters scattered wildly around the screen—when you view it on the screen with DOS's TYPE command (see your DOS manual if you're unfamiliar with TYPE). The reason is that DOS text files consist entirely of ordinary characters stored in ASCII code format, and have none of the special formatting codes peculiar to a particular program.

The simplest way to print a plain text file from DOS is by COPYing it to the printer. If your file is called OPUS.TXT, you type

copy opus.txt lpt1:⏎

♪ *Note: All the examples of sending escape sequences and control codes from DOS assume your printer is connected to LPT1. If you've connected via another port, substitute that port's DOS name for lpt1 in the DOS commands shown in the examples.*

If you want to get a little bit fancier you can use DOS' PRINT program. PRINT is a memory resident program that starts the printing process and then returns you to the DOS prompt immediately, so you can go on with your work as printing proceeds.

⚡ Tip: *COPY and PRINT work fine with the DeskJet, but you have to remember to send any setup commands yourself ahead of time. If you have a favorite font or use a standard set of margins, you can automate the entire printing process, including sending the DeskJet commands and printing the file itself, with a single batch file.*

Sending printer commands from DOS

Sending DeskJet commands directly from DOS is simple, as long as you know a couple of tricks. The main challenge is this: you can't type the critical control codes on the command line. Fortunately, there's an straightforward way to sidestep this obstacle. Before we get to the solution, though, let's spend a little more time explaining the problem (if you want the brass tacks, skip to the section "The ESCAPE solution" below). Here's the situation: When you type the keys that correspond to DeskJet commands, DOS itself responds immediately, taking some action and gobbling up the commands for good. To see what I mean, you might want to sit down in front of your computer and start the beast, so that the DOS prompt is on the screen.

As you'll recall from Chapter 8, typing the (ESC) key at the DOS prompt doesn't produce the escape character on your screen. If you're at the computer, try it. A slash appears and the cursor moves a line lower, but you won't see the ← that represents the escape character.

The same sort of thing happens when you try to enter most of the control codes. When you press the necessary keys ((CTRL) plus a letter key) DOS takes some kind of action, or does nothing, instead of placing the control code character on your screen.

For example, try pressing (CTRL) J, which is supposed to produce an ASCII code value of 10, the line feed code (you'll find a table of DeskJet control code in Chapter 22 on DeskJet programming.) When the DeskJet receives a code 10, it stops printing and advances the paper by one line.

But when you press (CTRL) J, you won't see a code of any kind on the command line. Instead, DOS follows the line feed command itself, and simply moves the prompt and cursor one line down on the screen.

Actually, you can enter one or two of the ten DeskJet control codes on the command line. But that's hardly enough to bother with.

The ESCAPE solution

If we can't enter our precious special codes directly in DOS, how, then, can we get the codes to the DeskJet? With special files containing the codes prepared ahead of time, that's how. At a minimum, you should create a file called ESCAPE containing the escape character and it alone. Using a technique you'll learn shortly, you'll be able to combine this file and characters you can type at the keyboard to send any escape sequence to the DeskJet from DOS.

♪ **Note:** *If you want to use DOS to send other DeskJet control codes such as the form feed command to start a new page, you'll need a separate file for each code. You'll find details in the "Batching It" section below.*

To create ESCAPE, you'll need a word processor or text editor that can store files in plain ASCII format, without any special formatting codes. All the major word processors—and most of the minor ones—have a command for saving files in ASCII format. Another absolute requirement is that your word processor or text editor must not automatically add a carriage return and/or line feed character at the end of every line. The ESCAPE file must consist of the escape character only, not the escape character plus a carriage return or line feed (see the tip below if your word processor fails this test).

In addition, your word processor or editor must allow you to enter non-keyboard characters such as the escape character. In most word processors, you do this by holding down the (ALT) key and typing the ASCII code for the character you want to enter on the numeric keypad. To enter the escape character, for example, you hold down (ALT), type 2 then 7, and release the (ALT) key. The escape character, ←, appears in the file.

⌒ **Caution:** *When entering characters using the Alt key, you must use the number keys on the numeric pad, not the ones on the row above the letters. It doesn't matter whether or not the Num Lock function is on.*

To create the ESCAPE file, start a new file and enter the escape character at the very first position in the file (don't move the cursor). Without doing anything else, save the file with the name ESCAPE. That's all there is to it. Similar files for other control codes are a little longer than one character.

✄ *Tip: If your word processor doesn't meet all the requirements listed above, you can create the ESCAPE file using a combination of a DOS function and a utility program. At the DOS prompt, type COPY CON ESCAPE and press ⏎. Now type **e** (actually, any single character would do) and immediately press* (F6). *Then press ⏎ to create the 1-byte ESCAPE file containing only that e. Now load a disk utility program such as the Norton Utilities and use the hexadecimal edit function to change the value recorded in the file from 65 for the e to 1B for the escape character, and then save the file.*

Using ESCAPE

Once you've created the ESCAPE file, you can use it to send any escape sequence to the DeskJet from DOS. Here's how:

1. At the DOS prompt, type

copy escape+con lpt1

2. Type in the remainder of the escape sequence. Remember, although an escape sequence starts with the non-typeable escape character, the rest of the sequence consists of ordinary keyboard characters that you can type in directly.

3. Press (F6) followed by ⏎ to finish your entry and send the escape sequence to the DeskJet.

✄ *Tip: You can automate the process of sending escape sequences from DOS using batch files. See "Batching it" below.*

For example, to send the escape sequence that turns on boldface type, you would type:

copy con escape+con prn
(s3B
(F6)
⏎

See Chapter 8 for a discussion of the most commonly used escape sequences, and Chapter 22 for a complete reference to all DeskJet commands.

Batching It

Whether you want to send DeskJet commands, download fonts, or print DOS text files without a word processor, *batch files* can help you do the job much faster. A batch file as a predefined series of standard DOS commands that DOS executes for you, so you don't have to type them in yourself each time. If you like, you can think of a batch file as a simple program that gets DOS to do your bidding.

To run a batch file, all you do is type its name on the DOS command line, and then press (↵), just as if you were running an ordinary program. When you execute the batch file, DOS reads the file and carries out its commands one line at a time, exactly as though you were pounding them out on the keyboard.

Let's take a simple example. Since you can send files to your printer using the DOS command COPY, a batch file that automatically prints two files might contain these commands:

```
copy c:file1 lpt1:
copy c:file2 lpt1:
```

If you named this batch file PRNTFILE, you would type PRNTFILE(↵) at the DOS prompt to run it. You could rerun the file as often as you wante the same files each time.

Obviously, batch files make using a set of a frequently used DOS commands much quicker and less prone to error. For our purposes, batch files are great for the DeskJet commands you use most often. For example, you might create one batch file for setting margins, and a collection of separate batch files for selecting your favorite fonts.

Creating DeskJet batch files

There are two basic ways to create batch files: directly from DOS using the COPY CON command, or via a word processor or text editor. The COPY CON method has the advantage of being instantly available, since you don't have to wait for your word processor to load. In fact, you don't even need to have a word processing program at hand. However, although the COPY CON method works for printing files, you can't use it to enter control codes or escape sequences. For that, you'll have to use a word processor. Besides, a word processor makes it much easier to edit your file, especially if the file is longer than one line.

Either way you go, the one essential—other than avoiding typing errors in the command—is that you name the file properly. The first eight characters of the filename can be anything you want, but you must use .BAT as the filename extension.

⌒ **Caution:** *All batch files must have .BAT as the filename extension. Valid batch file names include 1.BAT, E.BAT, COPYFILE.BAT, and so on.*

Creating a batch file with COPY CON

Here's how to use COPY CON to create the PRNTFILE.BAT batch file for printing two files, shown in the above example:

1. Switch to the disk drive and directory where you wish to store the batch file.

2. At the DOS prompt, type

   copy con prntfile.bat⏎

The cursor will jump down a line to the far left margin of your screen.

3. Type

   copy c:file1 lpt1⏎
   copy c:file2 lpt1⏎

4. Press F6

You'll see the characters ^Z on the screen.

5. Press ⏎. Your batch file will be saved on the disk, and you'll get the message **1 File(s) copied** from DOS to confirm it.

Creating batch files with your word processor

To create batch files with a word processor or text editor, program you use must be capable of saving files in plain ASCII format, without any special formatting codes. It must also let you to type in symbols like the escape character that aren't represented on the keyboard. Most of the well-known word processors, including WordPerfect, Microsoft Word, and PC-Write meet these criteria. For batch files, it's all right if your word processor automatically adds a carriage return at the end of each line.

With most programs, you use the (ALT)-numeric pad method described above in the section "The ESCAPE solution" to enter the codes you can't type. Some word processors have a special command for entering non-keyboard characters—you give the command first, and then use whatever method is provided for entering the codes.

Using the ECHO command

In batch files, you should use the DOS command ECHO to send your escape sequences and control codes to the DeskJet, not the COPY command. Some DeskJet escape sequences include the * character, which COPY interprets as a filename *wildcard.* Instead of sending the * to your printer, COPY will look for files on your disk whose name begins with the escape character and ends with the characters following the * in the escape sequence. ECHO correctly sends the * to the DeskJet. Note that you must type the DOS redirection symbol > before the printer designation (lpt1 in the examples). Do not use the redirection symbol with the COPY command.

Making a batch file

The overall process of creating a batch file with your word processor are no different than creating any plain ASCII text file: start your word processor, open a new file, type in the characters, and save the file.

For practice, try creating the batch file BOLD.BAT for switching to boldface type:

1. Start your word processor and open a new file. If your program wants you to name the file before you start typing, call it BOLD.BAT.

2. Without moving the cursor (it should be at the the first position in your new file, the top left corner of the screen work area), type *echo* and press the spacebar.

3. Next, use whatever method your program allows to enter the escape code, ASCII value 27. In most cases, you'll just hold down the (ALT) key while you press **2**, then **7** on the numeric keypad. When you let up the (ALT) key, a ← symbol representing the escape character should appear in your file.

If your program provides a different method for entering non-keyboard characters, use that method instead.

3. Now type the following string of characters: (s3B >lpt1. The ">lpt1" sends the command to the printer when the batch file is executed.

4. Without moving the cursor or typing any more characters (do not even press (↵)), save the file in plain ASCII format. If you haven't yet named it, call it BOLD.BAT.

You can use this technique to create batch files for all the commands you use regularly, including those that use control codes other than the escape character. For example, to create a file that sends the form feed control code to eject the current page from the DeskJet, you would:

1. Start a new word processor file called FF.BAT

2. Type **echo** and press the spacebar

3. Press (ALT) and type **12** on the numeric pad, then release the (ALT) key. The ♀ symbol, representing the form feed character, should appear on your screen.

4. Press the spacebar, then type **>lpt1**. The completed line should look like this:

```
echo ♀ >lpt1
```

5. Save the file.

Combining commands in batch files

You can combine as many separate commands as you like in a single batch file. For example, you could create a SETUP.BAT batch file that sends a form feed command, sets a 1" left margin, and switches to boldface type. The contents of this file would be:

```
echo ♀ >lpt1
echo ←&a12L >lpt1
echo ←(s3B >lpt1
```

A generic batch file for escape sequences

You won't want to bother with creating a separate batch file for every possible escape sequence you can send to the DeskJet. Instead, the method described in "The ESCAPE solution" above will do for escape sequences you use only occasionally. However, you can speed up this technique by creating a batch file to do all the repetitive typing for you.

Using either the COPY CON method or your word processor, create a new batch file called DJ.BAT. The file should contain this one line:

```
copy escape+con prn
```

To use this file, type **dj** at the DOS command line and press (↵). You'll be dropped down to a new line where you can type in the rest of the escape sequence. Press (F6), then (↵) to send the escape sequence to the DeskJet.

Batch files for printing text files

Batch files are handy for printing DOS text files. If you have a favorite font or use a standard set of margins, you can automate the entire printing process, including sending the DeskJet commands and printing the file itself, with a single batch file.

Using the word processor method, create a batch file named PRINTDJ.BAT that looks like this:

```
if %1==stop
echo ♀ >lpt1
echo ◄(s3B >lpt1
copy %1 lpt1
:stop
```

Once you've saved the file, you can print a letter called BOXTOPS.TXT with your preferred font, margins, and so on, by typing printdj boxtops.txt⏎ on the command line.

This batch file relies on a couple of tricks that we haven't covered yet. In the first line, the notation *%1* refers to the filename you type on the command line after "printdj". When DOS reads the batch file, it substitutes what you typed for every *%1* it finds in the batch file.

In the example batch file, the *if* statement on the first line determines whether you entered a filename to be printed. If you didn't type anything, this line causes DOS to skip everything else and pick up the batch file at the last line, labelled *:stop*. Since there are no further lines after the *:stop*, the batch file simply finishes without doing anything.

If you did type something following "printdj," it's on to the heart of the batch file. The next two lines in the sample PRINTDJ.BAT are for the DeskJet commands you want to send before printing the text file. The ones shown send a form feed command and select boldface type, but you can substitute any DeskJet escape sequence or control code you prefer, and you can add as many commands as you like. Each command must be on a separate line.

The line that begins with *copy* gets down to business and prints the file. As you can see, this line also includes a *%1*, which means that DOS will print whatever file you chose when you started PRINTDJ.BAT.

Batch files within batch files

Before you create your own version of PRINTDJ.BAT, there's one more potentially time-saving wrinkle you should know about first: a batch file can execute another batch file. If you've already created batch files for individual DeskJet commands, you don't need to retype the commands themselves in PRINTDJ.BAT. Instead, the file should look something like this:

```
if %1 == stop
FF
BOLD
copy %1 lpt1
:stop
```

That concludes our look at DOS batch files and ends this chapter as well. Although it's generally easier to control the DeskJet with your application program's built-in commands or with a printer setup utility, you can access almost every feature of your printer with the techniques you've learned here.

10

Word Processing

Word processing is the one software application all PC users have in common. It's also the one of primary interest to most DeskJet owners. After all, most people buy their DeskJets mainly to make their correspondence, professional papers, and reports look sharper and more visually interesting.

In this chapter, you'll learn how to get the most from the DeskJet using several of the most popular word processors. Depending on the word processor under discussion, you'll find an overview of the program's capabilities and limitations with respect to the DeskJet and instructions on how to set up the program for the DeskJet and access DeskJet fonts and print features as you create your documents. The chapter also includes a look at techniques for merging graphics with word-processed text, and covers programs that let you enter scientific and engineering symbols in your documents.

$495/WordPerfect Corp.
288 West Center
Orem, UT 84057
800/321-5906

Profile: WordPerfect 5.0

With release 5.0, WordPerfect has consolidated its wide lead in the PC word processing marketplace. The addition of better typographic features, style sheets, the ability to merge graphics with text, and an improved macro feature, have made WordPerfect something more than a word processor—it's now a force to be reckoned with in desktop publishing as well. Sure, some of WordPerfect's closest competitors have all these features. But with the majority of PC users already hooked, the new version of WordPerfect has what it takes to keep reeling them in.

DeskJet Capabilities

WordPerfect includes drivers for the DeskJet and the DeskJet Plus, offering support for whatever mix of HP's cartridge and soft fonts you have at your disposal. With a little effort, you can even set up the program to work with soft fonts from suppliers other than HP.

The only problem of note with the DeskJet driver available at the time of this writing is that text printed alongside graphics may be malpositioned (more on that in the section "Adding graphics to your documents" below). Otherwise, you can make use of all of WordPerfect 5's flexible typographic and layout features with the DeskJet. The simple layout on the opposite page was printed on a DeskJet straight from WordPerfect.

Setting up WordPerfect for the DeskJet

The process of setting up WordPerfect to work with the DeskJet starts after you've installed WordPerfect itself; unlike many other word processors, WordPerfect does not let you choose a printer when you install the main program. Instead, setting things up for the DeskJet according to the procedure outline here should be your initial act when you run WordPerfect for the first time. If you've already set up your copy of WordPerfect for another printer, you'll use exactly the same procedure to reconfigure the program for the DeskJet.

Catalog of Delusions

◆ *Imagines he is gradually swelling, his body becoming larger and larger.*

◆ Illusion that he was a *pump-log*, through which a stream of hot water was playing, and threatening his friend with a wetting.

◆ Illusion that he was an inkstand, and that, as he lay on the bed, the ink might spill over the white counterpane. In the person of an inkstand he opened and shut his brass cover—it had a hinge—shook himself, and both saw and felt the ink splash against his glass sides, and, angry at his friends' incredulity, turned with his face towards the wall, and would not speak a word.

◆ Now he is a huge saw, and darts up and down, while planks fly off on either side of him in utter completeness; and then he is a bottle of soda water, running to and fro; then a huge hippopotamus; then a giraffe.

◆ He seems to himself to be transformed into a vegetable existence, as a huge fern, and to be surrounded by clouds of music and perfume.

◆ His eyelashes became indefinitely prolonged, and began to roll as gold threads upon small ivory wheels, which revolved with great velocity.

◆ He has ludicrous visions of old and wrinkled females, who are found to be composed of knit yarn.

◆ *He fancies he hears numberless bells ringing most sweetly.*

(Excerpts from records of experiments with the homeopathic medicine Cannabis indica as recorded in the 10-volume Encyclopedia of Pure Materia Medica, by Timothy F. Allen, M.D., 1874-1880.)

Here's a summary of the setup process: The first step in the procedure is to choose the DeskJet as your printer. In response, WordPerfect will create a corresponding driver file that contains the information WordPerfect requires to work properly with your printer. This file is referred to as a *printer resource file*, and is stored on disk with your other WordPerfect program files. In later steps, you customize the printer resource file for the specific fonts you'll be using.

Selecting the DeskJet

To proceed with configuring WordPerfect for the DeskJet, you need is a copy of the Printer 2 disk that came in your WordPerfect package, the one labelled PostScript, Daisy Wheel, and Misc. Once you've located the disk, you're ready to select the DeskJet as your printer. Run WordPerfect, and beginning at the main screen, follow these steps:

1. Select the Print menu by pressing Shift-(F7).

2. Choose the Select Printer option by pressing **s**. The Print: Select Printer screen appears, allowing you to add or remove support for particular printers, or to change the way WordPerfect is set up for an existing printer.

3. Choose the Additional Printers option by pressing **2** or **a**. You'll see a message indicating that printer files can't be found.

4. Place Printer 2 disk in a floppy drive, and choose the Other Disk option by pressing **2** or **o**. You'll see the message **Directory for printer files:** at the lower left of your display.

5. Type the letter name of the floppy drive where you've placed the disk (for instance, **A:**, and press ↵. You'll see the Select Printer: Additional Printers screen, which is dominated by a list of the available printers on the disk.

6. Scroll through the list of printers to the DeskJet/DeskJet Plus entry. Select it by pressing ↵ or **1**.

```
┌──────────────────────────────────────────────────────────────────────┐
│ Printer Helps and Hints:  HP DeskJet/DeskJet Plus                      │
│                                                                        │
│ 7/21/89                                                                │
│ If you have a DeskJet Plus printer, select the cartridges and fonts option in │
│ the Select Printer : Edit menu.  Select the group type  "DeskJet+ Internal │
│ Fonts ".  Mark Courier Landscape Internal as initially present.        │
│                                                                        │
│ Support for Additional fonts is available by ordering the Printer 21   │
│ diskette.  To order, call (801)225-5000.  There is a $10 handling fee. │
│                                                                        │
│ Printing text and graphics side-by-side may cause the top of the text to be │
│ printed lower than normal.                                             │
│                                                                        │
│ When using landscape fonts, the minimum left margin is .7" and the minimum │
│ top margin is .3".                                                     │
│                                                                        │
│ Use DeskJet specific fonts; LaserJet fonts are not supported.          │
│                                                                        │
│ The R,T,U,V cartridges only work on the DeskJet Plus.                  │
│                                                                        │
│ When using the 22708C and 22708D, softfonts that are 14pt. and larger will │
│ not work on the DeskJet.  The 14pt. and larger fonts only work on the DeskJet │
│                                                                        │
│ Press Exit to quit, Cursor Keys for More Text, Switch for Sheet Feeder Help │
└──────────────────────────────────────────────────────────────────────┘
```

Figure 10-1: *The WordPerfect helps and hints screen offers tips on using your DeskJet to best advantage from within WordPerfect.*

At this point, WordPerfect will show you the name it has chosen for the printer resource file, and ask for your go-ahead to save the file. Note that the name ends in the extension .PRS.

7. If you're satisfied with the name, press ⏎ to confirm it. If you don't like the name WordPerfect offers, you can type in another at the *Printer Filename:* prompt, and then press ⏎. Either way, WordPerfect next displays a detailed Helps and hints screen with tips on how to to best use the printer model you've chosen, as shown in Figure 10-1. In the meantime, it saves the printer resource file to disk.

Selecting DeskJet setup options

The setup process continues with a couple of steps in which you configure WordPerfect for specific DeskJet options, including the communications port used to connect to the printer, the paper size you'll be using, and the paper feeder.

From the Helps and Hints screen, press (F7) to bring up the Select Printer: Edit menu, as shown in Figure 10-2. As you can see, the menu offers several setup options for the DeskJet, and displays the current settings for these options at the right of the screen.

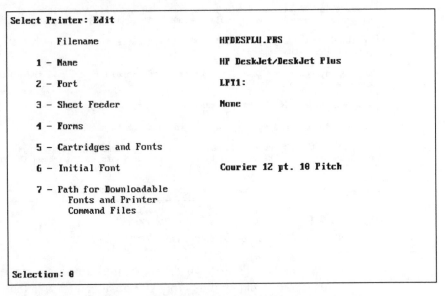

```
Select Printer: Edit

        Filename                    HPDESPLU.PRS

    1 - Name                        HP DeskJet/DeskJet Plus

    2 - Port                        LPT1:

    3 - Sheet Feeder                None

    4 - Forms

    5 - Cartridges and Fonts

    6 - Initial Font                Courier 12 pt. 10 Pitch

    7 - Path for Downloadable
        Fonts and Printer
        Command Files




Selection: 0
```

Figure 10-2: WordPerfect's Select Printer: Edit menu

Option 1, *Name,* lets you change the name that WordPerfect displays for the printer—feel free to rename the DeskJet at your whim, since doing so doesn't affect the way your printer works.

Option 2, *Port,* allows you to select the printer port to which you've connected the DeskJet. As a glance at the list of defaults on the right of the screen will show you, WordPerfect assumes you'll be connecting the DeskJet to LPT1: (parallel port #1), which is by far the most common situation. If you've connected to another port, select the Port option by pressing **2** or **p**. At the bottom of your screen you'll see a list of possible ports. Select the port you'll be using by pressing the appropriate number, and then pressing (↵).

Option 3 on the Select Printer: Edit menu, *Sheet Feeder,* can be ignored, since an add-on sheet feeder is not available for the DeskJet. Leave it set to "None".

Option 4, *Forms,* lets you choose which paper size you want to use. From the Select Printer: Edit menu, choose the Forms option by pressing **4** or **f**. Normally, you'll want to leave this set to the standard 8½"x11" letter size. The screen that appears lists the various paper sizes that WordPerfect will let you select when you print, including envelopes. Notice too that there's a column for paper orientation, indicating whether the paper can be printed in portrait, landscape or both.

If you wish to use a paper size or orientation not already defined in the Forms menu, you can edit an existing form type or add a new one. Refer to your WordPerfect manual for details. When you're through defining forms, return to the main Select Printer: Edit menu by pressing (ESC).

Defining fonts

Now it's time to define which DeskJet fonts you plan to use within WordPerfect. Option 5 on the Select Printer: Edit menu, *Cartridges and Fonts,* lets you tell the program which fonts you've installed. Press **5** or **c** to select the Cartridges and Fonts option. You'll see (what else?) a Cartridges and Fonts screen, as shown in Figure 10-3, listing three choices: DeskJet+ Internal Fonts, Cartridge Font, and Soft Font.

WordPerfect uses the same driver for the DeskJet and DeskJet Plus. If you have the Plus, you must tell WordPerfect that your printer has internal landscape fonts. Highlight the first choice on the Cartridges and Fonts screen, *DeskJet+ Internal Fonts,* and press **1** or **s**. Type a ***** to select the Courier Landscape Internal choice, indicating your printer has these fonts built-in. Press (F7) to return to the Cartridges and Fonts screen.

If you have font cartridges, highlight the *Font Cartridge* choice and type **2** to select the *Change Quantity* option. Type in the number of font cartrdiges you have and press (↵) (even though you can only use two at a time, you should set up the program so that it can use all your cartridges). Now, with the *Font Cartridge* choice still highlighted, press (F7) to display a list of the font cartridges that WordPerfect supports. Highlight one of the cartridges you have, and then press ***** to select that cartridge. Repeat this process for each of the font cartridges you'll be using. When you're through marking car-

```
Select Printer: Cartridges and Fonts

Font Category              Resource                   Quantity

DeskJet Internal Fonts     Plus Internal                 1
Font Cartridge             Cartridge Slot                2
Soft Font                  Memory                      256 K















1 Select Fonts; 2 Change Quantity; N Name search: 1
```

Figure 10-3: *The Cartridges and Fonts screen*

tridges, press (F7) to save your work and return to the Cartridges and Fonts screen.

⌒ **Caution:** *The R,T,U,V cartridges only work with the DeskJet Plus.*

If you'll be using any of the soft fonts sold by HP, the next step is to select them (if you have third party soft fonts, you'll have to do a little custom work as described in the section "Using PTR to customize your DeskJet printer driver" later in this chapter).

⌒ **Caution:** *At this writing, WordPerfect is unable to automatically download soft fonts to the DeskJet during a print job, as it can for LaserJet printers. Instead, you must download the fonts using a font utility or DOS commands (see Chapter 7), or with WordPerfect's Initialize Printer command.*

The first thing you should do is tell WordPerfect how much RAM cartridge memory you've installed in your DeskJet for soft fonts. At the Cartridges and Fonts screen, scroll down to highlight the *Soft Font* choice. Now press **2** or q to select the *Change Quantity* command and type in the total amount of memory in your printer's RAM cartridges. Press ⏎ to complete the command.

```
 Select Printer: Cartridges and Fonts

                                       Total Quantity:    512 K
                                   Available Quantity:    512 K

 Soft Font                                       Quantity Used

 ▓22708C Helv 08 pt.                                  27 K▓
  22708C Helv 08 pt. (ASCII)                          10 K
  22708C Helv 10 pt.                                  32 K
  22708C Helv 10 pt. (ASCII)                          12 K
  22708C Helv 12 pt.                                  58 K
  22708C Helv 12 pt. (ASCII)                          14 K
  22708C Helv 14 pt.                                  70 K
  22708C Helv 14 pt. (ASCII)                          25 K
  22708C Helv 30 pt.                                 243 K
  22708C Helv 30 pt. (ASCII)                          88 K
  22708C Helv Italic 08 pt.                           28 K
  22708C Helv Italic 08 pt. (ASCII)                   11 K
  22708C Helv Italic 10 pt.                           35 K
  22708C Helv Italic 10 pt. (ASCII)                   14 K
  22708C Helv Italic 12 pt.                           63 K

 Mark Fonts:  * Present when print job begins        Press Exit to save
                                                   Press Cancel to cancel
```

Figure 10-4: *Selecting soft fonts*

✂ Tip: *For maximum soft font flexibility, enter a very large number for soft font memory no matter how much RAM cartridge memory you've actually installed. That way you'll be able to access a large number of soft fonts from within WordPerfect using a single driver. The drawbacks are that you won't be able to use WordPerfect to download the fonts for you with the Initialize Printer command, and you'll have to make sure that you've downloaded the correct fonts before you print.*

Now, with the highlight still on the soft fonts option, press **1** or **f**. You're presented with a list of individual soft font names as shown in Figure 10-4. The list contains only the soft fonts marketed by HP. Mark each font you have in turn by highlighting the name and typing *****. Remember that there are separate fonts for upright and italics printing, and you must select them individually. On the other hand, each font you select will automatically be available in bold and in half-size versions.

As you mark fonts, notice that WordPerfect updates the amount of memory remaining at the upper right of your screen, based on how much you originally indicated as the available quantity. Once you've selected and marked all the soft fonts you wish, press (F7) twice to save your work and return to the Select Printer: Edit menu.

⌒ *Caution: HP soft fonts from packages 22708C and 22708D that are 14 points and larger will work only on the original DeskJet Plus.*

Now that WordPerfect knows which fonts will be available in your DeskJet, you can tell the program which font you want to use as your default. WordPerfect will print your documents using this font unless you specify another font explicitly. The relevant menu selection is *Initial Font.*

At the Select Printer: Edit menu, type **6** or **i** to choose the Initial Font command. You'll see a list of all the DeskJet fonts you've installed so far via the Cartridges and Fonts menu, plus the DeskJet's internal fonts. Scroll down to the font you want to use as your default, and press **1**, **s**, or ***** to choose that font. WordPerfect automatically returns you to the Select Printer: Edit menu.

Your final step in the font setup process is to tell WordPerfect where your soft fonts are stored, so that it can find them when it's time to download them. Of course, if you'll be using a downloading utility downloading the fonts yourself, this step isn't critical. At the Select Printer: Edit menu, choose the *Path for Downloadable Fonts* command by pressing **7** or **d**. You'll see a prompt asking you to enter the name of the path (disk and directory) where you've placed your soft fonts. If they're stored in the directory named FONTS on hard disk C:, for example, type **c:\fonts** and press (↵).

Saving your customized printer resource file

Once you've made all your DeskJet setup choices for printer port, paper handling, and fonts, save your changes permanently as follows:

1. Return to the Select Printer menu by pressing **0**, (F7), or just (↵).

2. Press **7** or **u** to select the *Update* command. As WordPerfect saves your newly modified DeskJet printer resource file, you'll see the Hints and Helps screen again. When the updating process is complete, return to the Select Printer menu by pressing (F7) twice.

3. Finally, to get WordPerfect to use the new driver, you must explicitly select it. At the Select Printer menu, press **1** or **s** to bring up a screen listing the printers you've installed. If the DeskJet is the only printer you have, it will be the only printer listed here. Scroll to the DeskJet's name in the list of printers, and press ⏎ or **1** to select it. You'll be returned to the main Print menu. From there, you can go back to writing in WordPerfect by pressing (ESC) or Exit ((F7)).

Adding fonts from other vendors

Although the Select Printer command within WordPerfect proper doesn't recognize third-party soft fonts, you can get WordPerfect to work with just about any font. The easiest way out is provided by some soft font vendors, who supply utilities that make the necessary modifications to your DeskJet driver (the printer resource file) for you. Check with your soft font supplier to see if such a utility is available. If not, the ultimate solution is a program called PTR that comes with the WordPerfect package.

Using PTR to customize your DeskJet printer driver

PTR works on existing printer resource files, so you should go through the steps above to create a preliminary DeskJet printer resource file. Then use PTR to add third-party soft fonts to that file. (Actually, you can call on PTR for all kinds of modifications to your printer driver, but we'll concentrate on font-related functions here.)

Since the PTR program isn't copied to your working disk with the other WordPerfect program files when you install WordPerfect, you must either run it from a floppy drive or copy it to your hard disk. PTR comes on a separate disk labelled, of all things, *PTR Program*. If you want to run PTR from your hard disk, copy the files PTR.EXE and PTR.HLP from the floppy disk to your WordPerfect directory (usually named WordPerfect50), or to the directory where you've told WordPerfect to store your printer resource files.

PTR gives you jillions of different choices, some of them quite obscure, but unfortunately, no instructions for the program come with WordPerfect. If you plan to make extensive modifications in your printer driver, you'll definitely want to beg a copy of the *WordPerfect Printer Definition Program Technical Reference* from WordPerfect. On the other hand, all the PTR options options are presented on a reasonably straightforward set of hierarchical menus, and if you're reasonably experienced with computers, you may be able to figure out how to add new soft fonts to your DeskJet driver. To get you started, I've outlined the steps you'll need to follow below.

✄ *Tip: Use* (CTRL) (F3) *to get help on the specific PTR function you're using.* (F3) *by itself displays an overall help screen.*

1. Start PTR with the name of the DeskJet driver file you're modifying as a parameter on the DOS command line. For example:

PTR HPDESPLU.PRS⏎

2. Highlight the DeskJet as your printer and press ⏎ to display the main PTR menu, shown in Figure 10-5.

3. Highlight the Fonts menu choice, then type **1** to select the Add option.

4. You'll now see a list of all the fonts already installed in the driver. When you add a new font, PTR requires you to choose a template font from the list. It doesn't really matter which font you use for the template, since you can change any aspect of the template in defining your new font. However, the closer your template is to the new font, the less work you'll have to do—so pick a template that is at least the same point size as the font you're adding. (In case you're worrying, the original font on which the template is based is not affected in any way.) To choose a template font, highlight it and press ⏎.

5. Name your new font. PTR will place the new name in the driver's font list.

6. Now it's time to define the new font so WordPerfect will know where to find it and how to use it. The new font should be highlighted, so just press ⏎ to start editing its definition. You'll be presented with a lengthy list of font characteristics, each of which opens onto other menus where you can make changes in various specific aspects of the font's definition. Crucial items include point size, character width, default leading, and

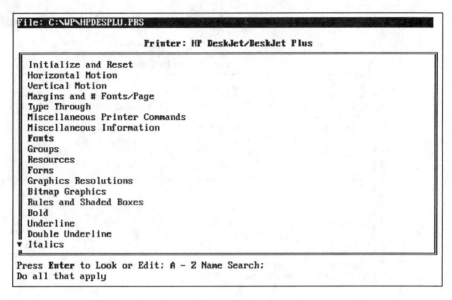

Figure 10-5: *The main PTR menu with the Fonts option highlighted*

proportions. Your soft font supplier should have provided you with the information necessary to complete all these menu choices.

One of the font-related menus, *Load and Select Strings*, deserves special mention. In order for WordPerfect to select your new soft font when you use it in a document, and to download it for you if you want it to do so, you'll also need to complete the choices on the menu.

Use the *Load Font* choice if you want WordPerfect to be able to download the new soft font for you when you give the Initialize Printer command, discussed in the section "Downloading soft fonts" below. Type in the download command in this format:

[27]"(*c*xD" DOWNLOAD("*filename.ext*')[27]"*c5F"

This command consists of three parts: an escape sequence that tells the DeskJet to expect a new font, the command that actually gets Word-Perfect to download the font file, and an escape sequence that instructs it to make the font "permanent." (see Chapter 7 for details on download-ing escape sequences and a discussion of permanent versus temporary

```
File: C:\WP\HPDESPLU.PRS

                    Printer: HP DeskJet/DeskJet Plus
                    Font: Steve's Font 12 point (PC-8)
                         Load and Select Strings

  ┌──────────────────────┬──────────────────────────────────────────┐
  │ Function             │ Expression                               │
  ├──────────────────────┼──────────────────────────────────────────┤
  │ Load Font            │ [27]"(*c8D" DOWNLOAD("STEVE.DJP")[27]"*c5F"│
  │ Unload Font          │                                          │
  │ Select Font          │ [27]"(10U"[27]"(s0u0p12v1s0b3t2Q"        │
  │ Deselect Font        │                                          │
  │                      │                                          │
  │                      │                                          │
  ├──────────────────────┴──────────────────────────────────────────┤
  │                                                                  │
  │                                                                  │
  │                                                                  │
  │                                                                  │
  │                                                                  │
  └──────────────────────────────────────────────────────────────────┘

  <- Name Side; Cursor Key Edit; Non Cursor Key New String;
  Ctrl Enter Edit in Window
```

Figure 10-6: *Entering font downloading and selection strings in PTR*

soft fonts). Enter a number between 0 and 32767 for the *x* in the command, using a different number for each font you define. Substitute the filename of your soft font for *filename.ext.* Don't enter the path, since WordPerfect expects all soft fonts to be located in the path you chose during printer setup.

In the *Select Font* choice, enter the PCL string that WordPerfect must send to select that font, as explained in Chapter 22. The string will look something like this (include the quotation marks in the string):

[27]"(1ØU"[27]"(sØuØp10h12v1sØb33t2Q"

You don't need to enter anything in the *Unload Font* or *Deselect Font* choices. Press ⒡ to finalize your entry.

When you're through defining the font, return to PTR's main Fonts menu by pressing ⒡, and add your next font. When you've added all the soft fonts you want, save your new version of the PRS file and exit the program.

WordPerfect and Fontware

Bitstream's Fontware Installation kit is a sophisticated font generating system with which you can create soft fonts from master typeface outlines in as many different sizes as you like. Bitstream offers a large library of typefaces for both body text and display applications. Unfortunately, the quality of Bitstream's DeskJet fonts isn't as high as the ones for the LaserJet family.

As of this writing, only the WordPerfect version of Fontware supports the DeskJet. The WordPerfect Fontware Installation Kit comes with three free typefaces: Charter, Dutch (similar to Times Roman) and Swiss (similar to Helvetica). You can buy as many additional faces as you can fit on your hard disk, or as you can afford, whichever comes first.

Although the WordPerfect Fontware Installation Kit is free, it doesn't come with your WordPerfect disk set. To order it by phone, call 800/222-9409 and request a copy.

Using DeskJet fonts within a document

WordPerfect gives you a lot of flexibility as to how you pick fonts for the text in your documents. To use the available options wisely, you need to understand the way WordPerfect uses two terms, *initial font* and *base font*.

The initial or default font is the font that WordPerfect will use for all your text unless you tell it otherwise. You defined the initial font when you created and installed your DeskJet printer driver—if you didn't explicitly name an initial font, WordPerfect automatically selected the DeskJet's internal Courier 12 point font for you. The base font is the font that's currently active as you're typing in WordPerfect. Until you choose a new base font, it's the same as the initial font.

Changing the initial font

You can change the initial or default font at any time. Your new choice will remain in effect, even when you exit WordPerfect, until you change it again later. Here are the steps in outline form:

1. Print — Select Printer — Edit — Initial Font

2. Highlight the desired font and press ⏎

3. Exit

Changing to a new font within a document

With WordPerfect's Base Font command, you can assign a new font to any text within a document with the Font command. To use the command, position the cursor where you want the font change to occur, then press (CTRL) (F8), then 4 to select the *Base Font* option. Select the font you want to use from the list that appears on your screen and press ⏎. The new font will remain in effect until your next Base Font command.

⌒ **Caution:** *You can't apply a new base font to a selected block of text.*

When you press (CTRL)(F8), you're presented with a menu at the bottom of your screen offering five choices, including *Size, Appearance, Normal, Base Font,* and *Print Color.* You can ignore the *Print Color* option, since the DeskJet is strictly a black-on-white mach

The "base" in the term base font refers to the fact that WordPerfect lets you modify some of the characteristics of the base font without explicitly selecting a whole new font. For example, if the base font is 12-point upright TmsRmn, you can use the Appearance command to switch to an italic version of the font, or the Size command to switch to a "Large" TmsRmn.

These modifications to the base font work OK with the limited fonts on standard dot matrix printers, but they give unpredictable results with printers such as the DeskJet or LaserJet. As you know by now, a DeskJet font is defined quite strictly as a particular typeface at a particular size and with a particular style (italics or upright). When, say, you request a large version of the base font, WordPerfect doesn't actually enlarge the base font. Instead, it looks for a font that's identical to the base font except for point size. You may not get the size you wanted; if no larger font is available, you simply can't print at a larger size. Similarly, while the DeskJet can print most fonts at half-size, that may not be what you have in mind when you ask for a small font with the Size command.

✄ ***Tip:*** *In general, it's always a better policy to explicitly select the new font you want with the Base Font command, even if all you want to do is change from an ordinary upright font to an italics version of the same typeface at the same size.*

Your results will be more predictable when you request bold type with the Appearance command, since the DeskJet can transform any font so that it prints in boldface. Still, a genuine bold font looks better. Other options of the Size and Appearance commands will work reliably with any font. These include underlining, redlining, and strikeout on the Appearance menu, and super- and subscript on the Size menu.

Undoing font selections

To remove a font selection, all you have to do is delete the font code, as follows:

1. Select Reveal codes by pressing (ALT) (F3).

2. Cursor to the code for the font change you want to delete.

3. Type (DEL) to delete the font code.

The text following the deleted font code will now be formatted with the same font used for the text that comes earlier in the file.

Changing leading

In Chapter 5, there's a discussion of why it's nice to be able to control leading, or the amount of space between lines of text. Fortunately, WordPerfect can automatically adjust the leading to an appropriate amount based on a line-by-line basis, based on the largest font used in the line. However, you may want to override WordPerfect's leading decision, since additional leading often helps to improve the appearance of a document. Type:

(SHIFT)(F8) **1 4 2**

Now enter the amount of leading you want. If WordPerfect is set to display units in inches instead of typographer's points, you can enter the leading value in points simply by typing a **p** at the end of the number. For example, if you want 15 points of leading, type **15p**. When you press ⏎, the program converts the point value into inches. (Note that WordPerfect measures leading from baseline to baseline.)

Adding graphics to your documents

With version 5.0, WordPerfect has added a powerful ability to merge graphics files created in other programs with text to create illustrated documents. Unfortunately, while WordPerfect graphics themselves print well on the DeskJet, nearby text gets knocked out of position, printing too high or too low.

✄ *Tip: WordPerfect can't position text properly on pages that include graphics when printing on the DeskJet. Until the problem is fixed by an update, you'll need to work around it by printing each page twice, one pass for text, one for graphics, as follows: Press* (SHIFT)(F7) *to start the printing process, then type* **G 1** *to select the Do Not Print option for graphics. Type* **2** *to print the page. When it emerges, place it back in the paper tray, with the printed side face down and its top toward the printer. Type* (SHIFT)(F7) **G 4** *to select High graphics quality, then type* **T 1** *to select Do Not Print for text. Type* **2** *to print the page again.*

In the process of importing a graphic image, you get all kinds of control over how the image will look—you can specify the location on the page where you want the graphic printed, the size for the printed graphic, whether you want text in the document to wrap around the image, whether you want a caption, whether there should be a box printed around the graphic and how thick it should be, and on and on.

In my view, these fancy new graphics capabilities make WordPerfect a true desktop publishing program, though it isn't as efficient for this purpose as the upscale DTP packages such as Ventura and PageMaker. In Daniel Will-Harris' *WordPerfect 5: Desktop Publishing in Style*, you'll find all you need to know about using WordPerfect for desktop publishing.

Drawing lines and boxes

WordPerfect's new graphics talents extend to letting you draw your own boxes and lines using the standard line drawing characters in the PC's screen character set. A caution is in order here: be sure you use a monospaced typeface such as Courier for these characters. Otherwise you may get broken boxes and lines that don't line up.

Embedding printer commands

If there's ever a time when your WordPerfect DeskJet driver fails you, and some special command is out of your reach, you can get direct access to the printer feature by embedding DeskJet commands directly in your document. Here's how to embed escape sequences and control codes:

1. Place the cursor where you want to embed the command (WordPerfect will send the command to the DeskJet immediately before printing the text to the right of the cursor).

2. Press the following keys in succession:

(SHIFT)(F8) **4 6 2 1**

3. Type in the command you want to send to the DeskJet. You can enter codes between 32 and 126 decimal directly from the keyboard. Enter codes below 32 or above 126 by typing in the numerals within angle brackets (<>). For example, to enter the escape sequence E_{S_C}*r1A type **<27>*r1A**.

4. Press (F7) to complete the command and go back to regular editing.

You can even send a whole series of commands stored in a separate file to the DeskJet from within a document. Create and save the file in WordPerfect, saving it as plain ASCII text in the same directory where you store downloaded fonts (check the Printer Settings menu by typing (SHIFT)(F7), then **S**, then **3** to make sure that the directory is the one selected for downloaded files). Then, to embed the file in another document:

1. Place the cursor where you want to embed the command. The commands in the file will be sent to the DeskJet immediately before the text to the right of the cursor is printed.

2. Press the following keys:

(SHIFT)(F8) 4 6 2 2

3. Type in the filename.

4. Press (F7) to complete the command and resume regular editing.

Previewing your document

In WordPerfect, you create and edit text in WordPerfect in the screen's standard text mode. That's fine for the text content, but now that WordPerfect is so handy with multiple fonts and graphics, you need a way to see how your document will look in print before you actually print it out. That way, you can see whether your layout settings have produced the intended result, without having to waste time and paper on a futile printout.

WordPerfect's new View Document feature meets this need. If you have a graphics monitor, you can use the command series (SHIFT)(F7), then **6** to bring up an image that closely approximates the way your document will appear in print. You can't change anything in this preview mode, but you can go back and forth between ordinary editing and the preview until everything looks right.

The preview mode displays one or two pages at a time. You can scroll around to see parts of the page image that don't fit on the screen, or change the magnification to zoom in for detail or zoom out for a bird's eye look at your whole page. The major limitation of the preview mode has to do with fonts. No matter what font you use in your document, WordPerfect will substitute a generic serif or sans-serif screen font. Still, even if you can't see what your characters will look like in details, you'll know where they will be placed on the printed page.

Printing your document

To access any of WordPerfect's print features, start by issuing the Print command by pressing (SHIFT)(F7). A full screen menu appears, offering a variety of print options, whose functions are summarized in this section.

Downloading soft fonts

If your document uses soft fonts, you must download these fonts before you can print it. You can do the downloading yourself or use a font management utility such as Backloader (see Chapter 7). Alternatively, you can use WordPerfect's own Initialize Printer command. From the Print menu, press **7** or **i** to select the Initialize Printer command. WordPerfect downloads the soft fonts in your DeskJet driver.

⌒ *Caution:* *Don't use the Initialize Printer command if you've added more soft fonts than your DeskJet can hold at one time to your driver. See the section "Defining fonts" above for a discussion of the pros and cons of doing just that.*

Selecting print options

Before you begin printing, you should make sure you've selected the print options you want for your printout. On the Print menu, you can select the text quality (draft or full quality) and graphics resolution (75 through 300 dpi). You can even shut off graphics printing altogether when you want a quick text draft, or vice versa.

The WordPerfect print spooler

To reduce the amount of time you spend waiting for your documents to print to a minimum, WordPerfect comes with its own print spooler. As described in more detail in Chapter 4, a print spooler provides a temporary parking place on disk or in memory for printer data. The spooler takes over the job of feeding the data from this temporary storage to your DeskJet as fast as the printer can digest it. With the spooler in control of the data transfer, WordPerfect can go on about its business, and you can get back to work. The print spooler continues to monitor the DeskJet, and whenever necessary interrupts WordPerfect just long enough to send the next mouthful of data to the printer.

Whenever you give one of the commands to print a document, you'll see the message *°Please wait°* at the bottom left of your screen while the document is transferred to the print spooler. When the transfer is complete, you can go back to the main program screen to do more editing while printing continues.

The WordPerfect spooler can accept several print requests, or "jobs," at a time. With the option 4 on the Print menu, Control printer, you can display the jobs that are currently waiting to be printed, cancel a job, or rush a job so that it prints before earlier ones.

Caution: Although it's possible to cancel the job that's currently being printed, doing so may foul things up enough that you'll have to re-initialize the printer. Also, remember that the DeskJet has a built-in 16K buffer, and will continue to print until that buffer is empty, even after the spooler stops sending new data. In other words, if something is really wrong with the printout, you may have to turn the DeskJet off and then reprint the entire document.

Printing options

To print the entire document that you're currently working on: From the Print menu, choose the Full Document option by pressing **1** or **f**.

To print a single page, place the cursor anywhere on the page you want to print before using the Print command. When the cursor is located properly, press (SHIFT)(F7) to select the Print command, then press **2** or **p**.

To print a WordPerfect document stored on disk, from the Print menu, press **3** or **d** to choose the Document on Disk command. At the prompt, type in the path and file name for the WordPerfect file you want to print, and press (↵).

Profile: Microsoft Word 5.0

$450/Microsoft Corp.
*16011 N.E. 36th Way
Redmond, WA 98073
206/882-8080*

Way back in the early days of PC computing, Microsoft Word anticipated the present popularity of two pieces of equipment: the mouse and the laser printer. At the moment, Word remains one of the few non-Windows word processors that lets you use a mouse. More to the point for this book, Word is still second to none when it comes to support for the cornucopia of fonts you can use with a DeskJet, though the other programs are catching up in this department.

Word was also the first major word processor with style sheets. A style sheet is a collection of "styles," each of which determines everything about the way a paragraph of text looks with a single command. Styles encompass such formatting attributes as indentation, line spacing, justification, font, and so on. For example, you might define one style for headings as a 30-point bold font centered on the page. Another style for body text paragraphs might be a 12-point regular-weight font with 14 points of leading, 1" margins, and a first line indentation of ½".

Despite its forward-looking features list, Word fell behind in sales early in the game to WordPerfect, and it has yet to catch up. Just to stay even in the race, Word has added a slew of features, most recently a macro capability and the ability to merge graphics with your text. In Word 5.0, the Print preView function that lets you see how your pages will look before you print them is now part of the main Word program, instead of a separate Windows application.

A new version of Word that will work within Microsoft Windows is in the works and should be out around the time this book is published. Word for Windows will have much the same feature set as its predecessor, but you'll be able to edit your document as it will look in print, just as in a desktop publishing program.

Word and the DeskJet

As far as the DeskJet goes, Word 5 comes with five predefined drivers for the DeskJet, one for the internal fonts only, the other four supporting different combinations of cartridge fonts. None of the newer font cartridges for the DeskJet Plus are supported. All the drivers allow you to print envelopes as well as ordinary paper, and to select graphics resolutions from 75 to 300 dots per inch.

Setting up for the DeskJet

Word's printer drivers are stored in PRD files (PRD stands for PrinteR Driver, I guess), with accompanying DAT files specifying soft fonts for downloading. To set up the program to work with your DeskJet, all you have to do is make sure that the correct PRD is active. If not, you can install it while you are working in Word itself.

To select a DeskJet PRD:

```
   holds that in choosing the "similar" medicine, the
   practitioner must take into account all of the patient's
   current symptoms, sensations, and physical findings, whether
   or they are thought to be associated with the chief
   complaint, and even if they don't seem to have pathological
   signficance. The underlying assumption of the homeopathic
   methodology is that symptoms are adaptive responses of the
   organism to stress or infection. Utilizing a medicine that
   mimics the symptoms of the sick person can therefore aid the
   body's inherent defenses, ultimately leading to an improved
   healing response.

   The third fundamental homeopathic principle is that the
   chosen medicine must be administered in extremely dilute

PRINT OPTIONS printer: HPDESK1           setup: LPT1:
       model: HP DeskJet (No Cartridges)  graphics resolution: 300 dpi
       copies: 1                          draft: Yes(No)
       hidden text: Yes(No)               summary sheet: Yes(No)
       range:(All)Selection Pages         page numbers:
       widow/orphan control:(Yes)No       queued: Yes(No)
       paper feed: Continuous             duplex: Yes(No)
Enter printer name or press F1 to select from list
Pg1 Co1            {¶}                              Microsoft Word
```

Figure 10-7: Word's Print Options menu on the lower portion of the display

1. Choose *Print*, then *Options* to display the menu shown in Figure 10-7. With the *Printer* field highlighted, press (F1) to display the available PRD files in the current directory. I disks, in which case you can copy it to your working program disk or to the hard disk.

2. Move the higlight to the *Model* field. Again, press (F1), and choose the "model" of the DeskJet you have. In the standard PRDs included with Word, there are two model names: *HP Deskjet (No Cartridges)*, which supports the internal fonts only, and *HP Deskjet (cartridges)*, with the letter names of the supported cartridges listed in the parentheses.

3. Check to make sure that the printer port selection in the *Setup* field is correct.

4. Press (↵) to confirm your choices.

Modifying your DeskJet PRD

✄ *Tip:* *If you're planning to use soft fonts with Word, save yourself a lot of trouble and buy them from a vendor who includes a utility that will make the necessary PRD changes for you.*

To customize Word's DeskJet driver for your own set of soft fonts and any other special requirements you have, you must run one or both of two utility programs that come on your Utilities disks, MergePRD and MakePRD. Instructions for using both programs are found in the *Printer Information for Microsoft Word* manual that comes with Word. So that you know what you're up against, we'll cover some of the fundamentals here.

Using MergePRD

MergePRD lets you combine fonts from several PRD files to create a single PRD file that supports all the fonts you have. You can also use this utility to delete fonts you don't have or don't use from a PRD file and to update a customized Word 4.0 PRD file.

When you start MergePRD, you begin by telling the program which PRD files you want to work with. This done, other menu choices let you see the fonts available in the existing PRDs, and select the fonts you want in your new merged PRD. To select a font for inclusion in your new PRD, you must type its number as displayed on the screen. You then name your new file, save it on disk, and exit the program.

Using MakePRD

If your PRD file needs more extensive customization—specifically if you want to add new soft fonts—you need the MakePRD program, found on Utilities disk 2. MakePRD converts the information in the current PRD file from computerese (binary) format into readable (though inscrutable) text. You load this text file into Word, where you make whatever changes you see fit, and then convert the text with your modifications back to PRD format. Figure 10-8 offers a sample of what you'll be up against.

With MakePRD, you can specify new soft fonts for use in Word, and describe them in detail so Word can use them properly. To complete this process, you'll need a considerable amount of technical information about your fonts from the font vendor. You can also redefine which printed characters correspond to which characters on the screen.

As you can guess, the fact that you can freely edit the text of the PRD file makes this an error-prone process. Essentially, you're writing a computer program. Just as in BASIC or C, one little typing error in a crucial location can disable the whole program. Be absolutely sure to save a copy of your original PRD before you start, follow the instructions carefully, and check over your work before you convert the file back to PRD format.

Downloading soft fonts from within Word

Word has a built-in downloading capability. To take advantage of this feature, however, you must create a gawdawful binary DAT file containing the names of the fonts that can be downloaded along with numeric descriptions. Don't bother with DAT files unless you're a true-blue programmer—stick with a downloading utility instead, or do the downloading yourself with DOS commands (Chapter 7).

```
  AutoSkipTop:1 UnprintableTop:384
  AutoSkipLeft:1 UnprintableLeft:360
  UnprintableBottom:491 UnprintableRight:360
  DownloadFlag:0
  GraphicsNotSupported:NIL
  FontsNotSupported:2 3 4 5 56 57 58 59
  BinsSupported:0 1 4
  IniFile:NIL
  ModelName:HP DeskJet (No Cartridges)

  InhibitCTT:0 InhibitRevLF:0
  LinedrawAutoMap:0 LinedrawNoShade:0
  LinedrawFlag:0 LinedrawFont:0 LinedrawAdjust:0
  ColorMod:0 ColorFlags:0 DuplexFlag:0 OrientationFlag:0
  AutoSkipTop:1 UnprintableTop:384
  AutoSkipLeft:1 UnprintableLeft:360
  UnprintableBottom:491 UnprintableRight:360
  DownloadFlag:0
  GraphicsNotSupported:NIL
                                                      DSKJET.DRV
COMMAND: Copy Delete Format Gallery Help Insert Jump Library
         Options Print Quit Replace Search Transfer Undo Window
Edit document or press Esc to use menu
Pg1 Co1          {}                              Microsoft Word
```

Figure 10-8: *This excerpt from the standard DeskJet PRD file should convince you that customizing a PRD is not for the faint of heart.*

Changing fonts in a Word document

To format text in your file with a new font:

1. Begin by highlighting the block of text you want printed in the new font.

2. Press (ESC) to activate the Command menu.

3. Choose *Format,* then *Character.*

4. Highlight the *Font Name* option, and press (F1) to see the list of available font choices. Select the one you want, then press (↵).

The alternative to this direct approach is to use style sheets. Define a style that includes the desired font along with the other formatting characteristics you want. Then, after you've typed your text, you can apply the style's entire collection of formatting characteristics, including your font choice, to any paragraph in your file. To assign a style to a paragraph, position the cursor in the paragraph, use the command sequence Format—Style—Paragraph, and select the particular style you want. Alternatively, you can press (ALT) and the two characters of the style name.

IBM DisplayWrite 4

Though it's not very popular in the retail software stores, IBM's DisplayWrite 4 word processor is widely used by larger companies that buy both computers and software directly from IBM. DisplayWrite lacks the sophisticated formatting capabilities of WordPerfect and Microsoft Word, but it can still give you excellent results from your DeskJet. However, even the latest version of the program, DisplayWrite 4 Version 2, lacks drivers for the DeskJet. That means that you have to hunt down the drivers you need from another source, or create them yourself.

DisplayWrite 4 printer drivers are stored in separate files known as printer function tables, or PFTs. Each PFT can support only a limited number of fonts, so you'll need multiple PFTs if you want to use many fonts. As you can guess, these driver files all end in the extension .PFT. You can install the PFT for the fonts you use most often when you install DisplayWrite itself, and then switch to other PFTs as needed while you are using DisplayWrite.

Hewlett-Packard's PFTs

Since IBM has dropped the ball on DeskJet support, HP has developed six PFTs for the DeskJet and DeskJet Plus printers. Here's the list of fonts and character sets that each of the HP PFTs supports:

DESK1.PFT Internal fonts, cartridges A, K, and L (PC-8, Legal, and linedraw)

DESK2.PFT Cartridge B (PC-8, Legal, Math8 A and B, pifontA, linedraw)

DESK3.PFT Cartridges 22706D, E, F, F, H, J, P, Q; soft fonts A and C (ASCII only)

DESK4.PFT Cartridges D, E, F, G, H, J; soft fonts A and C (PC-8, Legal)

DESK5.PFT Cartridges C, M, and L (PC-8, Legal, and ASCII)

DESK6.PFT Softfonts D (PC-8, Legal, and ASCII)

DwLaser

You've heard the saying about Mohammed and the mountain. Like the prophet, DwLaser takes the line of least resistance in getting around DisplayWrite's DeskJet limitations. Instead of trying to teach the program how to use the DeskJet's advanced features, DwLaser turns the DeskJet into an imitation of the IBM Quietwriter II, a printer DisplayWrite *does* know something about. After you've configured it for your fonts and various defaults, DwLaser runs as a memory resident program, monitoring printer output. When the program detects a Quietwriter command, it converts the command into DeskJet form.

DwLaser lets you select any HP-compatible font for use in your DisplayWrite documents. The package includes a collection of symbol fonts, providing special mathematical and scientific characters that aren't available in the regular DeskJet character sets.

Access: DisplayWrite Utilities

Hewlett-Packard PFTs

Hewlett-PackardDeskJet
Customer Support
Mail Stop 516
11311 Chinden Blvd.
Boise, ID 8371

DwLaser/ $195

Koch Software Industries
11 W. College Dr., Bldg G
Arlington Heights, IL 60004

MultiMate Advantage

MultiMate Advantage II is another word processor with large numbers of users in corporate America. While even the latest versions of MultiMate lack the advanced support for fonts and formatting found in programs like WordPerfect and Microsoft Word, you can create attractive documents with the program.

The biggest problem you'll face is with proportionally spaced fonts. MultiMate defines the length of a line in terms of a fixed character width, but the characters in a proportionally spaced font vary considerably in width. For this reason, the length of a printed line, and the location of the right margin, can change significantly from one line to the next. You'll have to experiment with fonts and right margin settings to find the combination that works best for you.

Using MultiMate drivers

MultiMate printer drivers are stored in files called Printer Action Tables (PATs), with supplementary font information in Character Width Tables (CWTs). The latest version of MultiMate Advantage II includes a set of DeskJet PATs, each of which supports a limited number of DeskJet internal and/or cartridge fonts. Once you've installed the PATs, all you have to do is modify a few options on the printer default screen and you're ready to go.

To install these PATs and select one of them as your default:

1. Copy the DeskJet drivers from the driver disk (available from Hewlett-Packard) to your MultiMate directory. Make note of the file names and the fonts each PAT supports.

2. Load MultiMate, and from the main menu, press **4** to select Printer Control Utilities.

3. Press **2** to select the Edit Printer Defaults command.

4. Go down the list of defaults and make the necessary changes. Pay special attention to these settings:

- At the Printer Action Table line, type in the name of the DeskJet PAT you want to use. The PAT named "DESKJET" supports the standard Courier and Courier Italics fonts.

- If you're using a PAT that supports proportionally spaced fonts, indicate this by entering a **y** in the appropriate setting on the right side of the default list. Also, note that MultiMate does not support justification with proportionally spaced fonts, so the justification setting should be set to **n**.

- The Paper Length setting should be set to 10 times the lines per inch setting for standard letter paper, 13 times for legal paper. In landscape mode, Paper Length should be 7.5 times the lines per inch setting.

5. Return to the main menu by pressing (F10).

Selecting fonts within a document

You can use up to 26 different fonts within a single document, but only if they're all supported by a single PAT. To select the PAT you want to use, press (ALT) **C**, then **?**, then (⏎). Now type in the name of the PAT you want to use. Within a PAT, each font is labelled with a letter (A, B, etc.). To change to a new font, place the cursor where you want the font change to occur, press Ins followed by (ALT) **C**, and then type the font letter.

Embedding printer commands

To give you control over additional printer functions, MultiMate lets you embed escape sequences and control codes directly into your document. Here's how to embed a printer command:

1. Move the cursor so that it's at least one space to the right of the left margin (if you're left margin is set to 8, you should have the cursor in column 9 or higher).

2. Press (ALT) **A**. The Greek letter μ (mu) will appear on your screen.

3. Type in the rest of the command. For control codes and the escape character, which can't be typed from the keyboard, enter the appropriate 3-digit decimal ASCII codes. For example, type **Ø27** for the escape character, **Ø1Ø** for the line feed control code. And if you're using a proportionally spaced font, you must enter *all* the characters of the command string as numeric ASCII codes.

Profile: WordStar Release 5.5

$495/WordStar International, Inc.
33 San Pablo Ave.
San Rafael, CA 94903
800/227-5609; 415/499-1200

Venerable old WordStar lives on, still distinguished by the touch-typing efficiency of its control key commands. But Release 5.5 is a thoroughly modern beast, with *de rigueur* pull-down menus, style sheets, the ability to merge graphics, a host of first-class utilities—and support for today's printers with their multitudes of fonts. And WordStar has one of the best DeskJet drivers—the developers have finely tuned it to the idiosyncracies of your printer.

WordStar printer drivers are stored in Printer Description Files (PDFs). At the time I wrote this book, Release 5.5 was being shipped with a PDF for the standard DeskJet, but you had to order a separate DeskJet Plus driver from the WordStar sales department. The standard driver recognizes only the A, B and C font cartridges. The DeskJet Plus PDF adds support for the newer cartridges, including P, Q, R, T, U, and V, most of which can only be used in the Plus. In addition, the Plus driver supports all the soft fonts available from HP. You can customize your DeskJet PDF for the particular collection of fonts you own, or even create several different PDFs, each with its own set of fonts.

If you own an earlier version of WordStar, you'd be well advised to upgrade to 5.5 if you want to get the best possible results from you DeskJet. According to the technical people at WordStar, changes have been made in the way the program as a whole works with many printers, including improvements in paper handling and character positioning. If you don't have the newest release of the program, you won't be able to take advantage of these upgrades.

♪ **Note:** *WordStar gained its ability to merge graphics with text by incorporating a version of Inset, a utility described later in this chapter.*

Customizing WordStar for the DeskJet

If you didn't install the DeskJet driver when you first installed WordStar, you'll have to do so to now, a simple process. WordStar 5.5 also makes it relatively easy to add support for third party soft fonts to your DeskJet driver. The necessary instructions for either of these procedures are found in a slim pamphlet that accompanies the main program manual. In outline, here's what you have to do:

1. Run the program WINSTALL, which you should have already installed on your hard disk (otherwise, it's on the Installation/Customization floppy).

2. At the opening menu, if you need to install new soft fonts, choose *Add third-party laser fonts (LSRFONTS)*, and skip to the instructions in "Adding soft fonts" below. If you just want to select from fonts already available, or otherwise modify the driver, choose *Modify or install a printer (PRCHANGE)*.

3. You should now be at the Installed Printer Menu. If you're creating a new DeskJet PDF, enter the name of the PDF file you wish to create, then choose the DeskJet or DeskJet Plus from the list of available printers on the Printer Selection Menu. If you're modifying an existing DeskJet driver, highlight the name of the PDF file you want to change and press ⏎.

4. You can now choose or modify the selections for printer port, print controls, and available fonts. As far as fonts are concerned, the *Add or delete fonts* option lets you select which of the fonts that are theoretically available for the DeskJet you actually want to place in this PDF. If you want to add soft fonts that don't appear on the list, you need to install them first, as described in the next section.

5. When you're through making changes, go back to the Installed Printer Menu. You'll be asked if you want the PDF you've just created to be the

default. There, you can create or modify another PDF, or exit back to WINSTALL by pressing (F10).

Adding soft fonts

Before you can add new soft fonts to your DeskJet PDFs, you must first install the fonts, as follows:

1. Run WINSTALL, and at the opening menu, choose *Add third-party laser fonts (LSRFONTS)*. Then choose *HP LaserJet and compatible fonts*.

2. Follow the instructions on the screen to add the fonts. You'll need technical information from the font manufacturer to complete the process correctly. Press (F1) for help at any time.

3. When you're finished installing the new soft fonts, go back to the WINSTALL main menu. To add the new fonts to a DeskJet PDF, select *Modify or install a printer (PRCHANGE)*, and continue with step 3 in the section "Customizing WordStar for the DeskJet" above.

Changing Printer Definition Files

If you like, you can create multiple PDFs for your DeskJet, each customized for a particular situation. The default PDF is automatically assigned to all your documents. Each time you create a new PDF you're given the opportunity to designate it as the default, and you can select a new default PDF from the WINSTALL Set Basic Editing Defaults Menu whenever you like. You can also change the PDF on a document-by-document basis. Press (CTRL) **P?** and choose the new PDF. Then press (CTRL) **QU** to reformat the document with the new PDF.

Using fonts within a WordStar document

To change fonts within your file, move the cursor to the place where you want the new font to start, then press (CTRL) **P=** or select *Choose font* from the Style menu. You'll see a list of the available fonts in the current PDF. Highlight the one you want and press (↵). The font you selected will now be in effect from the cursor location to the next font change, or to the end of the file.

For even quicker font changes, you can set up two default fonts in advance with the WSCHANGE program, and then switch back and forth between them by pressing (CTRL) **PA** for the first font, (CTRL) **PN** for the second.

Embedding printer commands

WordStar 5.5 offers several related methods for embedding your own printer escape sequences and control codes directly in your files.

1. To enter a command on a one-time basis, press (CTRL) **P!**. At the prompt that appears, enter control codes and the escape character by typing a carat (∧) followed by the character associated with the code, as shown in the table of control codes in Chapter 22. For example, you'd enter the escape character by typing **∧]**. You can type in ordinary characters directly. To include a carat in the command, enter **%∧**, and to enter a percent sign, type **%%**.

Alternatively, you can enter any code in hexadecimal notation by preceding the hex characters with **%x**. To enter the escape character this way, you'd type **%x1b**.

2. You can also define four reuseable print commands and insert them as often as you need them anywhere in your document. Besides cutting down on your typing at the outset, this is a great help if you want to experiment with different values in an escape sequence—just change the definition of the command, and the corresponding escape sequence changes everywhere in your document.

Use the WordStar dot commands **.xq, .xw, .xe**, and **.xr** to define the corresponding reuseable print commands, (CTRL) **PQ**, (CTRL) **PW**, (CTRL) **PE**, and (CTRL) **PR**. The dot command must be placed in your document above the point where you first use the corresponding print command. Type the dot command followed by the print command you want to define, expressed in hexadecimal notation. You can type a maximum of 24 hexadecimal characters.

For example, to define the (CTRL) **PE** command so that it selects the legal character set, you'd set up the **.xe** dot command for the escape sequence ᴱs_C(1U by typing **.xe 1B 28 31 55**. Then, to insert the command you've defined in your file, just position your cursor where you want the command to take effect, and press (CTRL) **PE**. You can redefine these dot commands as often as you like in a document.

3. You can also create default definitions for the **.xq, .xw, .xe**, and **.xr** dot commands using the PRCHANGE setup program. Using PRCHANGE, you can have separate definitions for each PDF (see above), and the printer commands can be longer than 24 characters.

Amí

The first popular word processor for Windows is Amí, whose name is supposed to make you think warm, friendly thoughts about the program. Whether or not you resonate in the expected fashion, Amí is a good word processor that you should consider if you have the computer power necessary to run Windows.

Because it runs in the graphical "environment" of Windows, Amí lets you edit and lay out your text on a mockup of your document as it will appear in print. You'll see each text character at its correct relative size and with all its attributes such as italics, boldface, and underlining. Your margins and indents, the breaks between lines of text, and any text columns occur on screen just where they will the printed page. You can see exactly what you're doing as you place charts and illustrations wherever you like.

If you're concluding that Amí is a desktop publishing program, I won't argue with you. But it's a word processor as well, with a much more complete set of text editing functions—and both keyboard and mouse commands to get at them—than you'll find in any program bearing the DTP label. You can use a draft mode for faster text editing, then switch to the page preview mode to concentrate on layout. Like any word processor worth its salt, Amí provides a search and replace function, something that's missing from Ventura and PageMaker. A 130,000-word spelling checker is also included.

Like any high-end word processor or desktop publishing program, Amí has style sheets, letting you control all aspects of the overall page layout and the format of individual paragraphs with a click or two of the mouse. There's also an automatic headers and footers feature. Amí comes in two versions, the standard package and an enhanced model called Amí Professional. Professional adds a thesaurus, mail merge, drawing tools, and a feature for formatting tables automatically.

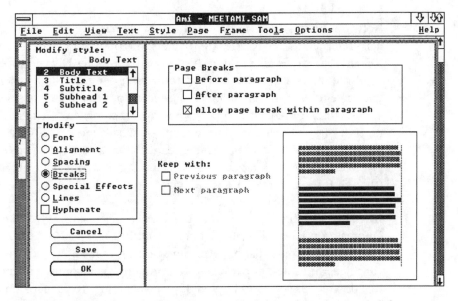

Figure 10-9: *Amí's comprehensive stylesheet system lets you define many typographic settings via a series of menus listed here under "Modify."*

Since Amí works within Windows, the program depends on the Windows DeskJet driver to communicate with your printer. Currently, that means you can't use ordinary DeskJet soft fonts in your Amí documents. Chapter 17 on Windows discusses ways to work around this limitation. Another Windows drawback is slower speed. Even in draft mode, Amí is slower than most character-based word processors because it runs in Windows.

PC-Write

My favorite word processor is PC-Write. This program has three big advantages: it's shareware, and inexpensive when you register; it has just about every text editing command you could ever want; and above all, it's amazingly fast. You can move from screen to screen or top to bottom of the file instantaneously, something that no other top-name word processor can claim.

Notwithstanding these strengths, But PC-Write has one major weakness, and it's an important one for DeskJet owners: the program makes it too hard to format your pages for printing. It's not that you don't have control; in fact, PC-Write offers a dizzying array of formatting options. The problem is that you have to type in formatting choices into your document as strange little codes, rather tby han just selecting your layout settings from a menu. T arere's no style sheets to ease the burden, either. What's more, PC-Write lacks the more advanced desktop publishing features that are showing up in WordPerfect and Word. You can't place pictures into a document for instance (though Inset, discussed later, will give you that capability).

Installing the program for the DeskJet is easy, since PC-Write has an automated printer installation routine and the DeskJet is one of the menu choices. During installation, you can select fonts from most of the HP font cartridges and soft font packages. The program even comes with a batch file that downloads soft fonts for you. If you want to use fonts that aren't already supported by the printer installation program, you'll have to rely on Quiksoft's technical support personnel to guide you through the process.

Sprint

Borland's Sprint is a more recent entry on the word processing scene, and has gathered a respectable following based on its speed, advanced macro language and formatting commands, and the ease with which you can customize almost any setting. That flexibility extends to printer support. Though Sprint comes with a prefab driver for the DeskJet, it also allows you to create you own driver with complete control over a huge number of different parameters, including downloaded soft fonts.

But you'll have to earn your right to that control. To create your own printer driver for Sprint, you type a series of arcane commands into an ordinary text file using the Sprint text editor, then pass the file through the SP-SETUP program. Though Microsoft Word uses a similar approach, this system is hardly at the leading edge of software technology. You should be prepared for a long and frustrating cycle of write-test-scratch your head as you work the bugs out of your driver.

Merging graphics with your text

Given the DeskJet's talents with both text and graphics, it would be nice to be able to mix both types of information together on a single page.

Of course, the most direct route to text and graphics integration is with a true desktop publishing program. But the DTP approach is overkill for many people, who may only want to spruce up a report with an occasional chart or add a little levity to a letter with a cartoon. Besides, even if you can justify buying and learning a full-scale desktop publisher like PageMaker or Ventura, it takes too much time to switch out of your word processor when all you really need is a company logo on your letterhead.

The ideal solution would allow you to stay within your word processor, so you can concentrate on editing text, but would let you bring in graphics as needed with a minimum of hassle. For owners of WordPerfect, Microsoft Word, WordStar, and TotalWord— and probably some other word processors as well—that day has arrived. All of these products now sport built-in graphics features that let you select pictures stored in disk files for inclusion in your document. All allow you to size and position the images fairly easily. And once you've imported the graphics, you can switch to a special preview mode that displays a close facsimile of how your finished document will look when printed, graphics and all.

 For those of you who use other word processors, the situation isn't nearly as straigrhtfoward. The simplest way to get a graphic and some text to share the same page is to run the paper through the DeskJet twice. In your word processor, hit the ⏎ key enough times to leave a gap for the graphic, then print you file. Put the page back in the paper tray face up, and then fire up your graphics program and print your graphic.

This technique might work in a pinch, but it's a guaranteed time-waster. Plan on making several attempts before you figure out how to space everything so that the picture doesn't sit right on top of your text.

Inset to the rescue

A much better way to go is with Inset, a utility designed just for this purpose. Inset helps ease the process of positioning your text and graphics so they don't conflict, and then handles the printing chores so that both print on a single pass of the page through the DeskJet.

To use Inset, you just type in the name of the graphics file between a pair of special "tag" characters in your word processor document, wherever you want the graphic to be printed. If the image is stored in a file called BALLOON in the INSET directory, for instance, the tag might look like this: [c:\inset\balloon]. Following the tag name, you must still leave some blank lines so that the image doesn't print on top of your text.

Inset is a memory resident program that you load before you start your word processor, popping up when you press a hotkey combination. At this point, you can call on various Inset menu choices. You can see the graphic you want to print and view its relative size and position on the page. You can resize the image at will, rotate it, or place a border around it. Inset actually includes a complete paint program, so you can edit the graphic itself or create new ones from scratch.

Access: Inset

$149/Inset Systems

12 Mill Plain Road
Danbury, CT 06811
203/794-0396

Word processing for special applications

These days, flashy graphics get all the attention in articles and advertisements on word processing. For many people, however, it's far more important to be able to incorporate the technical symbols within a document than it is to print pretty pictures. Whether it's a mathematical formula, a chemical symbol, a foreign language character, or even a musical note, your special character may be absolutely necessary for making your point on paper. You don't want to have to leave a blank space and then draw in the symbol by hand—how tacky. Ideally, you'd like to be able to have the special symbols appear right on the same line as your regular text, looking as if they were an integral part of the document.

The DeskJet's dot-by-dot printing method gives it the potential to generate just about any symbol you can represent in two dimensions, and to put that symbol anywhere you want it on the page. In practice, there are some limitations in printing special characters, but you can achieve excellent results with the right software.

As in everything you can print with the DeskJet, there are two major approaches to putting special characters on a printed page. The first way is in text mode, using specially designed fonts. If you can find a font that includes the symbols you need, all you have to do is download the font to the DeskJet, then use your word processor to type out the characters that correspond to the right symbols. Of course, you won't see the symbols you'll actually be printing on the screen, since you can't change the PC's screen character set, so you'll probably have to consult some sort of conversion chart that tells you which screen character produces which printed symbol.

Text mode printing offers the advantage of being substantially faster than the alternative, graphics mode. It's ideal for characters that fall on a baseline like regular printed text, and that don't vary in size depending on how they're used. If you want to print text in a European or romanized foreign language from the DeskJet, for example, fonts are definitely the way to go.

The big disadvantage of the font approach is that you can't freely resize or reposition the symbols as the situation calls for. In mathematics, for example, a square root sign is much smaller when you're taking the square root of 4 than when you're taking the square root of $425 + \dfrac{\delta}{xn}$. In chemistry, those benzene rings and double bonds may not look right locked unless you place them just so, outside the lines used by your word processor. For some foreign languages, you may need immediate access to more than the 256 characters that are available in a single DeskJet character set.

Theoretically, you can avoid these problems if you use the second way to print special characters, by switching the DeskJet into graphics mode. It's perfectly possible to pint text and text-like symbols using graphics. Your pages won't print as fast, of course. But the only limiation on what you can print, and where, is the capability of your software.

Lotus Manuscript

If Lotus had used a little better timing and savvier marketing, Manuscript might now enjoy a reputheaioneering word procepioneered the trend the trail into the realm of desktop publishing. Instead, while Manuscript is a richly-endowed general word processor, it got stuck in the "good for technical documents" category. It's true that the program can print mathematical equations, and that it has special features for formatting highly structured long documents such as technical manuals. Still, Manuscript has all the features you'd want for writing letters, reports, and non-technical documents, and it has the same kind of page layout talents as the newest versions of WordPerfect and Word. You can create columns, merge graphics into your text, change fonts freely, control typographic details such as leading, and view a WYSIWYG mockup of your printed document on the screen. The program's design is unusual and takes some getting used to, but it's actually quite straightforward and consistent. The opposite page shows a simple example of what Manuscript and the DeskJet can do.

All that said, I've chosen to cover Manuscript in this section on special word processing applications apppprecisely because of its strengths in printing mathematical symbols and other special characters. As a look at the opposite page will show you, Manusoutput can print complex equations at any size that will fit on the page. To enter an equation in Manuscript, you place an ion arker" into your document, then type in a long-winded series of abb e symbols into a special window. The equation on the sample page required

Lotus Manuscript:
A Prodigious Document Processor

Manuscript can print equations——

$$\nabla_{32°} = \int_{x' \to 0}^{\infty} (x^{0.5} - c)\,\partial x$$

and graphics——

on the same page.

the entry **nabla sum [32 degree] = int sub [x prime ->] super infinity (x super 0.5 - c) partial x**. Other options in the equation window let you control the spacing and size of the equation in print. Equations can be dropped into text or printed in separate blocks, as on the sample page.

Manuscript's support for the DeskJet is good. The printer is listed on the installation menu, and you can configure the program for all the standard HP cartridges and soft fonts. However, third-party soft fonts are not currently supported. Graphics and equations print well.

Total Word

Total Word is the top-of-the-line word processor from Volkswriter, the creators of the very first word processor for the original IBM PC. Like Manuscript, Total Word claims to be a professional-level word processor for every need, with special features for technical documents that WordPerfect and Word don't possess. The program goes Manuscript one better in the scientific department, in that it can print organic chemistry symbols—benzene rings and all the rest—as well as equations.

Unlike Manuscript, Total Word prints technical characters as text rather than as graphics. This has its good and its bad points. On the one hand, text mode is always faster than graphics. On the other, you can't freely resize the symbols, and you have to build some of them out of separate components. Total Word does let you save macros containing the commands needed to create these composite characters, so you don't have to reconstruct the characters each time.

Amazingly enough, the program comes with a full set of downloadable fonts for the DeskJet, including those necessary to print a wide range of mathematical symbols anchemistry chemsitry building blocks.

Exact

Exact is a one-of-a-kind memory resident utility that lets you add equations to your documents with just about any word processor. To use the program, you position the cursor where you want the equation, press a hotkey, and enter a series of commands in a special graphics window that pops up over the document. As you enter the commands, the equation takes shape before your eyes. When you decide that it looks right, Exact places a corresponding marker in your document. At print time, Exact detects the marker and issues the necessary commands to print the equation in the proper place.

Used with the DeskJet, Exact is unable to place an equation within a line of regular text. Instead, the program skips down a line, switches your printer into graphics mode and prints the equation, then skips another line and switches back to text mode. This arrangement works fine for many situations, since equations are often printed so between blocks of explanatory text.

The worst thing about Exact is the price it exacts for the privilege of its use. For $495 you can get buy Manuscript or Total Word and get a complete technical word processing solution. If you're permanently hooked on another word processor, however, Exact is your only option.

Access: Word Processors and utilities

Lotus Manuscript/$495
Lotus Development Corp.
55 Cambridge Parkway.
Cambridge, MA 02142
617/577-8500

PC-Write/ $99
Quicksoft
219 First Ave. N. #224
Seattle, WA 98109
206/282-0452

Ami/$199
Ami Professional/$495
Samna Corp.
5600 Glenridge Dr.
Atlanta, GA 30342
404/851-0007

Exact/$495
Technical Support Software
72 Kent St. #110
Brookline, MA 02146
617/734-4130

Total Word/$495
Volkswriter, Inc.
411 Pacific St.
Monterey, CA 93940
408/373-4718

Sprint/$199.95
Borland International
1800 Green Hills Rd.
Scotts Valley, CA 95066
408/438-5300

11

Desktop Publishing

∾

Desktop publishing, the hottest personal computer fad in the mid-1980s, is now an established technology that has irrevocably transformed the face of publishing. From established publishing houses and public relations firms, on down to go-it-alone novelists and eccentric yellow journalists, people have been turning away in droves from traditional manual pasteup methods and towards personal computers and desktop publishing software. Armed with these tools, they're creating printed documents of every imaginable description: books, manuals, flyers, brochures, magazines; documents with multiple columns, illustrated documents, documents that combine a multitude of fonts.

Desktop publishing on the DeskJet

The DeskJet is your economy-fare ticket to the marvels of high-quality desktop publishing. With a DeskJet, anyone with a little patience can turn out documents that look as good as what you get from any of the popular desktop laser printers, including those ballyhooed PostScript machines. Take the pages you print on your DeskJet down to a professional printshop, and you can transform them into newsletters, flyers, or even books that hold their own in the looks department against all comers. All you need is the right software.

You doubt my claims? I draw your attention to the sample printed on the opposite page. It may not be a model of classic design, but it shows how the DeskJet can handle complex layouts combining a variety of text and graphics elements. It's reproduced directly from an actual DeskJet printout made from Ventura Publisher with the help of Publisher's Powerpak, a utility described later in the chapter.

That's not to say that the DeskJet is the best printer around for desktop publishing. But its only major limitation compared to more expensive laser printers is that it's considerably slower.

The evolution of desktop publishing

By most reckonings, the desktop publishing era officially began with the advent of two related products: Apple's LaserWriter printer, and PageMaker software for the Mac. With PageMaker helping you combine text and graphics in complex page designs, and a LaserWriter to print out your documents with exquisite clarity, your printed output could rival the results of traditional graphics arts and typesetting techniques.

But while PageMaker and the LaserWriter were radical technological improvements, people had already been publishing their own documents since the earliest days of the personal computer. From the earliest days of the PC, most word processing programs have included fairly sophisticated print formatting capabilities in addition to their text editing features. Using a word processor and a good daisy wheel printer, hundreds of intrepid souls were putting together manuals, flyers, and booklets, sometimes even distributing

Naturalist's Journal

Beagle Blowings

—*C. Darwin*

I have not as yet noticed by far the most remarkable feature in the natural history of this archipelago; it is, that the different islands to a considerable extent are inhabited by a different set of beings.

My attention was first called to this fact by the Vice-Governor, Mr. Lawson, declaring that the tortoises differed from the different islands, and that he could with certainty tell from which island any one was brought. I did not for some time pay sufficient attention to this statement, and I had already partially

At sail in the Archipelago

mingled together the collections from two of the islands. I never dreamed that islands, about 50 or 60 miles apart, and most them in sight of each other, formed of precisely the same rocks, placed under a quite similar climate, rising to a nearly equal height, would have been differently tenanted; but we shall soon see that this is the case. It is the fate of most voyagers, no sooner to discover what is most interesting in any locality, than they are hurried from it; but I ought, perhaps, to be thankful that I obtained sufficient materials to establish this most remarkable fact in the distribution of organic beings.

Bugs of Gold

—*E. A. Poe*

The winters in the latitude of Sullivan's Island are seldom very severe, and in the fall of the year it is a rare event indeed when a fire is considered necessary. About the middle of October, 18__, there occurred, however, a day of remarkable chilliness. Just before sunset I scambled my way through the evergreens to the hut of my friend, who I had not visited for several weeks—my residence being, at that time, in Charleston, a distance of nine miles from the island, while the facilities of passage and re-passage were very far behind those of them commercially. And at the high end of the software spectrum, a variety of programs designed for page layout had preceded PageMaker by many months. (Desktop publishing programs are also known as *page layout* software, since they let you precisely control the layout of each page of your printed documents.)

All the same, it was only with PageMaker, the LaserWriter, and a little later, Ventura Publisher for the PC, that desktop publishing became the next big epoch in personal computing. With several years to mature, the big name desktop publishing programs have now become real typographic and graphics arts powerhouses.

Word processing meets desktop publishing

As it evolves, desktop publishing software is being given more and more built-in text and graphics editing capabilities. You can't throw away your word processor or graphics programs yet, but you don't need them as often as you once did. On the other hand, those in the word processing camp haven't rolled over and died when it comes to document formatting. Today's word processors have extended their existing formatting talents to handle the cornucopia of fonts you can use with present-day printers like the DeskJet. Many of them even let you to mix graphics with text.

At this point, top-notch word processors and desktop publishing programs already have so much in common that we're clearly heading toward an eventual merger of the two genres. For the time being, you can tell them apart with the following rule of thumb: Whatever else it does, a word processor is supposed to help you shape the *content* of your text, by providing plenty of text editing features. By contrast, a desktop publishing program's paramount concern is your documents' *appearance*, even though it may offer good text editing capabilities.

WYSIWYG Desktop publishing

Before the PageMaker revolution, page layout programs for personal computers were much harder to use. In those dark ages, layout software relied on complicated special codes that you had to embed within your text.

PageMaker and its kin changed all that. Among many innovations they introduced, the single most significant one was the ability to lay out your document by manipulating an on-screen mockup. This screen version of the document looks exactly like the final printed version, within the limits of your monitor's resolution. You can see each character of your text just as it will actually be printed—the size and typeface typeface. If a page contains a graphical image, you see the image alongside the text, just where it will appear in print.

The advantages of this WYSIWYG, "what you see (on screen) is what you get (on paper)," approach are obvious. As you make changes in the layout, you see the results immediately, and can decide right then whether you like them. If you make a mistake, you know it, and can make the necessary changes without waiting for a printout. For these reasons, WYSIWYG programs—led by PageMaker, Ventura, and, at the low end, PFS:First Publisher—have left the older page layout software in the dust.

Code-based desktop publishing software

Although WYSIWYG desktop pubslishers have far outpaced the "code-based" programs in popularity, some representatives of the older genre are still with us. Many of these are low-budget horrors, but several extremely sophisticated code-based packages, such as LaserScript, PC Tex, MicroTex, and EROFF, have enthusiastic adherents among professional typesetters.

A session with a code-based program works like this: Instead of seeing what your printed page will look like as you create it, you have to work "blind" in an ordinary word processor, with nothing but plain text characters on the screen. Your job is to imagine in your mind's eye how you want the document to look, and then type in a code for each facet of the layout you've visualized. One code might indicate which font to use for a given passage of text, another might determine where on the page a graphic was to be printed.

When you think you have all the codes right, you pass the file through a special formatting program. The formatter processes the text and codes and adds in any graphics files you've called for, turning the whole shebang into printer data for the finished pages. The problem is that likelier than not, the printout won't come out the way you expected, and you'll have to go back to your word processor and try to find and correct the mistakes you made in entering formatting codes.

Look but don't touch

The latest versions of some code-based programs give you a compromise between the "print it and weep" approach and full WYSIWYG editing in the form of a *preview* mode. As you develop your document's format, you can hit a couple of keys to see an image of the document. You can't make any changes while you're looking at the preview, but you can switch back and forth fairly quickly as needed until the document looks right, and then print.

The preview mode solution is also the road taken by the major word processing packages as they've beefed up their typographic, graphics, and layout features. WordPerfect, Microsoft Word, Total Word, and WordStar all now come with a preview command.

But the line they have yet to cross have is in letting you edit a WYSIWYG version of your document on screen. Like code-based programs, some word processors still require you to manually type in special formatting codes within your text to produce the layout effects you want. In more modern programs such as WordPerfect, it's a little easier, since you can use keyboard commands to make your formatting changes. But these commands simply insert the formatting codes into your text for you (if you want to see the codes in Wordperfect, just press (ALT) (F3)). Even if you're allowed to look at a WYSIWYG preview of your document, you still have to make your layout changes while you work with plain text on the screen.

Actually, though, I know of several programs marketed as word processors that provide plenty of font and graphics features, and allow you edit a WYSIWYG image of your document to boot. For my money, if it waddles like a desktop publisher, and quacks like a desktop publisher, it's a desktop publisher, even if it also has strong text editing features. The two programs that best fit this category are Samna's Amí and NBI's Legend, both of which require Microsoft Windows.

How desktop publishing programs work

Several common themes run through most of the WYSIWYG desktop publishing programs. For one thing, their basic mission is to assemble files that come from a variety of sources into complete documents. To serve this purpose, all DTP programs can import a number of file types. Almost universally, the process of importing a file starts when you define a *frame* to hold the file. Whether or not you can see the outline on your screen, a frame is a two-dimensional rectangle into which you "pour" a passage of text, a picture, or in some programs, a table. In some programs, each entire page is treated as a frame, into which you can place text, graphics, or other frames.

Each frame exists semi-independently from the rest of the document, in that you can change its size or move it around on the page or from page to page at will. Graphics images are confined to a single frame, while a passage of text that is too long for one frame can flow to another, and then another.

Style sheets are another feature common to most page layout programs. A style sheet is a collection of preset formatting options ("styles" or "tags") that you can apply as a group all at once to a given document element. In a program with a stylesheet feature, for example, you might define a style for headlines, calling for the text to be printed in the center of the page in a 30-point Helv font, with half an inch of space automatically left below the headline. Then, after you select a line of text that you want to use as your headline, you just give a single command to assign the style. Presto—instant headline! The big centered headline jumps out at you immediately.

Most desktop publishing programs also give you tools for creating simple line graphics, such as straight and diagonal lines, rectangles, and ovals, with or without shading. With these tools, you can create basic borders and highlights, without having to import a new file for each little line or box you want in your document.

Because of the almost geographic nature of page layout, it helps to be able to move from one part of the screen page to any other very quickly. For this reason, every WYSIWYG desktop publishing requires a mouse.

Choosing a desktop publishing program

To figure out which route to desktop publishing is best for you, start by asking yourself how far you're likely to carry your involvement with page layout. If you're at all serious about desktop publishing, or think you might eventually be, the only two programs you probably need to consider are Ventura Publisher and PageMaker. Unless you'll be creating extremely complex documents, one of these heavyweights should satisfy all your page layout requirements.

On the other hand, Ventura and PageMaker are expensive, and they can take a long time to learn. If you don't expect to do professional-level desktop publishing, but you want more formatting power than an old-style word processor can deliver, you have two choices. Either buy a high-end word processor with desktop publishing features, such as WordPerfect 5.0, Microsoft Word 5.0, or WordStar 5.5; or get a good-quality, low-end WYSIWYG desktop publishing package, such as First Publisher, GEM Publisher, Springboard Publisher, or Amí to use in conjunction with your word processor.

Ventura versus PageMaker

If I didn't know that you own a DeskJet, I'd have no qualms about recommending Ventura Publisher over PageMaker. I consider it the best page layout program overall for most serious desktop publishers. As things stand at this writing, however, the situation is complicated by the fact that Ventura does not come with a driver for the DeskJet. Although there are ways to get Ventura to work with a DeskJet, they involve extra work and extra expense (I'll discuss the alternatives in the profile on Ventura later in this chapter). By contrast, PageMaker works fine with the DeskJet right out of the box.

Putting aside that critical caveat for the moment, let's quickly run through some of the other ways the two programs differ:

Type of documents: From day one, the big dividing line was supposed to be that PageMaker was good for short documents, Ventura for long ones. When the two programs first appeared, there was a grain of truth in that analysis, but that's about all. A better way to put it is that the early PageMaker was lousy for long documents. In its latest incarnation, PageMaker has improved its long-document talents substantially, but it's still does its best work with newsletters, flyers, and the like. The one area in which PageMaker really excels is in special graphics effects. If you use color extensively, and particularly if you incorporate lots of scanned images into your work, PageMaker is the way to go.

Ventura is unparalleled at producing long structured documents, but it's just as good as PageMaker at newsletter-type formats—in fact, once you learn to use Ventura, you'll find that you can layout out a fancy newsletter in Ventura more quickly and with greater accuracy than you can in PageMaker. Overall, Ventura offers far more extensive typographic and layout controls than does PageMaker. It also automatically generates indexes and tables of contents. If you add the optional Professional Extension, it can generate tables automatically and format complicated mathematical equations, All these features are totally absent in PageMaker.

Style and ease of learning: Because PageMaker is set up to give you the feeling of working with real paper and graphics arts tools, it's easier to learn, especially if you have a background in traditional layout work. Also, it has somewhat fewer and less complex menu choices. Ventura takes a world-of-its-own approach that I find eminently logical, but that takes longer for most people to learn.

Speed: Ventura runs much more quickly than PageMaker, an advantage that has a big impact on how much you can get done and how soon you get frustrated. Despite its sophistication, Ventura can run at acceptable speeds on old-style PCs and XTs, while PageMaker requires an AT-class computer at a minimum.

Operating environment: PageMaker works within Microsoft Windows, which means you can run it simultaneously with other Windows programs such as Corel Draw, Micrografx' Designer, PC Paintbrush for Windows, or Amí or another Windows word processor. If you have enough memory, you can switch to one of these outside programs without shutting PageMaker down, edit a graphic or text file, and then switch back to PageMaker where you can import the file. Ventura is based on a special version of GEM, but you never have to start the GEM environment separately. GEM is much faster than Windows, but it doesn't allow you to run different programs at the same time.

Cost: PageMaker and the standard version of Ventura Publisher are comparably priced—both cost almost as much as a DeskJet. But to take advantage of the advanced features of Ventura's Professional Extension, including table generation, mathematical equations, advanced hyphenation, and more, you'll have to shell out a few hundred dollars more.

Desktop publishing on a budget

If you don't want to pay through the nose for Ventura or PageMaker, don't think you'll be stuck with ugly documents that people will turn up their noses at. With a top-notch word processor, or with one of the burgeoning crop of entry-level desktop publishing programs, you can churn out lovely output that looks just as good as if you composed it with one of the big league programs. Unless you attempt a really complicated layout, only a publishing professional will know the difference.

Word processors like WordPerfect or Microsoft word are perfectly adequate for documents with multiple fonts and occasional graphics. They have the big advantage of letting you do all your work, from outlining your ideas to printing your final copy, with a single program (of course, you also need a graphics program if you plan to create your own pictures). On the other hand, you'll find it time-consuming and frustrating to flip back and forth between the preview mode and your text while you try to figure out how to get the layout to look right.

Since most desktop publishing programs only give you rudimentary text-editing features, you have to type in your text in a word processor, then fire up the DTP software and import the text file. This extra step is a bother, but once you complete it, your document is "live" on the screen, and you can proceed with laying it out very efficiently. If necessary, you can make minor changes in the text directly, without having to flip to a preview mode time and again. Also, since the DTP program handles the layout for you, you can get by with a word processor that has fewer frills and costs less.

Which of these two approaches should you use? It's largely a question of personal preference, but it also depends on how much high-quality printing you do. The more you use your printer for documents where appearance counts, the more I'd recommend the separate word processor/desktop publisher method.

✂ *Tip:* *If you're looking for a good inexpensive word processor to team up with a desktop publishing program, PC-Write is your best bet. It has all the editing features of the big-name packages and then some, yet it's much faster than any of them. And it creates plain ASCII files that are perfect for importing into your desktop publisher.*

Low-end DTP shootout

Let's assume you've decided to buy one of the inexpensive desktop publishing programs—which one should it be? Your choices include PFS:First Publisher, GEM Desktop Publisher and Springboard Publisher, among others. Then there's Amí, even though the latter program isn't marketed as a desktop publisher. All four of these packages work fairly well with the DeskJet.

First Publisher

First Publisher is by far the most popular of the quartet, and warrants your attention for that reason alone—you can count on finding plenty of other people to swap files with, and to help you over any rough spots you might encounter. Overall, the program makes an excellent way to dive into desktop publishing. You can set up multiple columns of variable width, and have text flow automatically from one column to the next. You can import bitmap graphics from a variety of file formats and then resize or rotate them, or touch them up to remove stray pixels. And you can add lines and boxes anywhere on the page to set off elements of your layouts.

First Publisher imports text files from WordPerfect, Microsoft Word, Wordstar, and a variety of other word processors, retaining formatting details such as boldface, italics, and indentation. Unfortunately, the program supports only cartridge DeskJet fonts, but the same limitation holds true for Springboard Publisher and Amí. A factor that you may consider as either a plus or a minus is that First Publisher runs as a standalone program, without requiring either Windows or GEM as the other programs I've mentioned. On the positive side, you don't need to devote extra disk space to Windows or GEM, and you don't need to run them before you start desktop publishing. To the negative, this go-it-alone attitude may mean more trouble in working with other programs.

GEM Desktop Publisher

GEM Desktop Publisher is an good choice if you think you might eventually be interested in Ventura, but want to test the waters with a simler, less expensive program first. Like Ventura, GEM Desktop Publisher runs in the GEM operating environment, so the look of the screen and the way the menus and options work are very similar in both programs. Actually, GEM Desktop Publisher makes clever improvements over Ventura in several common functions, such as adjusting the magnification of the screen, making them easier to use than they are in Ventura. As far as page layout power is concerned, GEM Desktop Publisher's popgun pales in comparison to

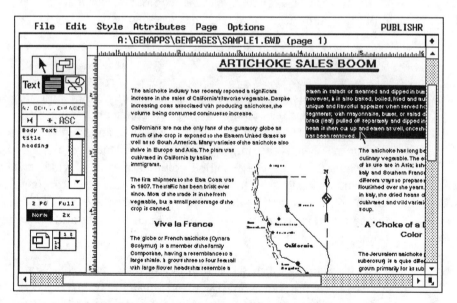

Figure 11-1: *GEM Desktop Publisher looks and acts a lot like Ventura. In this screen, the paragraph tagging function has been used to select a paragraph so that it can be reformatted via a previously defined stylesheet.*

Ventura's awesome weaponry. But that's just an indication of how strong Ventura is, not really a knock against Desktop Publisher. You can prepare perfectly acceptable newsletters, manuals, flyers, the whole nine yards. And GEM Desktop Publisher is fast, because GEM is—it's a good choice if you have a standard PC or XT. My biggest complaint is that the program lacks an "undo" feature, but then again, so does Ventura.

Springboard Publisher and Amí

Springboard Publisher and Amí are both Windows programs, with all the attendant benefits and drawbacks (see Chapter 17). You don't need to buy Windows separately to use either program, since both come with a limited "run-time" version of Windows. However, if you have the full-blown version of Windows, you can use your desktop pubisher and a separate graphics program, spreadsheet, and word processor simultaneously. That way, you

Figure 11-2: *Springboard Publisher has a unique graphics import feature that allows you to examine the graphic before you import it, and to clip only the portion of image you want to import (in this example, the rose).*

can transfer pictures, charts, and text to your final document as you need them, without having to repeatedly exit one program to start the next. Whichever version of Windows you use, you'll need a fast computer: Windows bogs down all its programs, you need an AT-class computer or better to get acceptable performance.

Feature for feature, Springboard Publisher is a stronger product than the better-known First Publisher. Its page layout features are reminiscent of Ventura's. You can type text on the background page, or draw as many "frames" to hold text or graphics as you like. You can change the layout for every page, or have frames repeat from page to page. Like Ventura, the program automatically generates as many pages as necessary to hold the text you import.

Springboard Publisher also offers a complete built-in paint program similar to PC Paintbrush or MacPaint. You can't paint in color, but that shouldn't bother you given the DeskJet's one shade of black ink. If you're not feeling artistic, you can choose from a large collection of bitmapped clip-art that Springboard sells for use with the program (see Figure 11-2). The one major shortcoming of the program is its lack of style sheets, which in other programs let you a whole range of formatting choices (for font, line spacing, character style, and so on) with a single command.

My favorite low-end desktop publisher is Samna's Amí. Samna prefers to call this program a word processor, and the description is fair: Amí has stronger text editing features than the other desktop publishing programs. You get keyboard good cursor control, an effective search and replace feature, even a built-in spelling checker. In other words, you don't need a separate word processing program. But even if you prefer to keep on entering text with your old DOS word processor, you might want to consider Amí for desktop publishing. Amí is at least as capable at page layout and text formatting as Springboard Publisher, First Publisher, or GEM Publisher, and in some ways superior. For instance, it includes the vital stylesheets feature that Springboard and First Publisher lacks. If your computer is fast enough to run Windows, and you're not ready for PageMaker or Ventura, put Amí at the top of your list when you shop for a desktop publisher.

Special situations

Database publishing: dbPublisher is the first program dedicated to desktop publishing of database files. It's an expensive and complicated beast, but extremely powerful. Another choice is Xerox FormBase, covered briefly in Chapter 16 on forms software. At the low end, Ashton Tate's ByLine is the best choice. Again, it reads dBase and Lotus 1-2-3 files directly.

Mathematical equations: Currently, the only popular desktop publishing program that lets you add complex mathematical equations to your documents is Ventura Publisher with the Professional Extension. If you're not ready to spend that much money, you can do a passable job at formatting equations with some word processors—see Chapter 10 for details.

Access: Desktop Publishing Software

First Publisher/$129
1901 Landings Dr.
Mountain View, CA 94039
415/962-8910

Springboard Publisher /$129
Springboard Software, Inc.
7808 Creekridge Circle
Minneapolis, MN. 55435
612/944-3912

GEMDesktop Publisher /$299
Digital Research, Inc.
Box DRI
Monterey, CA 93942
408/649-3896

Amí/$199
Amí Professional/$495
Samna Corp.
5600 Glenridge Dr.
Atlanta, GA 30342
404/851-0007

dbPublisher/$695
Digital Composition Systems
1715 W. Northern Ave.
Phoenix, AZ 85201
800/527-2506; 602/870-7667

ByLine/$295
Ashton-Tate
20101 Hamilton Ave.
Torrance, CA 90502
213/329-8000

Profile: Ventura Publisher

$895/Xerox Corp.
101 Continental Blvd.
El Segundo, CA 90245
800/822-8221

Ventura Publisher is one of the most marvelous software programs ever devised. With Ventura, a PC, and a comatilbe printer, you can make short work of your most complex layout tasks. The catch for DeskJet owners is that innocent-sounding phrase "comaptible printer." But we'll get to that painful subject in a moment.

First, let's tick off the highlights of Ventura's features list, which is as long as two or three of your arms:

Ventura is unsurpassed for longer documents. It automatically creates as many pages as are necessary to hold the document's text. It can combine multiple smaller "chapters" into longer complete manuscripts. It can automatically number chapters, pages, lists, figures, footnotes, and so on, and can generate tables of contents and indexes automatically as well. Graphics images can be attached to particular passages of text; when a document revision changes the layout of the text, the attached graphics automatically move in concert with the text.

The program has a comprehensive, superbly designed style sheet system for instantaneous text reformatting. Yet although features such as this excels at structured documents with repeating elements such as headers, it's also flexible enough to handle free-form layouts with aplomb and ease.

Ventura imports text and graphics files from almost every major word processing and graphics program, so there's rarely a problem in assembling documents from whatever component files you're starting with. In the process of importing text, Ventura leaves intact the character formats in the original document, such as bold, italics, underlining, so you don't have to add them again. Even better, Ventura preserves the original files as separate entities in their original formats. This way, even after you've imported a text or graphics file into Ventura, you can make changes to the file using the program that originally created it. The next time you load Ventura, the edited version of the file automatically becomes part of the Ventura document.

Ventura lets you move and size layout elements quickly and easily with the mouse, or with perfect accuracy by typing in numeric coordinates. If you need a precisely aligned graphic, the by-the-numbers approach actually gets you there much faster than the mouse does—but many DTP programs provide only the mouse method. Ventura has an excellent set of simple line-graphic tools. You can draw lines, rectangles, and ovals.

If you install the optional Professional Extension, Ventura can generate tables automatically, produce sophisticated mathematical equations with a minimum of hassle, and access a 2-megabyte hyphenation dictionary for near-perfect hyphenation.

Just as important as all these features is the fact that Ventura is extremely fast for a large program running in graphics mode— fast enough that it's practical to use it on a standard PC or XT. I'd still suggest an AT-class computer or better, however.

Ventura and the DeskJet

For DeskJet owners, alas, there's one terribly nasty fly in the ointment. To date, Ventura's talented programmers haven't come up with a driver for the DeskJet (if you're hazy on what a driver is, see Chapter 3 for a quick review). It can't be that Ventura only works with page-oriented printers like the LaserJet or PostScript machine—the program turns out quality pages on other line-by-line printers like the Epson series. Whatever the explanation, DeskJet owners have to face the fact that Ventura has ignored them.

Where there's a will, there's a way, they say, and the old saw fits this situation perfectly. If you can't live without Ventura, and you're not ready to exchange your DeskJet for a more expensive laser printer, there are now several add-on software packages that will fix you up.

The Ventura solution

To get the most out of Ventura and your DeskJet, look to a PostScript interpreter package. To use one of these products, you install Ventura as if you had a real PostScript printer. When it's time to print, you trick Ventura into feeding its printer output into the PostScript interpreter. The interpreter converts the printer data into instructions the DeskJet can understand, and sends them on to your printer. Though the process is slow, the results are excellent. A DeskJet driven from Ventura by one of these PostScript interpreters even does a standard LaserJet one better, by printing Encapsulated PostScript files. If you're interested in the idea, Chapter 20 is devoted to a discussion of three of these PostScript interpreters.

Publisher's Powerpak

Another eminently workable alternative is Publisher's Powerpak from Atech Software. This product provides Ventura printer drivers for over 200 printers that Ventura itself doesn't directly support, including the DeskJet, along with a font generator that scales master typeface outlines to any size supported by Ventura as you print. The three typefaces supplied with Publisher's Powerpak imitate Times Roman, Helvetica, and Courier, and you can add additional typefaces at extra cost. Each can be printed in a variety of special styles, such as thin, condensed, and hollow (outlined). Powerpak works as advertised. Installation is effortless (I never once looked at the manual), and you use the standard techniques to print from within Ventura. My only criticism is that the fonts aren't quite as sharp as those produced by products such as MoreFonts (Chapter 7) or GoScript (Chapter 20). The sample Ventura newsletter reproduced earlier in this chapter was printed on a DeskJet using Publisher's Powerpak. Versions of Pubisher's Powerpak are also available for First Publisher, Windows, Microsoft Word, and WordPerfect.

A similar solution is LaserTwin, the LaserJet emulation utility profiled in Chapter 4. With LaserTwin, you configure Ventura to print to a LaserJet, and the program converts Ventura's output into DeskJet format. The results are just as good as if you'd printed your document on a real LaserJet.

Access: Ventura/DeskJet utilities

Publisher's Powerpak/$199.95
Atech Software
5962 La Place Court #245
Carlsbad, CA 92008
619/438-6883

LaserTwin/$179
Metro Software, Inc.
2509 N. Campbell Ave., # 214
Tucson, AZ 85719
800/621-1137

There are several drawbacks common to all these alternatives for getting Ventura to work with a DeskJet. The first is speed—the process of making Ventura's ordinary output palatable for the DeskJet takes time. Another problem is that none of these programs can digest fonts in any of the standard formats. That means you'll be limited to the fonts the vendor provides. Specifically, you can't use any of these products with normal DeskJet fonts, nor, in the PostScript interpreters' case, with standard PostScript fonts either.

Ventura tips and tricks

My first tip is a plug for another book. If you want to know more about Ventura than the manual reveals, the best single source to call on is Ted Nace's *Ventura Tips and Tricks, 2nd Edition.* This chunky volume packs a wealth of practical how-to advice on handling almost every conceivable page layout chore with Ventura. It fills you in on all of Ventura's little quirks, sets you straight on a host of behind-the-scenes technicalities that can affect your work, and covers the diversity of hardware and software you can use with the program. A must for serious Ventura users.

Adding new fonts

At the moment, the only way to use Ventura with a DeskJet is via a third-party software package (Publisher's PowerPak, LaserTwin, or one of the PostScript interpreters). For this reason, you have to rely on the vendor of that package to set you up with additional fonts. Since all of these programs are designed with Ventura in mind, the optional fonts are supplied in Ventura-compatible format, and come with the instructions you'll need to install them into Ventura.

Speeding up your printer

The DeskJet isn't the world's fastest printer, and there's nothing you can do to boost it's performance directly. Still, you can drastically reduce the time you spend twiddling your thumbs while waiting for your Ventura documents to pop out. Just install a print spooler utility such as LaserTORQ or the one that comes in the Super PC-Kwik utilities bundle. See Chapter 4 for more details on spoolers.

Profile: PageMaker

$795/Aldus Corp
411 First Ave. S. #200
Seattle, WA 98104
206/622-5500

PageMaker is the program most closely associated with desktop publishing—in fact Aldus president Paul Brainerd is responsible for coining the term. Although PageMaker's PC version looks and works almost identically to the groundbreaking Macintosh version, it hasn't the enjoyed the same market dominance, what with Ventura's overwhelming popularity. Nonetheless, it's a great piece of software that does its intended job well.

PageMaker's name is apt, because the program's strength lies in its ability to lay out individual pages. The screen looks much like a real pasteup table, with icons for various commands designed to resemble a graphics artist's tools as much as possible. The pasteup metaphor is functional as well as cosmetic, since you assemble text and graphics onto a screen page much as you would on paper. Unlike Ventura and most other DTP programs, PageMaker doesn't ask you to draw frames for your text and graphics before you import them. Instead, you "paste" each element onto the page directly where it will go.

PageMaker readily imports text and graphics in all the common formats. Several new features for modifying and printing imported graphics have been added in version 3, making PageMaker your best choice if you plan to work extensively with color or scanned images. There's a drawback to PageMaker's approach to imported files, however. The program merges the contents of imported files into one central document, instead of maintaining each file as a separate entity. Once PageMaker has imported a file, any changes you make to the original with another program won't show up in the PageMaker document. There is a function for re-exporting text, however.

Although PageMaker doesn't offer the depth of typographic control you get in Ventura, it offers enough to keep most desktop publishers occupied and happy. You can control leading, kerning, letter spacing, and word spacing, and create hanging and nested indents. You also get a variety of simple drawing tools for adding lines, rectangles, and ovals to your documents. Unique features include the ability to print documents larger than a single piece of paper, by printing each page in sections that you then paste together;

an on-screen pasteboard, an area in which you can park text or graphics temporarily; and the ability to position graphics so that they straddle adjacent pages. PageMaker also has one simple yet vital advantage over Ventura: an Undo function that cancels the effects of your most recent command if things didn't turn out as you expected.

In version 3, PageMaker has also acquired some new features essential for producing long documents. It can now automatically generate as many new pages as are needed to fit the document's text. Equally important, PageMaker 3 owners enjoy a well-implemented style sheet feature for much quicker text formatting.

One other major attribute of PageMaker that you should consider is the fact that it runs within the Microsoft Windows. That makes it considerably slower than Ventura, and that speed difference is enough to make an impact on how productive you can be. You can compensate to a degree by buying a faster computer and more memory, but that will cost you a pretty penny.

On the other hand, Windows has the major advantage of allowing you to run multiple programs at the same time. Say you're putting together a business report, and you need a chart showing the price of eggs in Wisconsin over the past 12 months. From within PageMaker, you can switch over to Excel to format the chart. Then you go back to PageMaker, which is still idling right where you left it, and import the chart. Later, when you realize you need an illustration, you start up Corel Draw or Micrografx Designer, lay down your artwork, and hop back to PageMaker exactly where you left off. Another Windows plus is that Windows manages your fonts for all your application programs. Tell Windows which fonts you have, and all your programs know automatically (at the moment, however, you can't use DeskJet soft fonts with Windows).

Using PageMaker with the DeskJet

As far as DeskJet owners are concerned, PageMaker has one major advantage over Ventura: since PageMaker runs in the Windows environment, it works with the standard Windows DeskJet driver. Once you've installed Windows for the DeskJet, you can print any PageMaker document, with the exception of ones that contain imported Encapsulated PostScript files. Your font choices are limited with the standard Windows driver, however. If you want more flexibility, you can obtain PostScript-like scalable fonts with Publisher's Powerpak, SuperPrint, or one of the PostScript emulation packages. These alternatives are discussed in Chapter 17 on Windows and the DeskJet.

12

Graphics Software

∾

One of the best things about the multi-talented DeskJet is that it prints high-resolution graphics just as effortlessly as it does text. As usual, all you need is some good software.

Graphics software covers the gamut, from crude low-budget wonders to expensive feature-laden packages that suit the needs of the professional graphics artist. Somewhere in that range, you should be able to find a program that's just what you need to express your visual creativity.

DeskJet issues

If computer art for art's sake is your passion, you can print your masterpieces directly from the program in which you create them. In this case, you'll need to be sure that the graphics software you select works well with the DeskJet.

More often, though, your pictures will end up as illustrations in a larger document that you put together with a desktop publishing program. If this is how you plan to use graphics, your concerns will be to ensure that your art files transfer easily to the desktop publishing program, and that the latter program is DeskJet-compatible.

Paint versus draw programs

A great divide separates two fundamentally different types of graphics software. On one side of the gulf are the "paint" programs, on the other the "draw" programs. The distinction between the two is rooted in the method each type of program uses to represent images within your computer, but this technical difference has important artistic repercussions.

Paint programs get their name from the way they let you apply colors and patterns to your screen much as if you were spreading paint onto a canvas. With complete abandon—within the boundaries of your screen—you can roll on a swath of deep purple here, splash some spots of hot pink there, and drip tiny droplets of gold (of course, all of these colors would show up as different shades of grey when printed on the DeskJet). And don't let the name fool you. You *can* draw—lines, boxes, circles, what have you—with a paint program, just as easily as you can with a draw program.

The key point is that a paint program lets you directly control the placement of every individual dot that makes up the picture. Of course, if you're using a wide "brush" to slather on your colors, you may not take advantage of this dot-by-dot control. But it's still true that you are directly responsible for where the paint ends up in your picture. As a result, an image created in a paint program can be beautifully detailed—even to the point that it starts to look like a real painting, depending on the resolution of your program, screen, and printer.

That brings up the subject of graphics resolution vis-a-vis the DeskJet. The DeskJet's top resolution, of course, is a high 300 dots per linear inch—that's enough dots for some stunningly sharp pictures. Unfortunately, in many paint programs, the maximum resolution you can achieve is limited to the resolution of your screen. Even on a VGA monitor, that's only 640x480 dots for the entire screen, a far lower resolution than the DeskJet's. As a result, the graphics you create in these programs tend to look rough and jagged when printed. However, you can buy paint programs that let you create 300 dpi pictures by enlarging the image on screen—of course, you can only work with part of the picture at a time with this method.

Working at 300 dpi, a paint program lets you create far more richly detailed pictures than a draw program. But even the high-resolution paint programs have some drawbacks. Talking technical for a moment, paint programs render pictures in bitmapped form (see Chapter 3), where each dot of the image is stored in the computer's memory. That consumes a tremendous amount of memory and hard disk space for pictures of any size. In addition, if you try to enlarge or reduce the picture to fit a particular space, the quality of the image may deteriorate. That's because the program has to add and subtract dots where it thinks it should, and its guesses may not be very good.

One important use of paint programs is in editing scanned images. A digital scanner works much like a photocopy machine, passing a beam of light over an image on paper and converting the reflection into a pattern of dots. Instead of printing the dot pattern or bitmap on a new piece of paper, however, the scanner simply stores it in a file on your hard disk. At this point, you can incorporate the scanned image into a document in your desktop publishing or word processing program. For example, you might want to scan in your signature, and merge it into a form letter you're sending out.

Though you can use your scanned image files without modification, bringing them into a paint program first for editing is often a good idea. You may well find you need to remove stray dots, lighten overly dark areas, and do other touch-up work. If you like, you can add shading, or even go hog wild and make the scanned image part of a larger painting.

Paint programs that work well with the DeskJet include HotShot Graphics, ColorRIX, and, of course, all the members of the PC Paintbrush family.

Draw programs work much like paint programs in some ways, but quite differently in others. As you'd expect by the name, draw programs do a great job at drawing lines. But even here, they make work somewhat differently than you'd expect. In a paint program, you just draw your lines, and every spot on the picture that the mouse pointer touches becomes a dot in your picture. The line doesn't exist as a separate entity, and if you wish to change it in any way, you have to erase the old dots and draw in new ones.

In a draw program, the software translates your mouse movements into a mathematical description of the line you trace. It stores this description as a separate object unto itself, rather than as a series of individual dots. Now, if you want to change the line as a whole, you can, by shrinking it, stretching it, moving it as a whole from place to place, or—in the case of the more advanced drawing programs—by reshaping the contour of the line with precision control.

Draw programs handle all the elements in a picture, whether they are lines, triangles, circles, or boxes, in this way, treating them as independent objects stored as mathematical descriptions in the program's memory. These descriptions are converted into dots for display on your screen, or when the picture gets printed.

This *object-oriented* or *vector* approach to graphics has many implications for your artwork. The most important advantage is that it allows the program to automatically adjust things so that the drawing prints at the highest possible resolution on whatever printer you own, independently of the image you see on the screen. This means that you can work on your drawing at actual size even on a relatively low-resolution monitor, and still get excellent quality when you print. All the program has to do is retranslate all those mathematical descriptions into a new dot pattern matching the printer's resolution.

In like manner, you can freely resize any object in the picture, or the entire picture, without any degradation of quality—again, the program just recalculates the objects. Another positive is that these mathematical descriptions consume far less memory and disk space than do the dot-by-dot paint graphics.

On the downside, you don't have anywhere near the control over details of color and shading as you do in a paint program. Draw programs do let you color the lines themselves, of course. But though you can apply colors and shades to empty parts of the picture, you can only do so within boundaries specificially defined by lines. You simply can't daub on a little color here and there. As a result, images created in draw programs can consist of very complex shapes, but they have simple, poster-like color schemes, lacking the life-like realism that's possible with paint programs.

These days, most of the action in PC artwork is on the draw side of the great graphics divide. The advantages of precision control over line contour, and the ability to print at the highest possible resolution are just too great for most artists to ignore. Besides, the simpler color and shading of draw-type images actually works better than the complexity of the paint type variety for the kinds of illustrations most people use.

At this writing, at least five professional-quality draw packages are jockeying for your attention, and there are still several less expensive intermediate-level programs that are good for occasional use. All work well with the DeskJet. Note, though, that some of the most advanced features of the draw programs rely heavily on the PostScript language, which shines when it comes to object-oriented graphics. Since the DeskJet isn't a PostScript printer, you'll be unable to use these features. But as you'll see in Chapter 20, it's possible to add PostScript capability to your DeskJet.

Profile: PC Paintbrush

$99.95 (for PC Paintbrush IV)/**ZSoft**
450 FranklinRd., Suite 100
Marietta, GA 30067
404/428-0008

In the divided world of PC graphics programs, PC Paintbrush is still the leader of the paint pack. The PC Paintbrush file format for paint-type graphics, PCX, has become firmly established as far and away the most widely used bitmapped format on IBM-compatible microcomputers.

Over the last few years the original PC Paintbrush program has evolved into a whole family of Paintbrushes. There have been too many versions of the program for me to keep them straight without my crib notes, but all of them share the basic strengths: comprehensive graphics editing tools, good performance, and support for just about any type of screen, mouse, and printer you can name, including the DeskJet.

The screen tools common to all versions of PC Paintbrush let you paint swatches of colors or patterns with a brush, draw lines, boxes, and circles, cut, copy, and paste parts of you picture, and type text. A "spray can" tool lets you apply color or paint lightly, in a sort of a mist effect, without obscuring the entire background—this is a great way to lighten up parts of a scanned image that are too dark. The program gives you access to loads of different colors and patterns, and you can create your own if the pre-defined ones aren't enough.

At the time I wrote this book, ZSoft was in the process of giving birth to yet another generation of Paintbrushes which will have lots of new features. First to emerge are the lower-end PC Paintbrush IV and PC Paintbrush IV+. Both of these reasonably-priced programs now have most of the talents that were previously available only in the chief of the clan, Publisher's Paintbrush. The list of new features includes the ability to import TIFF files (the kind created by most scanners), grey-scale editing for enhancing black-and-white images, and other sophisticated special effects such as blending, smudging, and tiling. Type handling capabilities have also been significantly improved, and you can now use outline fonts created in Publisher's Type Foundry, a sister product, in either program.

Figure 12-1: *PC Paintbrush IV. The new release is marked by improved grey-scale editing features, enhanced type handling, and better on-line help,*

The biggest difference between PC Paintbrush IV and PC Paintbrush IV+ is the size of the images each program allows. In ordinary Paintbrush IV, you're limited to whatever you can fit into the standard DOS memory space of 640K. Paintbrush IV+, by contrast, can park portions of your pictures in extended or expanded memory, or on your hard disk, letting you create much larger pictures. In addition, the + version lets you control your scanner directly from within the program, so you don't have to leave your work when you want to scan. The old version of Paintbrush + could import Lotus 1-2-3 charts in the .PIC format, but this feature has been dropped.

PC Paintbrush + for Windows has yet to undergo revision, and it isn't nearly as strong a program as the non-Windows versions. It does give you all the standard editing tools, and it has the important advantage of being able to run at the same time as other Windows programs such as PageMaker. On the other hand, it doesn't have the grey-scale features of its siblings, and like all Windows programs, it's a bit sluggish.

Publisher's Paintbrush used to be the king of the hill, but it doesn't have that much to offer above the new versions of PC Paintbrush IV and IV+. Until this program gets a thorough upgrade, stick with one of its less expensive relations.

All versions of Paintbrush come with a utility program called Frieze which lets you capture screen images and save them in PCX format. Once you've captured a screen, you can edit with Paintbrush, or import it into a word processor or desktop publishing document. See Chapter 19 for the scoop on screen capture.

All versions of PC Paintbrush work fine with the DeskJet. The non-Windows editions come with their own DeskJet drivers, which allow you to choose between draft quality (150 dpi resolution) or high quality (300 dpi) printing modes.

Profile: GEM Draw Plus

Digital Research, Inc.
Box DRI
Monterey, CA 93942
408/649-3896

If you're looking for a quick, competent, no-frills drawing package, start your hunt with GEM Draw Plus.

As its full name suggests, GEM Draw Plus runs in the GEM graphical environment, sort of a scaled down version of Microsoft's Windows. Like Windows, or the Apple Macintosh, GEM relies heavily on the mouse, and on a series of drop-down menus available from a menu bar across the top of the screen. In Draw Plus, as in many GEM programs, a pallette of icons on the left side of the screen gives you quick access to the commands and features you'll use most often. If you've ever used Ventura Publisher, GEM Draw Plus will be instantly familiar, since Ventura is also based on the GEM environment.

Figure 12-2: *GEM Draw Plus lets you open two windows simultaneously and copy images between them.*

GEM Draw Plus may not have the sophistication of fancier draw programs such as its stablemate Artline or Corel Draw, but it can just about everything you need. You can place circles, arcs, rectangles, and polygons in a snap, and you can draw freeform lines to your heart's content. Once you've created one of these objects, you can resize it, rotate it, flip it vertically or horizontally, or combine it with others as a conglomerate that you can then work with as a unit. There's even a command that instantly creates a shadow effect for any object, making it easy to add the illusion of depth to simple 2-dimensional shapes.

GEM Draw Plus is an especially good choice as a drawing program if you use Ventura Publisher or GEM Desktop Publisher for page layout. Since both of these programs also work in the GEM environment, they can import Draw Plus' object-oriented .GEM files perfectly, and without any intermediate translation step.

A small but high-quality collection of clip art accompanies the program. You can also buy GEM Draw Plus as part of a package deal called the GEM Presentation Team, which includes a charting program and a more extensive supply of business-oriented clip art as well.

GEM Draw Plus is fast as well as capable. As a rule, GEM programs run significantly faster than Windows programs because the GEM environment is inherently less complicated. If you're still using a standard PC or XT, GEM Draw Plus is definitely preferable to a Windows alternative.

This program's biggest drawback is its lack of an "undo" feature. If you change something and then realize you liked it better before, you're stuck with manually putting things right.

At this point, although the DeskJet is supported by the GEM environment, the DeskJet driver is not shipped with the standard GEM installation kit. Instead, you have to order it separately on a "printer pack" from DRI.

Profile: Zing

$199.95/Enabling Technologies, Inc.
6005 Dearborn St, #1304
Chicago, IL 60605
312/427-0408

If you want your illustrations to have a little depth, you should look into Zing, a 3-D drawing program from Enabling Technology. Zing allows you to create graphical objects that appear 3-dimensional on your screen and to manipulate them in an imaginary 3-D workspace. You're not just adding perspective to a two-dimensional image. Instead, Zing drawings actually have fronts, backs, sides, tops, and bottoms, and you can see them from any angle you like.

Since Zing approximates all curved surfaces with a series of short lines, contoured objects appear unnaturally blocky, like Bizarro in the old Superman comics. However, the 3-D effect is often interesting enough to offset this, and careful shading can make it less noticeable.

Figure 12-3: *Zing lets you combine "3-dimensional" images and rotate them through space.*

As you might imagine, the process of drawing a new 3-D object on a flat screen is considerably more complex than is making a conventional PC graphic. However, if you're not inclined to devote the time required for creating your own 3-D artwork, you don't have to. Enabling has a large library of 3-D clip-art available in thematic packages (Holidays, Geography, and so on). To get you started, Zing includes a sampling of a few images from several of the categories.

What's most fun about Zing is the way you can combine clip-art images and those you design yourself into complete 3-D scenes, positioning each object where you want it in your 3-D workspace. You can resize and rotate each object or the entire scene to view it from below and in front, from directly above, or from any other angle you like (see the illustration in Figure 12-ggg). You can also manipulate the apparent lighting on your scene, emulating twilight, overhead lighting, a single light source, and a variety of other scenarios.

If you're interested in designing your own 3-D artwork, be prepared for a period of adjustment to the new techniques involved. For objects such as bowls and bottles that are symmetric about two axes, you use a "lathe" tool to draw a cross-sectional view of the object. Objects that are symmetric around only one axis take shape on a "jigsaw", on which you draw a front face of the object and specify its thickness. To create objects that are completely assymetric, you must build them up from smaller symmetric objects.

Despite a wide selection of sophisticated commands, Zing is crude compared to the 3-dimensional drawing programs you can expect to see in the future. For the time being, though, it's a fun way to relieve the flatness of PC graphics.

Profile: Five high-end draw programs

After years of taking a back seat to the Macintosh when it comes to high-quality graphics, the PC and its extended family have suddenly evened the score. As of this writing, there are five professional-quality drawing programs, any one of which can be used to produce artwork that rivals the creations of a traditional graphics artist, yet can be printed on your DeskJet.

Though all five of these "illustration" programs offer many improvements over simpler draw software such as GEM Draw Plus, one of these differences is the real key to their superiority: the method they use to let you place lines very accurately, and then modify the lines after you've drawn them.

In their inner workings, all these upscale illustration programs use an efficient method of representing lines mathematically; lines defined by this method are called *Bezier curves*. To form the outline of a Bezier curve, you only need to know where a few points on the curve are located: the points where the line starts and stops, and the points where the curve changes direction, known variously as the *anchor points, handles,* or *nodes.* On the screen, the anchor points appear as big squares or rectangles directly on the path of the curve.

At each direction-changing anchor point, you must also know the angle of deflection, and how far the curve extends in that direction. These characteristics are represented on screen by the length and direction of dashed lines which extend out on either side of the anchor points and end in *control points.*

Once you've defined the anchor points and the control points, the program just connects the anchors with a smooth curve. Of course, you never see the formulas involved. Instead, you simply draw on the screen. Some programs let you draw freehand; after you've drawn a line, the program converts it to a Bezier, calculating where the anchor points and control points should go. In other programs, you place the anchor points by hand, one at a time. This method may sound less intuitive than the freehand approach, but it can actually be more precise and quicker. To modify the shape of the line, you can move the anchor point itself, or manipulate the control points to lengthen or shorten the deflection lines or change their angles. Figure 12-4 shows how this process looks in Artline.

Figure 12-4: *This screen from Artline exemplifies how all the high-end illustration programs work. The small dark box on the curve of the pear's leaf is an* anchor point, *while the small lines extending on either side of it end in* control points. *Using the mouse, you can drag the anchor to change the location of the curve at that point, or drag the control lines to change the curve's shape.*

All this sounds quite complicated, and it does take awhile to get the hang of these bizarre Beziers. But if you keep at it, you'll soon find that working with Bezier curves becomes a fairly intuitive process, and it definitely lets you place curves exactly where you want them to go.

Because so many images are already available in bitmapped, paint-type files, an *autotrace* feature is common to many of the illustration programs. Autotracing converts the outlines of the bitmap into Bezier curves, allowing you to print the image at the highest resolution your printer can produce, and to edit it with the other drawing tools provided by the software.

Since they're targeted at professional graphics artists, most of these illustration programs have strong tools for manipulating text. That way, you can compose an entire brochure or flyer in one program, without resorting to manual pasteup or even a desktop publishing product.

The emphasis is on jazzy headlines and captions, not long stretches of copy. Typically, you can use a wide assortment of fonts, and you can dress them up with all kinds of fancy special effects. For instance, you can fill the characters with patterns or colors, create bold outlines around them, rotate, stretch, or squeeze them, or array them along a curve. In three of the programs, you can even edit the character outlines just as if they were ordinary graphics, adding ornate embellishments, or enlarging the first character in a logo for emphasis.

Choosing an illustration package

Four of the five programs are designed for Microsoft Windows and one for GEM, which is sort of a pared down version of Windows. Both Windows and GEM assume primary responsibility for interacting with your printer, relieving the actual program you're using from this burden. This being the case, the results you can expect when printing your graphics on the DeskJet from any of these illustration packages depend mostly on the quality of the DeskJet driver that comes with the environment (Windows or GEM).

Unless you're independently wealthy, you obviously can't buy all five of the high-end draw programs—so which one is best? There's a short answer and a long answer. With a relatively small market for these packages, at least compared with word processors, The stakes are high, With one possible exception, each of them has its strong points.

Corel Draw

Like everybody and her sister, I choose Corel Draw as my hands down favorite among today's crop of upscale drawing programs. Corel Draw has just about every graphics feature you could imagine, and a whole bunch more beyond that. And Corel Draw is the fastest of the Windows-based illustration packages, almost as responsive as GEM-based Artline.

Corel Draw's core drawing features are second to none. The program responds quickly and accurately as you draw your Bezier curves freehand, giving you a better sense of control over the placement of your lines than in most of the competition. Even more important, there's a complete set of functions for editing the Beziers, and they work. In addition, you get tools for drawing ovals and rectangles in a single step, and you can resize, rotate, or skew the objects in your drawing with the mouse or with numeric precision.

Draw currently sports a decent autotrace feature, but it's somewhat inferior to the one in Designer. A separate more capable autotracing program will soon be released by Corel Systems, I'm told, though at this writing the company hasn't decided whether to include it for free with Corel Draw.

Corel's prowess with text is nothing short of phenomenal. The program comes with a whole slew of built-in typefaces that are nearly identical copies of the most popular PostScript originals sold by Adobe Systems. You're restricted to using typefaces in the Corel format, but as a reward you get to print them in any size on any printer that works with the program, the DeskJet included. Purchase Corel Draw, and your like the DeskJet, that means you've instantly acquired an entire library of typefaces What's more, you can tell the program to convert the type outlines into graphics objects, and then edit them just as you would any other shape in your picture for really classy text effects.

As if that wasn't enough, the newest version of Corel Draw, 1.1, has been filled out with still more type-oriented features than version 1.0. To start with, the package includes even more imitation PostScript typeface outlines in the Corel format. In addition, a new utility takes outline printer fonts from all the major vendors—that includes Adobe Systems' specially coded PostScript fonts—and converts them into Corel Draw's own format. Once the conversion is made, you can modify the text with any of Corel Draw's text features. The conversion utility hasn't always worked perfectly for me, but no other graphics package even attempts this feat.

For easy integration with other programs, Corel Draw imports and exports long list of different kinds of graphics file formats—it even does a better job with Illustrator files from the Macintosh than the PC version of Illustrator does.

Figure 12-5: A screen from Corel Draw, taken from a full-page monitor. You draw with the outlines in the top window, and see the results as they'll print in the preview window below.

To top it off, all these capabilities are wrapped up in a screen package that's attractive and easy to use. The major drawing tools have been combined into an efficient, uncluttered icon bar, while ordinary menus give you access to less commonly used commands for printing and fine tuning.

Designer

Micrografx Designer was the first PC illustration package, and the program has won a lot of converts over the last couple of years. Designer boasts many strengths, including a wide range of excellent drawing tools, strong import-export capabilities, and the best built-in autotrace function I've used. Designer is unique among the drawing packages in letting you set up drawings with independent *layers*. You can turn the display of a given layer on or off as necessary, making it much easier to work with complex, richly textured illustrations. On the convenience side, it's the only program that lets you

Figure 12-6: I don't know who spent the hours that were necessary to create this complex, professional-quality illustration in Designer, but even in the black and white reproduction here you can get some idea of its intricate detail.

customize the screen palette of tools so that it contains icons for the commands you use most often.

The current version of Designer, 2.0, does have one important weakness, and that's its limited text capabilities. While you can use any Windows font in a piece of Designer artwork, you can't modify the characters with many of the fancy embellishments available in the other programs. You can't outline them, you can't place them along a curve—in fact, you can't change from one font to another, or even from italics to bold, within a block of text.

Of course, if you just need artwork for its own sake, or as illustrations in text-heavy documents, these textual limitations shouldn't matter to you. Still, Micrografx is hard at work to overcome them. Version 3.0 should make Designer competitive in the text arena when it appears in late 1989.

Arts & Letters

Everyone who writes about the Arts & Letters Editor is always harping on the large library of clip-art images that come with the program. The conventional wisdom has it that Arts & Letters is the program of choice if you don't want to draw your own pictures, but would rather capitalize on prefab drawings, perhaps editing them to suit the document you're working on.

I find three things wrong with this argument:

First, ignore the clip-art altogether, and you'll find that Arts & Letters stands on its own as an excellent drawing package with a couple of features not available in the competition. No other program offers as many different ways to limit which lines go where in advance, helping ensure that your results are as you expect them. No other program has A&L's blend tool, which lets you smoothly transform one shape into another. The latest version of Arts & Letters, 2.0, gives Corel Draw a good run for the money in the special effects department, with features such as "calligraphic" pen shapes and the ability to automatically fit text to a curve. File import/export capabilities have also been beefed up, and the program handles color much better than before—though that's hardly a concern when you're printing on the DeskJet.

Second, Arts & Letters' clip art system isn't as well-designed as the ones in Artline or Designer. Instead of showing you the clip art images stored on disk on the screen before you place them into your work, Arts & Letters makes you look them up in a book. When you locate the picture you want, you have to type in its catalog number into a little window.

Finally, just because Arts & Letters has lots of clip art doesn't mean it has the clip art you want. My advice is to shop for your clip art and your drawing program separately. Of course, if it turns out that you like what you see in

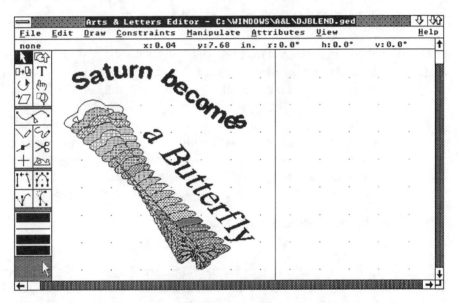

Figure 12-7: *Amazingly, Arts&Letters 2.0 lets you transform one shape into another through a series of gradual intermediates. You can also fit text to any shape, as shown crudely with the words "Saturn becomes" above.*

the Arts & Letters clip art catalog, and that you're just as happy with the features of the Arts & Letters editor, this program would make a great choice.

Artline

Feature for feature, DRI's Artline doesn't quite measure up to the other programs in the list, but don't count Artline out until you've looked it over closely.

Based on the same lean GEM environment that gave Ventura its reputation for speed, Artline runs quickly enough for practical use on a standard PC or XT, a feat none of its competitors can manage. Another strength is that it works directly with the high-quality Bitstream typeface outlines, allowing you to convert the characters you type into shapes you can edit just like other graphics elements. The facing page is a reproduction of a DeskJet printout from Artline showing some of the text effects you can produce. Artline also has easiest to use system for managing libraries of clip art and stored images. As shown in Figure 12-4, a little window pops up on the screen showing you a reduced version of one image at time.

Artline's fundamental drawing tools work reliably. You can't draw freehand, but I find that the point-by-point method of placing curves lets you be more accurate the first time around, which makes it quicker. The biggest problem I've encountered is that you can't have more than 128 points (anchor and control points) in a single curve, a limit that you can easily reach when you're doing complex artwork. Also, Artline so far lacks an auto-trace tool, so it takes much longer to convert bitmap graphics into draw format than with the other programs.

Adobe Illustrator

Bringing up the rear in the high-end drawing sweepstakes is the entry from Adobe Systems, the company that started the whole professional-quality drawing craze with Illustrator for the Macintosh. The Windows version of Illustrator certainly has the basic tools you need to make good looking pictures on your PC. Still, it offers far fewer amenities and advanced features than Corel Draw, Designer, or Arts & Letters, and suffers from limited text handling features. And since Illustrator only supports PostScript printers, you'd have to use an add-on PostScript interpreter, the kind discussed in Chapter 20, to print with the DeskJet at all.

But Illustrator's real downfall is its terribly slow performance. Even on a super-fast PC with an 80386 microprocessor, you have to wait much too long for each little command to take effect. Until Adobe improves Illustrator's performance, you should shy away from this program.

GEM *Artline* by CCP

Access: Professional Illustration Software

**Arts & Letters Graphics
  Editor/$695**
Computer support Corporation
15926 Midway road
Dallas, TX 75244
214/661-8960

**Adobe Illustrator,
  Windows version/$695**
Adobe Systems, Inc.
1585 Charleston Rd.
Mountain View, CA 94039
800/344-8335; 415/961-4400

Corel Draw/$495
Corel Systems Corp.
1600 Carling Ave.
Ottawa, Ontario
K1Z 8R7 Canada
613/728-8200

GEM Artline/$495
Digital Research, Inc.
Box DRI
Monterey, CA 93942
408/649-3896

Micrografx Designer $695
Micrografx, Inc.
1303 Arapaho Rd.
Richardson, TX 75081
800/272-3729; 214/234-1769

13

Charting Software

For the workaday business professional, the most important graphics are the ones that relate to the bottom line. Sure, a drab report on fourth quarter shoe sales looks a little snappier when adorned with a cute clip-art picture of a shoehorn. What you really need, though, is a compact, high-impact, easy-to-understand chart summarizing the sales trends graphically. That way, those who read your report can understand the essence of your message at a glance; they'll have a much easier time deciding how much leather to buy.

Because the DeskJet prints charts with just as much clarity as it does text, it makes a superb printer for managers, scientists, teachers, or anyone who has to put together reports and papers that are rich in graphical information content. Of course, you'll need the appropriate charting software. To create charts most efficiently, you want software that can read your numbers directly and automatically turn them into bars, pie chunks, or lines of the correct size and shape. The ideal charting software will let you pick from a wide variety of chart types, and will automate the process of adding labels, legends and titles. More, it will let you embellish the chart with graphics, text, and boxes and arrows anywhere you like. And as long as you're asking for the moon, why not wish for a program that makes the whole process easy?

In this chapter, I'll touch on some of the most popular PC business graphics programs and how they measure up to the ideal. First, though, I have a few words about strategies for integrating charts into other documents.

Charts in reports

When you're ready to add a finished pie chart or bar graph to a textual document, you have two choices. The quickest and simplest alternative is to print out the chart on a separate page, directly from the software you used to create it. You then just insert that page where it belongs in your report.

If you want to get fancier, you can integrate your charts with the text of your report into a single complete document. When your chart is on the same page as the text that describes it, your readers will have no trouble relating the two. To use this strategy, you need a desktop publishing program that can read in both your text and your charts. Of course, designing an integrated report takes more time than simply printing your charts on separate pages.

Charting with your spreadsheet

Some people forego business graphics software, preferring to rely on the charting features of their spreadsheet instead. After all, if you use spreadsheet software to generate the data represented on the chart, it makes a lot of sense to create the chart itself in that same program. Otherwise, you're forced to export your data from the spreadsheet, start up the charting program, import the data—and then commence work on the chart. If your luck really goes sour, you'll realize you set up the data the wrong way to begin with, and you'll have to go back to the spreadsheet and start all over. Even if your charting program has "hot links" to the spreadsheet file, so that changes in the data are automatically reflected in the corresponding chart, you must still return to the spreadsheet to make the changes in the first place.

Nowadays all the major spreadsheet programs include charting modules of their own, most of which give you an acceptable range of options and produce excellent printed output. The 3 in Lotus 1-2-3 stands for graphics, meaning basic charts suitable for typical business applications. 1-2-3 charts are fairly rudimentary, though they've been improved somewhat with Releases 2.2 and 3.0. Excel, Supercalc, and especially Quattro Pro deserve high marks for their charting abilities. In fact, a complete drawing program for embellishing your charts is built right into Quattro Pro, giving it presentation graphics tools that are in the same league as those of the full-fledged charting programs discussed in this chapter.

However, even Quattro lacks some of the more sophisticated features of the top-notch charting packages such as Freelance Plus or Harvard Graphics. If you want your charts to stand out as really unique, you'll need to turn to the genuine article.

Harvard Graphics

By far the most popular of today's general-purpose charting software for the PC is Harvard Graphics. You can create more sophisticated other programs if you have the time, but Harvard has has the all-important virtue of being easy to use.

The key to Harvard's simplicity is its reliance on a large number of templates covering most of the common types of charts. It's considerably easier to modify these templates for your own use than to create a new chart from scratch as you usually must in other high-quality packages.

Other Harvard strengths include its large variety of chart types; support for a huge number of printers, including the DeskJet; and a spelling checker, a great touch for hurried businesspeople who want to avoid embarrassing slip-ups. Another important plus is that you can create permanent links to spreadsheet and ASCII files. Once you've established the link, Harvard automatically redraws the corresponding chart whenever the data in the file is changed, minimizing the time you spend transferring data into the program. In addition, however, Harvard lets you perform a variety of calculations on imported data so you don't have to go back to the program of origin when changes are necessary.

Weak drawing features are the one significant limitation of the program. You can't draw freehand, you can't flip or rotate objects, and you can't even zoom in on your work when it needs touching up.

Freelance Plus

Freelance Plus always finishes second to Harvard Graphics in sales, but not because it's a less capable product. In fact, Freelance has a considerably broader list of features than its archrival, including an exhaustive selection of chart types, a far more complete set of drawing tools, and a sophisticated presentation planning and file management system. In addition, its links to 1-2-3 spreadsheet data are superior—you can display an entire worksheet on the Freelance screen as you're developing a chart. The package comes complete with an extensive series of templates comparable to Harvard's and a larger clip-art collection.

Perhaps because it has more features, Freelance Plus isn't quite as simple a program as is Harvard Graphics. While this may help to account for its lesser popularity, Freelance isn't difficult to use, and it even has some creature comforts that Harvard lacks. For instance, while both programs require you to set up your charts on a non-graphics screen, Freelance makes the process more convenient with point-and-click popup menus. On the down side, Freelance is slower at displaying graphics, and doesn't let you recalculate imported data.

Graph Plus

Graph Plus is the preeminent business graphics package for Windows, with features comparable to those of Harvard Graphics and Freelance Plus.

Graph Plus has its own mini-spreadsheet for entering data from scratch or for editing data imported from a real spreadsheet file. Unfortunately, Graph Plus doesn't permit direct links to spreadsheet files, which means that you have to reimport the data each time it changes. Once you've entered the raw data, however, Graph Plus can manipulate them with a variety of mathematical functions, including simple arithemtic calculations and linear, logarithmic, and exponential regressions.

No matter what display format best suits your data, Graph Plus should have the right chart type on its lenghtly list. Sophisticated charting options include dua *y*-axes, log-log and semi-log scales. You also get extensive drawing functions, a good clip-art library, and the ability to import scanned images.

As a Windows program, Graph Plus works fine with the DeskJet for charting graphics. Its downfall is in the area of text. As with all Windows programs that rely on the standard Windows printer drivers to access fonts, a Graph Plus chart can only print with the limited array of cartridge fonts. However, you can avoid this restriction and print fonts of any size by installing the SuperPrint driver described in Chapter 17.

GEM Presentation Team

GEM Presentation Team comprises a threesome of programs which together cover the same bases as do Harvard, Freelance, and Graph Plus. The package includes GEM Graph, for charts and graphs, GEM WordChart, for word charts,

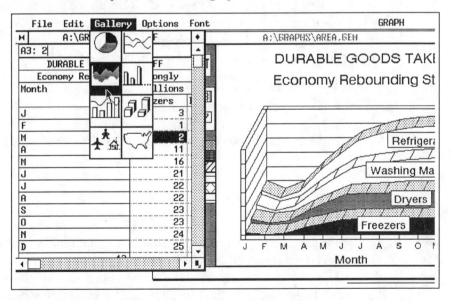

Figure 13-1: GEM Graph. The drop-down Gallery menu shown here lets you select the chart type via an icon. You can display both your data and the corresponding chart at the same time.

of course, and GEM Draw, a simple drawing program covered in more detail in Chapter 12. However, the combined features fall far short of the comparably-priced competition.

Presentation Team's main strength is its simplicity. Based on the GEM environment, all three programs run in a Windows-like graphical display which always shows you what your printout will look like. Since you're working on a WYSIWYG screen, you have the luxury of having your chart always in view as you select options from menus and dialog boxes. Creating Word Charts is particularly easy, since you can change the appearance of your text with a quick click on a toolbox that's always on screen. Compared with Windows programs such as Graph Plus and Pixie, GEM Presentation Team is faster on the screen due to its GEM heritage.

Unfortunately, this ease of use and quickness isn't matched by sophistication. GEM Graph, for example, provides only the basic types of charts, and has limited data importation features. Although you can transfer your charts to Draw Plus to touch them up with clip-art or your own drawing, you're then no longer able to edit the chart itself in GEM Graph. GEM Graph does have one nice feature found in few other programs: you can use clip art symbols for the bars in your bar charts. The program stacks up as many of the symbols as are needed to obtain the proper bar height.

If GEM Presentation Team cost less—say under $200—I would heartily recommend this suite of programs for those who need charting features occasionally or who want a truly easy business graphics solution. However, it's not sophisticated enough to compete with the other packages in its price class.

Pixie

Another Windows option is Pixie, a dandy little graphing program with a difference. Pixie's contribution to software evolution is the concept of "live" chartmaking. Other charting programs make you start with raw numbers, and show you your finished chart only after you've chosen all sorts of options from menus and dialog boxes. Since you don't actually see the effect of each design decision until the final chart appears, it's easy to make mistakes that force you to go back and try again.

Pixie takes a different tack. The program presents you with a generic version of the type of chart you want to generate. You then manipulate this template on the screen with the mouse until it shows off your own data in the way the best communicates your message (figure 13-1 gives you an idea of how this works). The process is much more intuitive than the traditional dialog box routine, and the direct feedback you get at each step along the way gives you a much greater sense of control. On the downside, Pixie is a fairly limited program, with far fewer customization options than the Harvards and Freelances. Also, while Pixie's template approach is easier to learn, some people claim that the traditional charting methods are faster once you're used to them.

Figure 13-2: *Creating a bar chart in Pixie. To change the size of a bar, just drag it with the mouse. A small window shows the corresponding value.*

PFS:First Graphics

If you're looking for a simple and relatively inexpensive charting program, the best non-Windows alternative is PFS:First Graphics from Software Publishing, the same company that publishes Harvard Graphics. First Graphics offers 15 different types of charts to work with. The list includes a number of chart types that aren't available in other DOS-based programs in this price range, such as high-low-close, trend, and overlapped bar. You can add a 3-dimensional effect to your charts, a feature not provided on the other inexpensive DOS charting programs. Five fonts are included, and you can scale these to 100 different sizes, again a far wider range than the competition permits.

First Graphics directly reads Lotus 1-2-3 files, so you don't have to translate them into ASCII format first. You can still import ASCII data too, of course. The program is easy to use and relatively fast at displaying graphs on the screen. Overall, First Graphics is an excellent low-cost way to get started with business graphics.

Access: Charting Software

Graph Plus /$495
Micrografx, Inc.
1303 E. Arapaho Rd.
Richardson, TX 75082
800/272-3729
214/234-1769

PFS: First Graphics/ $149
Harvard Graphics /$495
Software Publishing Corp.
1901 Landings Dr.
Mountain View, CA 94309
415/962-8910

Freelance Plus/$495
Lotus Development Corp.
55 Cambridge Parkway
Cambridge, MA 02142
617/577-8500

GEM Presentation Team/$495
Digital Research, Inc.
P.O. Box DRI
Monterey, CA 93942
800/443-4200

Pixie/$195
Zenographics
19752 MacArthur Blvd.
Irvine, CA 92715
714/851-6352

14

Spreadsheets

∾

Until fairly recently, a printed spreadsheet was about as interesting as the white pages of your phone book. All that changed with the introduction of Microsoft's Excel, the first major spreadsheet program to wed desktop-publishing design capabilities to PC number-crunching. Nowadays, features that let you select fonts, add boxes and lines, print charts and spreadsheets on the same page, and create more sophisticated charts in general are cropping up in many spreadsheet packages and add-on utilities.

The twin assumptions behind this rush to better output quality are sound. First, when facts and figures look good, the important points jump out at the reader. Second, slick-looking printouts are simply more impressive. Whether or not it's fair, the people you want to influence are likely to take you and your numbers more seriously when your report looks professionally published instead of banged out on a typewriter.

The DeskJet is an excellent spreadsheet printer. It serves equally well for quick draft copies for your own use and for polished final reports for your clients or superiors. Of course, the DeskJet isn't fast enough if you need to print lots of very long spreadsheets. However, most printed reports summarize large amounts of data in a few pages, and that's an application for which the DeskJet is ideal.

Basics of spreadsheet printer control

Back in the old days—a year or so ago—most spreadsheets offered precious little in the way of print formatting commands. In 1-2-3, for example, about all you could control was the position of characters in a cell: flush left, centered, or flush right. However, if you were dedicated to better formatting control, there was a way to get it. Most programs had a Setup String command that allowed you to type in an escape sequence which the program send to your printer immediately before printing the spreadsheet itself. In addition, you could embed escape sequences directly within your spreadsheets. If you wanted to print a certain cell in boldface, for instance, you could type in the necessary escape sequence directly into that cell in front of its data.

Today's presentation-quality spreadsheet programs are making most of this painful printer programming unnecessary. With Excel, with Quattro, and with 1-2-3 supplemented by Allways or Impress, you can switch fonts or type styles simply by marking a range of cells and choosing a menu command. Nevertheless, if you ever need to send out a DeskJet command that your spreadsheet program won't issue for you, you can still use the old method.

⌒ **Caution:** *Excel does not permit you to enter escape sequences yourself.*

The technique is essentially the same in every major spreadsheet program. To enter a printer command at the prompt for the setup string, you type in the initial escape sequence or control code in decimal notation, preceding the code digits with a backslash (\\). You then type the remaining characters of the command from the keyboard. For example, to enter the escape sequence for boldface printing, $^{E}s_{c}$(s3B, you would type in **\\027(s3B**. You use the same method to enter escape sequences with a cell, but you must precede the escape sequence or control code with a special character, typically one or two vertical bars (|).

Profile: Lotus 1-2-3

$495, 2.2; $595, 3.0/Lotus Development Corp
55 Cambridge Parkway
Cambridge, MA 02142
617/577-8500

Lotus 1-2-3 is the best-selling computer program of all time, and was largely responsible for the early popularity of the IBM PC. After long delays, Releases 2.2 and 3.0 are finally here. Release 2.2 is an incremental upgrade of 2.01, the long-running bestseller. Linked spreadsheet files and better graphics are two significant improvements. In addition, 2.2 incorporates Allways, an add-in that lends presentation-quality output to the product (Allways is described in more detail below). Release 3.0, on the other hand, is a substantially new product with a slew of powerful analytic features, but it requires an AT-class computer or better and a minimum of 384K extended memory above and beyond DOS's standard 640K.

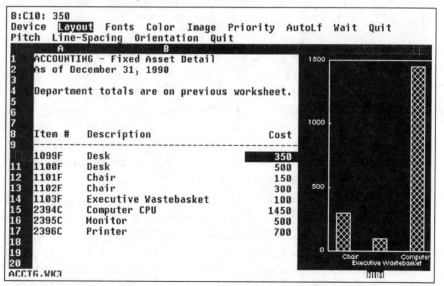

Figure 14-1: *1-2-3 Release 3 lets you control many print features with the menus shown here. You can see a graph and worksheet side by side as you work, and print a graph and worksheet range on the same page.*

Ignoring Allways for the moment, Release 2.2's printer controls are little changed from earlier versions. To send printer commands to your DeskJet, you must type them in as escape sequences as outlined above. To place an escape sequence in your worksheet, you must place it in an empty cell on an empty row. The cell must in the leftmost column of the portion of the worksheet you'll be printing. Precede the command by two vertical bars (|) (you won't see the first bar on your screen).

⌒ *Caution:* *You cannot embed printer commands in 1-2-3 Release 1A.*

Release 3.0 is a bit more savvy, allowing you to control many print characteristics from a series of simple menus. Specifically, the menus let you set margins, page length, fonts (including boldface and italic type), pitch, line spacing, and page orientation from the menus. You can still use the old system of embedding the commands in your spreadsheet, but you shouldn't combine both methods in the same document.

Allways and Impress

If you're a died-in-the-wool afficianado of 1-2-3, you no longer have to Allways and Impress are very similar programs that bring the look of desktop publishing to staid old 1-2-3. With either product, you can freely select fonts and typestyles for your spreadsheets, add lines and boxes for emphasis, and merge charts with spreadsheet text and numbers. Each program lets you see your work before you print it on a WYSIWYG display. Both products are add-ins, meaning that they merge themselves seamlessly into 1-2-3 itself, gaining direct access to the main programs data and menuing functions.

Both Allways and Impress support the DeskJet well. At this writing, however, you must request a special DeskJet driver for Impress from the publisher after you purchase the program. Each of the add-ins comes with its own fonts (Allways supplies three typefaces, Impress eight) that are translated into graphics for printout on the DeskJet. That means you don't have to worry about matching the program driver to your own font collection and there's no downloading hassle. Print speed is acceptable, and you can always churn out faster draft printouts with the DeskJet's own fonts using the standard 1-2-3 Print command.

Two big differences may help you decide between Allways and Impress. One is simply monetary: Lotus has been bundling Allways at no charge with 1-2-3 since early 1989, so if you bought your spreadsheet since then you already have Allways. On the other hand, Impress has the decided advantage of a "live" WYSIWYG spreadsheet display. You can work on your spreadsheet while you view it just as it will appear on your printed page. Allways makes you switch back and forth between text mode and a print preview.

✂ *Tip:* *If you don't need the fancy presentation-quality output of Allways or Impress, but would like to control your DeskJet more easily from within 1-2-3, look into the Funk Software's Worksheet Utilities. Also an add-in, the Utilities include PrintSet, a handy tool for creating reuseable libraries of print settings and escape codes. Instead of typing in a line of escape code gibberish, you can select predefined escape codes by description from a scrolling menu. Other components of the package add a formula editor, a search and replace function, and an autosave feature to 1-2-3.*

Access: 1-2-3 Printer Add-Ins

Allways/ $149.95
Worksheet Utilities/$99.95
Funk Software 222 Third St.
Cambridge MA 02142
800/822-3865

Impress/ $139.95
PC Publishing
1801 Avenue of the Stars, #815
Los Angeles, CA 90067
800/634-4555

Profile: Quattro Pro

$495/Borland International
1800 Green Hills Rd.
Scotts Valley, CA 95066
408/438-5300

Borland's Quattro Pro is brand new at the time of this writing. It's a blunderbuss spreadsheet program that combines a wealth of advanced analysis tools with knock-their-socks-off printed output. And it delivers the goods in the confines of ordinary DOS memory—you can build large spreadsheets even if you don't have oodles of expanded memory.

Quattro Pro works superbly with the DeskJet (see the sample chart on the opposite page, printed by a Quattro on a DeskJet Plus). The program comes with a slew of high-quality Bitstream fonts (see Figure 14-2) so both spreadsheets and graphs can have typeset-quality text (you can forget about those little stick-like characters on standard 1-2-3 graphs). Quattro doesn't download the fonts to your printer, but instead translates them into graphics, whether it's printing a spreadsheet, a chart, or both. In fact, because it prints all final-quality output in graphics mode, Quattro can rotate any spreadsheet

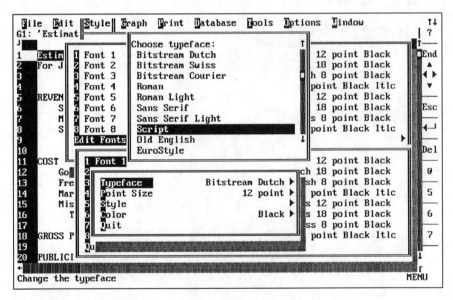

Figure 14-1: *Selecting a typeface with Quattro Pro's menus*

or chart, complete with all its text, into the "sideways" landscape. If you want a sideways spreadsheet printed in 8-point Old English, you've got it.

For faster spreadsheet output, you can print in a draft mode that uses the DeskJet's text fonts. In this case, you can use the method outlined in the section "Basics of spreadsheet printer control" above to insert escape sequences with the Setup String command, as shown in Figure 14-3, or in individual cells. When embedding an escape sequence in a cell, precede the whole thing with a vertical bar character (|).

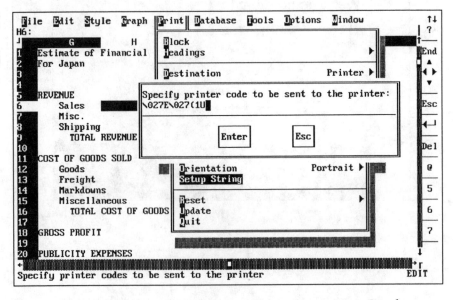

Figure 14-3: *Typing in a printer setup string in Quattro Pro. Use the menu sequence Print—Layout—Setup String to display this window.*

Excel

As so often happens in the world of high technology, Excel's ballyhooed innovations in presentation-quality spreadsheets have already been eclipsed by newer products. Excel gives you far more control over the format of the characters in your printed spreadsheet than does 1-2-3 alone, but not as much as you get with 1-2-3 plus Impress or Allways, or with Quattro Pro. And Excel still can't combine spreadsheets and charts on the same page. As a Windows program, Excel must live within the limits of the Windows DeskJet driver. Unless you use one of the Windows workarounds discussed in Chapter 17, this means you can only use internal and cartridge fonts in your spreadsheet printouts.

Supercalc 5

Supercalc is another top-notch spreadsheet package. It packs a features list comparable to that of 1-2-3 Release 3.0 into DOS's 640K memory space, which means you can use it effectively on a standard PC or XT. The sophistication of Supercalc 5's printouts is only a notch below what you can produce with with Quattro Professional or the 1-2-3 add-ins, with a variety of striking chart formats available from a comprehensive menu system.

In SuperCalc, you control the layout of printed spreadsheets via the Output Options menu, which lets you choose margins, set line width and page length, select page orientation, and set up headers and footers. SuperCalc supports the DeskJet for these basic features, but only the built-in and cartridge fonts can be directly accessed from the program. However, if you're facile with escape sequences, you can insert them freely in your spreadsheets and reports. As in Lotus 1-2-3, you can type in keyboard characters directly and enter non-keyboard control characters by typing the character's 3-digit ASCII code preceded by a backslash (\Ø27 for E_{s_c}, for examle). Unlike 1-2-3, however, SuperCalc also lets you enter non-keyboard by typing the equivalent ASCII keyboard sequence from the control code chart in Chapter 22. For example, you can enter E_{s_c} by typing Ctrl-[or a form feed character by typing Ctrl-L. Printer commands can be up to 240 characters long.

You can enter printer commands in three different places in a SuperCalc spreadsheet. To define a command that will be sent at the beginning of the print session, enter it at the *Setup* choice on the Output Options menu. You can also embed printer commands wherever you need them in the spreadsheet itself. Place the command in an otherwise empty row in the first column that will be included in the printout. As in 1-2-3, you must precede the command with two vertical bars. So, to turn on boldface printing, enter ‖\Ø27(s3B in the cell, pressing ⏎ to finalize the entry.

Finally, if you want to change printer setup for the headers or footers, you can enter printer commands directly within the header. In this case, you must precede the command with a vertical bar and two colons (| ::) and follow it with two colons and vertical bar. So, to print a header in boldface, you would enter the escape sequence in this format:

| ::\Ø27(s3B:: |

The two colons on either side of the command are necessary because SuperCalc uses a vertical bar by itself to indicate placement (right, center, or left) of the header or footer text. So, to print only the center portion of a header in boldface, the complete header entry would look something like this:

October 24, 1990| | ::\Ø27(s3B:: | Report Title | ::\Ø27(sØB:: | |Page 1

Access: Spreadsheets

Supercalc 5.0/$495

Computer Associates
1240 McKay Drive
San Jose, CA 95131
408/432-1727

Excel for Windows 2.1/$495

Microsoft Corp
16011 NE 36th Way
Redmond, WA 97017
206/882-8080

15

Database Software

∾

The DeskJet isn't fast enough for high-volume database printing, but it's an excellent printer for the kind of several-page summary reports that managers most often generate. In fact, the DeskJet has one advantage over its faster cousins in the LaserJet family when it comes to printing database reports. Its built-in ability to scale fonts to half their normal size means that you can print the internal Courier font at 6 points high and 20 characters per inch, for a readable 160 characters per line and 90 or so lines per page.

Current database management systems offer a lot of control over where your data appears on the page, but little or none over the appearance of the printed data itself—er, themselves. If you want to dress up a report with bold or italic type or even a few different fonts, you'll have to send the necessary escape sequences to the DeskJet yourself. (see Chapter 22 for a complete discussion of all the DeskJet commands you can use). Fortunately, however, most database software makes it relatively easy to accomplish this task.

Tip: If you do plan to change fonts within a report, remember that most database software uses a row/column system rather than absolute measurements such as inches or points to determine where to print each item. If you change fonts, and especially if you switch to a proportionally spaced font, you'll throw your margins and your column alignment out of whack unless you're very careful. It's safer to use font changes only for titles and other headings. If you stick with one monospaced font for the body of your report you can still add emphasis to important data with italics and boldface.

Profile: dBase

$895 /Ashton-Tate
20101 Hamilton Ave.
Torrance, CA 90502
213/329-8000

While the dBase programming language remains a widespread database standard, Ashton-Tate's dBase product has fallen on hard times. dBase IV's initial release was bug-ridden and slow, and the company is struggling to create an update that will restore its position of leadership. At this point, many dBase developers continue to use dBase III Plus, or have switched to a dBase-compatible database development product such as Nantucket's clipper. Others have jumped ship altogether for competing products such as Paradox, which I'll discuss in the next profile.

Printing in dBase

Whether you're working from the dot prompt or writing a program, all versions of dBase let you output information using the ? command, the ?? command, and the @..SAY.. command. Output from any of these commands goes only to the screen until you explicitly direct it to your printer by giving the command SET PRINT ON, or, in dBase IV, SET DEVICE TO PRINTER.

To use one of the output commands to print normal alphanumeric characters, you just enter the characters between a pair of single or double quotation marks. For example, the command **? "Call me Ishmael."** will print *Call me Ishmael.* on your page.

The difference between the three output commands is as follows: the ? command sends a carriage return and line feed before printing its output, so that the output appears at the left margin of a new line. By contrast, the ?? command outputs to the current cursor position. With @..SAY, you can specify exactly where you want the output to appear on the page in rows and columns. To print *Call me Ishmael* on the 10th row at the 12th column, you would give the command **@ 10,12 SAY "Call me Ishmael."**

After you're through printing, issue the command SET PRINT OFF or SET DEVICE TO SCREEN.

Using your own escape sequences

The only way to achieve full control over the DeskJet from dBase is to send the necessary escape sequences and control codes yourself using any of the dBase output commands (?, ??, or @..SAY..). You can't type the escape character or the other control codes from your keyboard, but you can use the CHR() function to enter the corresponding ASCII code instead. For example, escape character would be CHR(27), while the form feed character would be CHR(12).

To complete an escape sequence, you add a + after the CHR(27), then the remainder of the characters between quotes. So, to ouput the complete escape sequence that turns on boldface printing, you'd enter the command:

? CHR(27) + '(s3B'

dBase IV offers a new ??? command meant specifically for sending commands to your printer. With this command you output any of the non-keyboard control code characters by typing a predefined name between curly braces. These names should be easier to remember than the corresponding ASCII codes. For example, to send the above escape sequence with the ??? command, you would enter **??? "{ESC}(s3B"**. Since this command automatically sends its output to the printer you don't have to give the SET DEVICE TO PRINTER command first. Of course, since you're certainly going to be printing text immediately, you'll have to issue the SET command anyway if you want to see the output on paper.

Using variables for printer commands

With the dBase STORE command, you can define any escape sequence as a reuseable, easy-to-remember variable. That way, you only need to type in the escape sequence once. In the remainder of the current dBase session or program, you can use the variable in output commands as often as you like. dBase will substitute the full escape sequence and send it on to your printer.

For example, if you to print certain portions of a report in boldface, you could define two variables, one for bold type, one to restore ordinary weight type, as follows:

```
STORE "CHR(27) + '(s3B'" TO DJBOLD
STORE "CHR(27) + '(s1B'" TO DJBOLDOFF
```

Note that the entire escape sequence is enclosed in double quotes, and that the part of the sequence made up of keyboard characters is in single quotes. Follow this format when entering any escape sequence.

Then, to print a title in bold, followed by a piece of data in ordinary type, you'd enter the following lines:

```
SET PRINT ON
? &DJBOLD
? "Report Title"
? &DJBOLDOFF
? "First report field"
```

Note that the variables must always be preceded by the & character. Otherwise, the program would print the actual characters you typed between the double quotes of your escape sequences—you'd see *CHR(27) + '(s3B* in your report.

You can further automate your printer control by storing the variable definitions in a disk file for later use. Name all the variables with the same first few characters, the obvious choice being *DJ* as in the examples. Then use the SAVE..ALL LIKE command follows to collect them in a file called DJCMDS:

```
SAVE TO DJCMDS ALL LIKE DJ*
```

When you want to recall the definition file, use the command restore from djcmds additive. You'll then again be able to send printer commands via expressions such as **? &DJBOLD**.

⌒ *Caution: Be sure to include the ADDITIVE clause when reading in variable definitions stored in a disk file. ADDITIVE merges the variable definitions from the file with whatever variables are already defined. If you enter the RESTORE command without ADDITIVE, you'll lose all your current variables.*

Creating printer control programs

Another way to automate the sending of escape sequences from dBase is to create a miniature dBase program for each sequence. For example, you might create a program file named DJBOLD.PRG containing the lines:

```
SET PRINT ON
? CHR(27) + '(s3B'
SET PRINT OFF
```

Then, to switch the DeskJet to boldface printing, you would run the program by entering the command **DO DJBOLD** at the dot prompt.

Printing reports: basics

The Create Report menu system in dBase III Plus makes it easy to print reports. However, although the menus let set basic formatting characteristics such as the margins, the number of characters per line, and the number of lines per page, but you can't directly select fonts or control spacing of individual report fields. For ultimate control of your report's appearance, you must write your own report-printing program, placing the desired printer commands where you want them in the program.

As a compromise, however, you can include printer commands at the beginning of a report with one of two methods. Escape sequences may be embedded in the report when you specify the fields to be printed at particular locations. For example, if you wanted to print the contents of the LASTNAME field from your database file in boldface, you would enter **CHR(27) + '(s3B)'**

+ FIELD1. With this technique, however, you can't use the variable system described earlier to minimize your typing.

The second approach lets you send a printer command immediately before the report itself is printed. With this method, you define the basic layout of the report via the Create Report menu options, then save the report definition. Next, you create a simple dBase program that sends as many printer commands as you like and then prints the report. For example, if your report file is named SALES90, you might write the following program to print the entire report in boldface type:

RESTORE FROM DJCMDS ADDITIVE

SET PRINT ON	recalls the escape sequence variables you defined and saved earlier.
?? &DJBOLD	djbold is a variable the escape sequence for bold type
REPORT TO PRINT FORM SALES90	this command prints the report
SET PRINT ON	
?? &DJBOLDOFF	djboldoff represents the escape sequence to restore normal weight type

In dBase IV, using the Create Report menu command generates an actual dBase program. You can edit this program with dBase's built-in editor or your word processor to insert whatever printer commands you like, including the Restore command needed to recall a previously saved file of variable definitions.

Profile: Paradox

$725/Borland Internation
1800 Green Hills Rd.
Scotts Valley, CA 95066
408/438-5300

Among heavyweight relational database management systems for the PC, one of the top contenders is Borland's Paradox. Although Paradox doesn't come with a predefined DeskJet driver, there are several ways to enter escape sequences and other printer commands in your database printouts.

Whatever combination of these methods you use, enter the commands as follows: for control codes and the escape character numbered lower than 32 decimal in the ASCII code, type in the ASCII code value as a three-character string of numerals preceded by a backslash. So, to enter the escape character, type **\027**. Other characters in the command can be typed in directly from the keyboard.

To select the default printer setup for an entire printout, use Paradox's Custom Configuration Program. Access the Reports menu, then select the *Setups* option. You'll be shown a table of the printer setups already defined. Each setup includes the name of the printer, the printer port to which it is connected, and a Setup String field for the commands that Paradox will send to your printer at the start of each print job. To create customized printer setups for your DeskJet you can edit existing setups or create as many new ones as you like. Just type in your commands in the *Setup String* field using the backslash-ASCII code method described above to enter the escape character and other non-keyboard characters.

To select a default printer setup, enter an asterisk at the end of its name in the Setups table. Thus, if you want Paradox to print your reports in landscape orientation and in condensed 20-pitch type by default, the complete entry for this setup would look like this:

Name	Port	Setup String
DJ-LandscapeCond*	LPT1	\027E\027&l10\027(s20H

You can also control the format of a particular group of fields within a report by creating a pair of special fields containing your the printer commands.

Define the basic layout for your report first. When you have all the fields where you want them—and only then—use the command sequence Field — Place — Calculated to create a new field immediately to the left of the field whose format you want to change. At the *Expression:* prompt for the field, type a quotation mark ", then enter your escape sequence, and then type a second quote mark. When you press ⏎ to complete the "calculated" field, the command string will appear in your report, shoving the adjacent field to the right. But though your report layout will now look misaligned on the screen, it will print just fine, since the characters in the printer command don't actually print. Insert a second printer command field into the report where you want to switch back to your regular print settings. There's no way to simply cancel the commands you sent in the previous calculated field; instead, you must enter from scratch all the commands necesasry to restore the previous printer setup.

⌒ *Caution:* *If you use any command that changes the spacing increments, be sure to switch back to the defaults before the end of a line in your report. Otherwise, you'll get varying margins.*

Defining printer commands ahead of time

If you use one or more text formatting commands regularly in your Paradox reports, you don't have to type them in character by character every time—you can have Paradox do it for you. This trick takes advantage of Paradox' ability to link tables (database files) by blank fields. Start by creating a new table named DESKJET. The table must consist of only one row. The first field should be named something like *PrinterLink,* and should be left completely empty. Define as many additional fields as you need for the printer commands you'll be using, and in each field type in an escape sequence and name the field to correspond to the function of the command. For instance *BoldOn, BoldOff,* and so on.

At the very end of the table you wish to print, create a new field also named PrinterLink (or whatever you named the first field in your DESKJET table). Link the report table to the DESKJET table. Now, go on to design your report. After the data fields are laid out, use the Place command to add fields from the DESKJET table wherever you want to introduce a printer command.

Printing graphs

You can print Paradox graphs on the DeskJet by configuring the program for the LaserJet Series II. The only problem you may encounter involves positioning of the graphs when you print them in Paradox's landscape mode.

When Paradox prints a landscape page, it doesn't actually switch the printer into landscape mode. That's good, because the DeskJet can't print graphics in landscape. Instead, Paradox itself stands the chart on end, and sends the resulting rotated dot-by-dot image to the DeskJet in normal portrait mode.

Since the DeskJet responds to exactly the same graphics commands as does the LaserJet, a chart looks the same when printed by either printer. The problem is that its position is shifted slightly to the right (on a landscape-ori-endted page). If your chart is especially long along the horizontal axis, its right side may even show up on a second page. That's because the DeskJet has a larger unprintable areas at the top and especially at the bottom of a vertically-oriented page then does the LaserJet. When you print the rotated chart, the top of the page becomes its left margin, which will be located at a slightly more rightward position than with a LaserJet. And there'll be less room for the chart at the right margin. You'll have to restrict yourself to slightly fewer data elements in order to print some types of charts successfully on a single page.

Profile: Q&A

$349/Symantec Corp.
10201 Torre Ave.
Cupertino, CA 95014
408/253-9600

While there's no substitute for full-scale database management systems such as dBase when you really need to, extracting information from these relational juggernauts often requires a daunting programming session. If you need access to lots of information quickly and without the hassle of programming, a simpler file management system makes more sense.

Q&A is one of the best of these "file managers." With space for up to 16 million records, indexing on up to 115 fields for speedy search and sort operations, and a slew of powerful statistical and financial calculation functions, this program is no milktoast when it comes to data management.

Of course, you can import dBase, DIF, ASCII, and 1-2-3 files into your Q&A databases. In addition, Q&A includes a capable word processor built right in. However, Q&A's name hints at its most unique feature: the Intelligent Assistant, a program module that lets you make changes to the database or ask it questions in plain English. You can type "Change Nina's position to 'regional sales manager' and add $5,000 to her salary," or ask "Who are the sales people whose evaluation is above 6, ranked by evaluation?"

As far DeskJet support is concerned, Q&A is about equal to other database programs. While the program comes with an excellent system for laying out your own custom reports so that fields appear where you want them on your printouts, it isn't much help when it comes to selecting DeskJet fonts or otherwise giving you that "desktop published" look. However, you can embed printer commands within your reports to embellish them a bit. Each module of the Q&A system has a Print Options menu with a *Printer control codes* field where you can enter an escape sequence that will be sent at the beginning of the printout. Enter the escape sequence in this field as a sequence of decimal numbers. For example, if you want to print the report in bold type, you would enter the numbers **27 40 115 51 66**, for $^{E}s_{c}$(s3B. You can embed printer commands within a Q&A word processor file by typing ***PRINTER**, then the decimal codes, then another *****. So, to print the word important in bold, you would type

*PRINTER 27 40 115 51 66 *important*PRINTER 27 40 115 48 66*

in your document (the second sequence shuts off bold printing).

16

Forms Software

❦

Every business needs forms. Forms for invoices, forms for requisitions, forms for bills of lading. Retail shops need inventory forms, employers need time sheets, medical offices need forms for medical histories and insurance billing. And everyone needs tax forms.

With a computer and a high-resolution printer like the DeskJet, you no longer have to rely on (and wait for) a professional printing service to produce forms that are custom-tailored to your needs. It's fairly easy to create forms using a general-purpose desktop publishing program, a basic drawing package such as GEM Draw Plus, or even a word processor equipped drawing tools such as WordPerfect. After all, forms mainly consist of boxes, lines, and text, simple elements that you can produce in hundreds of programs. If you design many forms, however, your work will be considerably easier if you turn to a specialized forms software package.

Although the forms software genre is fairly new, it's maturing quickly. You're no longer forced to design forms via a trial-and-error cycle of entering codes onto a text-mode display and then printing out a draft to see if you got it right. Instead, in all the leading packages, you work with an accurate full-screen facsimile of the printed form using a mouse, just as in a drawing or desktop publishing program (PerFORM gets its graphical talents from GEM, while JetForm and FormBase are Windows programs). You're also provided with special tools for adding evenly spaced lines, duplicating fields and aligning boxes and other elements of the form, making the work faster than it would be in a general-purpose program. What's more, you can import graphics and place them wherever you like on the form.

But forms software isn't just for designing forms, it's also intended to let you fill them out on your screen, and to keep the information in them organized in database fashion. To fill out a form on the screen, you usually use a separate smaller program to open the form file. When you've typed in all the information, you can save the completed form on disk as a new file, or print it out if you need a paper copy. When you lay out the form, you're able to designate the order in which fields are to be filled in, specify default entries or constraints (for instance, that a field must contain a number between 10 and 100), and create fields whose entries are automatically calculated from other fields.

The best of the forms packages also provide strong database features. You can import a database file to print its records on your forms, or export the data you've entered in your screen forms to a database file. In FormBase's case, in fact, you can even use the program as a standalone relational database manager, sorting and searching for data across multiple files.

Forms and the DeskJet

You wouldn't think of using the DeskJet to print a large supply of forms all at once—the printer is just too slow for that. On the other hand, the DeskJet is excellent for forms design. You can produce a master copy of your form on the DeskJet, then take it to a copy shop or professional printer for economical duplication. In addition, the DeskJet is serviceable for forms that you print as you fill them out.

All three of the forms software packages mentioned here work fairly well with the DeskJet, but none of them excel. The standard DeskJet drivers for both Windows or GEM limit you to cartridge fonts. In JetForm's case, in fact, you can't even use the DeskJet's cartridge fonts—even though it is a Windows program, JetForm can access the DeskJet only with a generic dot-matrix printer driver supplied specially with the package.

Choosing a forms package

All three of the forms packages mentioned here are powerhouses, and you can't go wrong with any of them. All let you design multipage forms of great complexity, and are certainly up to any simpler task. All three products are quite competent at exchanging data with existing database systems through the delimited ASCII and dBase file formats.

JetForm

Indigo's JetForm is a top-rated forms generation and fillout package that runs under Windows. The program boasts a complete set of drawing tools specialized for forms design and is strong on data checking features to ensure that screen forms are filled out accurately. Like PerFORM, JetForm offers both graphical and text-mode form fillout utilities. If several people fill out forms in your organization, you need buy only one copy of the main JetForm program, and then equip each person with a copy of the cheaper fillout utility. JetForm lets you import several types of graphics for use in your forms, including TIFF images and PC Paintbrush files. The program reads TIFF images directly, but you have to convert other graphics into a proprietary JetForm format using a separate program first. The program will also generate a variety of types of barcodes.

PerFORM

Unlike JetForm and Xerox FormBase, Delrina's PerFORM runs under GEM instead of Windows. That makes it a good deal faster on the screen than the other two programs, and makes it the only package to consider if you have a standard PC or XT. However, it also means you can't use simultaneously other programs to exchange data as you work. PerFORM reads and writes dBase files and can append new records to them. Not only that, it can generate the dBase index files (NDX files) necessary to keep your data immediately accessible. If you're graphically oriented, you'll appreciate the fact that PerFORM imports more kinds of graphic file formats than its two main competitors, and does so more readily. The program also includes a barcode printing feature. A sample form printed on the DeskJet by PerFORM is shown on the facing page.

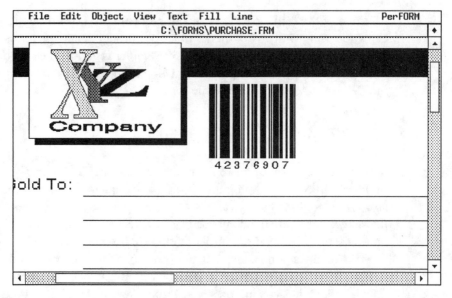

Figure 16-1: *A PerFORM form on the screen, showing a bar code generated by the program*

❀ **Tip:** *Barcode printing is hardly the most common use of the DeskJet, but certainly an option. If you want to print bar codes but don't need a full-blown forms package, look into Delrina's BarCODE Composer, which lets you build bar codes and transfer them to Windows programs or Ventura. Some bar code readers have trouble detecting the DeskJet's ink, but in many cases you'll be reproducing the original printer output via a copy machine or professional printer anyway.*

PERIOD END	MONTH	DAY	YEAR	PERSONNEL #				NAME	DIV

FOR INTERNAL USE ONLY

Description of Work	TIME DISTRIBUTION FOR PERIOD																Total Hours
	1	2	3	4	5	6	7	8	9	10	11	12	13	14	15	
	16	17	18	19	20	21	22	23	24	25	26	27	28	29	30	31	
Excused From Office																	
Holiday																	
Personal Illness - Approved																	
Total Hours (incl. overtime)																	
Overtime																	

Total Hours

List of Expenses and Dollar Value (attach receipts)			
Description	$	Description	$
	Total Expenses		

Overtime Approved By	Time Report Audited

PAGE   OF

Created using PerFORM from Delrina Technology Inc.

FormBase

Xerox FormBase is an exhaustively complete package, as much a database manager as it is a forms designer. Such integration of data input, management, and presentation functions is certainly the wave of the future for database software. However, if you already have a functioning database system, you probably won't want to switch; in this situation, all the extras may not be very important to you. Still, the package has a super-sophisticated set of calculation and validation functions that can speed fillout of complex forms. A separate form fillout utility isn't offered, so you must enter data with the full program. Although FormBase can import graphics, it does so only through the Windows clipboard. That limits the kinds of images you can display, and it also means you have to load another program first, cut the image to the clipboard, and then paste it in. FormBase does not currently print barcodes.

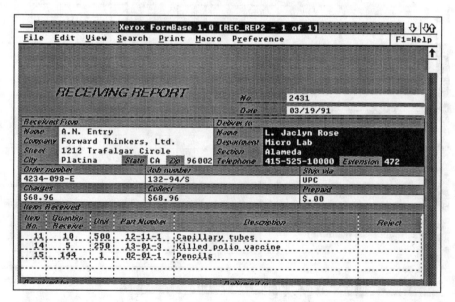

Figure 16-2: *You use the main FormBase program to fill out forms as well as design them.*

Access: Forms Software

PerFORM 2.0/$495
BarCode Composer/$99.95
Delrina Technology, Inc.
4454 Genesee St.
Buffalo, NY 14225
716/835-0405

JetForm Design/$495
Indigo Software
400-560 Rochester St.
Ottowa, Canada
K1S 5K2
800/267-9976

Xerox Formbase/$495
Xerox Corp.
101 Continental Blvd.
El Segundo, CA 90245
800/822-8221

17

Microsoft Windows

After years of languishing as a slow, clunky Macintosh imitator, Microsoft Windows is suddenly hot stuff. A lot of quality programs are being written to take advantage of Windows' graphics-based displays and convenient mouse-assisted menus, and a lot of people are buying the software.

One of Windows' big drawing cards is the notion of *device independence*. When a software developer creates a Windows program, he or she doesn't have to worry about how to make the program work with all the different monitors, mice, and printers that are on the market. Instead, the developer just concentrates on getting the program to work with Windows. When the user of the program wants to print, for example, Windows takes care of interacting with the user's particular printer.

This arrangement works great, as long as someone has developed a Windows driver for the printer in question. The driver gets installed into Windows, not into a particular Windows program, and all Windows programs will work with the printer once the driver installation is complete. But by the same token, if the driver has any limitations, all your Windows programs will have to put up with them—the quality of the driver determines how effectively you can take advantage of that printer's features.

Windows and the DeskJet

Which brings us to the practical questions—how good is the Windows driver for the DeskJet? What DeskJet features can and can't you use from Windows?

As I write this book, the most recently released DeskJet driver for Windows handles graphics well, and it allows you to access most of the HP cartridge fonts, including the ones designed for the DeskJet Plus. But the driver has one serious limitation: it does not recognize soft fonts from HP or any other vendor. That's a major flaw, given the limited variety and expense of cartridge fonts.

If you're willing to pay for the privilege, there's a superior alternative to the standard Windows driver in the form of Zenographics' SuperPrint. Driven by Windows via SuperPrint, the DeskJet can do almost everything a PostScript printer can, including print in multiple fonts. See the profile of SuperPrint for details. Publisher's Powerpak (Chapter 11), LaserTwin (Chapter 4) and the PostScript interpreters (Chapter 20) are other ways to bypass the limitations of the Windows DeskJet driver.

Installing the Windows DeskJet driver

To get Windows and your DeskJet working together, the first thing you need to do is to install the Windows driver for the DeskJet. How you do this depends on when you do it.

First-time Windows installation

If you're installing Windows itself for the first time, you simply follow the standard installation procedure outline in your Windows manual using the Setup program on your "Setup, Build and Displays 1" disk. Just make sure that you have the latest version of the DeskJet driver before you start. If your copy of Windows doesn't include a current DeskJet driver, obtain a copy from HP or Microsoft, and have it ready on a floppy disk.

When you set up Windows for the first time, the printer installation step comes after you've already chosen the correct computer type, display adapter, keyboard, and mouse. We'll pick up the story at the point when you see this message box:

```
┌─────────────────────────────────────────────────────────┐
│  WHEN YOU'RE READY TO                             PRESS   │
├─────────────────────────────────────────────────────────┤
│  Install a printer or plotter                      ▐I▌   │
│  Continue Setup                                      C    │
├─────────────────────────────────────────────────────────┤
│  Exit without completing Setup                  CONTROL+X │
└─────────────────────────────────────────────────────────┘
```

Figure 17-1: *Windows printer installation begins*

Follow these steps to complete installation of the DeskJet driver:

1. Press **i** or ⏎ to bring up the printer installation menu, as shown in Figure 17-2.

2. If the DeskJet driver you'll be using is listed in the menu, you just move the highlight to the correct driver name (DeskJet or DeskJet Plus). Then press ⏎ to confirm the choice and install the driver.

If you have a new version of the Windows DeskJet driver on a floppy disk, select the last choice in the list, "Other." When you press ⏎, you'll be asked to insert the disk containing the driver into your floppy drive. Do so, and then press ⏎ again.

```
Select an output device (printer, plotter, etc.) from the following list.

  - Use the DIRECTION (↑,↓) keys to move the highlight to your selection.

HP 7580A [HP Plotter]
HP 7585A [HP Plotter]
HP 7580B [HP Plotter]
HP 7585B [HP Plotter]
HP 7586B [HP Plotter]
HP ColorPro [HP Plotter]
HP ColorPro with GEC [HP Plotter]
HP DeskJet
HP DraftPro [HP Plotter]
HP DraftMaster I [HP Plotter]
HP DraftMaster II [HP Plotter]
HP LaserJet [PCL / HP LaserJet]
HP LaserJet Plus [PCL / HP LaserJet]

          (To see more of the list, press the DOWN(↓) key.)

 ┌──────────────────────────────────────────────────────────┐
 │ WHEN YOU'RE READY TO                            PRESS     │
 ├──────────────────────────────────────────────────────────┤
 │ Confirm your choice                             ENTER     │
 │ Exit without completing Setup                CONTROL+X    │
 └──────────────────────────────────────────────────────────┘
```

Figure 17-2: *Pick out the DeskJet on the list of printers you'll see as you install Windows.*

The names of the printers will now appear on your screen. Choose the correct model, and press ↵ to complete the driver installation.

✂ *Tip:* *You don't have to worry about selecting the wrong printer port at this step, since you can always reassign the selection via the Windows Control Panel. See the discussion of the Control Panel below or refer to your Windows manual for details.*

3. Setup now asks you to tell it which printer port the DeskJet is attached to. Select the port name—it's most likely LPT1:—from the list on the screen and press ↵.

✂ *Tip:* *If you plan to SuperPrint, Publisher's Powerpak, LaserTwin, or one of the PostScript interpreter programs discussed in Chapter 20, you'll want to install the appropriate driver as well as the regular DeskJet driver, as instructed in the product's manual.*

4. If you plan to use Windows with other printers as well, you may install all the appropriate drivers at this time. Setup presents a new dialog box asking you whether you want to install another printer or continue to the next part of the installation process. If you do want to install

another printer, press **i** or blank (↵), and repeat steps 2 and 3 above. Otherwise press **c**.

That completes the printer part of the Windows installation process. Continue with the rest of Setup to generate a working copy of Windows on your disk.

Adding a DeskJet driver to an existing Windows setup

There are two main reasons you'd want to add a new printer driver to Windows after you've already installed Windows itself. Clearly, if you buy a new printer, you have to make Windows aware of it somehow. But it's also important to be able to replace an older driver with an updated version that adds new features and corrects earlier flaws. In the DeskJet's case, the Windows driver has already gone a couple of rounds of evolution, and the new version is considerably more flexible than the original one.

Thankfully, adding a new printer driver to an existing copy of Windows is a simple task. If you haven't noticed already, Windows requires you to install the entire system over again whenever you change displays or mice. Not so in the case of new printers—you just run the Windows Control Panel and make a few quick menu selections.

The Control Panel is a vital little program that lets you alter a number of Windows features, including screen colors, mouse response time—and what we're interested in here, printer setup. The biggest problem with the Control Panel is that many Windows users don't realize it exists. Instead of building Control Panel functions into the main Windows menu, Microsoft designed Windows so that you have to run the Control Panel as an independent program.

1. To start the Control Panel, get Windows going, and then locate the file CONTROL.EXE among the files in your Windows directory. Launch the program by double clicking or highlighting the name and pressing (↵). Figure 17-3 shows the Control Panel.

2. To add a new DeskJet driver to your Windows setup, pull down the Installation menu at the left of the Control Panel box. Now select the *Add New Printer* command.

Figure 17-3: *The Windows Control Panel*

3. Place the disk with the driver you want to install into the floppy drive. If you use a drive other than **A**, type in the appropriate drive name in the dialog box. OK the box by pressing ↵ or clicking on *OK*.

4. A new dialog box will appear offering the names of the printers covered by the drivers on the disk as shown below. Highlight the name of the printer you want to install, and press ↵ or click *Add*.

Figure 17-4: *Choose the DeskJet driver you want to install from this dialog*

5. The next dialog box asks whether you want to copy the printer driver to your Windows directory. Click *Yes* unless you've already copied it

there yourself (in that case, click *No*). As soon as you select either option Windows completes the driver installation.

Changing printer setup with the Control Panel

After you've installed the right driver for your printer you must make a few adjustments to the system using the Control Panel before you'll be ready to print from Windows. You can modify these same settings whenever you need to change the way an existing printer driver works. Here are the settings you can alter from the Control Panel:

- Printer port. If you want your printer data to reach the DeskJet, you have to tell Windows which communications port the printer is connected to. If you've opted for a serial connection (against my recommendations, mind you), you'll need to set a variety of serial communication parameters.

- The default printer. When you install Windows with the Setup program, the first printer you install becomes the default printer, the one your Windows programs will use automatically unless you instruct them to do otherwise. If you've installed two or more printer drivers, you can designate a different printer as the default.

- Printer-specific options. Most Windows printer drivers give you a variety of options pertinent to the particular printer you're using—in the DeskJet's case these include which fonts are installed and which graphics resolution to use. The selections you make serve as defaults. Windows will automatically use them to configure your DeskJet at print time, unless you override the selections with the Printer Setup command in the program.

- Serial communications settings. If you've chosen to connect the DeskJet to your PC's serial port, Windows' serial settings must match the printer's.

To modify any of these options, start the Control Panel (see the previous section) and proceed as follows: To assign a communications port, open the Setup menu on the Control Panel and choose the *Connections* option. You'll see a dialog box listing all the printers you've installed on the left, and all the available communications ports on the right, as shown in Figure 17-5.

Select the printer you want to work with from the list on the left, then assign a communications port for that printer on the right. Repeat the process for as many printers as you wish, then OK the box to confirm your choices.

Figure 17-5: Indicate the printer port to which you've connected the DeskJet

⌒ **Caution:** *Windows won't permit you to assign more than one printer to the same communications port. But if you have only one parallel port, a common situation, you'll probably want to use the same port for all your printers, changing the cabling as necessary. Or perhaps you've installed both a standard DeskJet driver and a PostScript driver for use with one of the PostScript interpreters described in Chapter 20. In this case, Windows thinks you have two separate printers even though the DeskJet is the only one physically connected to the printer port. In either of these situations, the less-than-ideal solution is to use the Control Panel to change communications port assignments whenever you decide to call on a different printer or printer driver. If you switch back and forth between two or more drivers frequently, just leave the Control Panel running, so you can get to it quickly.*

If by some chance you've chosen a serial port connection, your next stop is the Communications Port box, also accessed via the Control Panel's Setup menu. Open the Connections dialog and make any changes necessary to match the printer's settings for speed, parity, and so forth. You can ignore this dialog box if you've connected your DeskJet to your PC via a parallel port, yet another reason to use a parallel connection if at all possible.

To select the default printer, open the Setup menu on the Control Panel and choose the *Printer* option. A dialog box appears allowing you to select which of the installed printers you want as the default. When you OK the box, you'll go immediately to a dialog box presenting options for the printer you've just chosen. As shown in Figure 17-6, you can select default paper size, page orientation, and graphics resolution, and you can indicate which cartridge fonts you've installed. OK the box when you've made your choices.

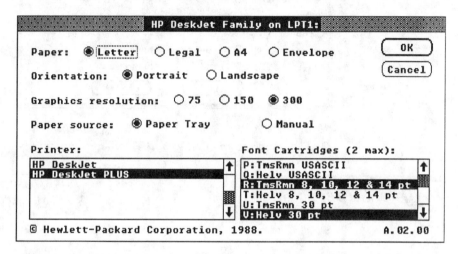

Figure 17-6: These are your configuration options for the Windows DeskJet driver.

To modify default setup options that are specific to your printer, you start by selecting the default printer as just described. You need to go through the motions even if the right printer is already the default—just reselect it. Once you've OK'd the default printer dialog, you'll see the same dialog box shown in Figure 17-6.

Finally, if you've connected the DeskJet to your PC via a serial cable, use the Control Panel's *Communications* option to set Windows' serial communications parameters to match the DeskJet's. The default settings, shown in Figure 17-7, should be correct if you've installed the DeskJet according to the instructions in your *Owner's Manual.*

```
┌─────────────────────────────────────────────────┐
│ Communications Settings                          │
│                                                  │
│ Baud Rate:   9600                                │
│ Word Length  ○ 4    ○ 5    ○ 6    ○ 7    ◉ 8      │
│ Parity       ○ Even      ○ Odd       ◉ None      │
│ Stop Bits    ◉ 1         ○ 1.5       ○ 2         │
│ Handshake    ○ Hardware  ◉ None                  │
│ Port         ◉ COM1:     ○ COM2:                 │
│                                                  │
│        ( OK )          ( Cancel )                │
└─────────────────────────────────────────────────┘
```

Figure 17-7: *Windows serial settings matching the DeskJet setup recommended in the* Owner's Manual

---

Profile: SuperPrint

$195/Zenographics
19752 MacArthur Blvd.
Irvine, CA 92715
714/851-6352

There are printer drivers and then there are *printer drivers*. Zenographics' SuperPrint, which bestows PostScript-like superpowers on ordinary-mortal printers like the DeskJet, is squarely in the latter category.

SuperPrint works exclusively with Windows. While the regular Windows driver for the DeskJet does a reliable job of translating what you see on the screen into print, the driver only works with internal and cartridge fonts, it can't handle PostScript-like graphics effects, and printing is very slow. SuperPrint overcomes all of these limitations.

In text mode, even if you buy every cartridge font HP makes, you're restricted by the DeskJet to a finite number of preset font sizes. Despite the similarity in appearance of, say, TmsRmn 10 point and TmsRmn 16 point type, you must have a separate font for each size if you want to use them both. What's more, you can't use any font larger than the maximum permitted in the DeskJet's text mode. While the DeskJet driver for Windows reflects these limitations, SuperPrint lets you scale master outline typefaces to any size you want as you print. Currently, SuperPrint can scale outlines from Bitstream, a major supplier of high-quality typefaces; within several months, you'll also be able to use typeface outlines from other important vendors, including Adobe and Agfa Compugraphic, Zenographics claims.

Sophisticated graphics effects pose another stumbling block to the DeskJet, and to the regular Windows DeskJet driver. You can't reproduce greyscale patterns, for example. Again, SuperPrint steps in to provide the missing capabilities. Perhaps most important of all, the SuperPrint driver is many times faster than the standard Windows driver for the DeskJet.

Reduced to fundamentals, the DeskJet's limitations are the result of too little computing firepower. PostScript printers commit a special microprocessor, lots of memory, and sophisticated internal software to the task of generating beautiful printed pages. The DeskJet just doesn't have those resources, and the ordinary DeskJet driver doesn't try to imitate them.

But SuperPrint does. Tapping directly into the inner sanctum where Windows stores an image of the file to be printed, SuperPrint enlists your PC's processor and memory to carry out PostScript-like image-processing and page-formatting functions, rather than turning over these duties to your printer. There's no PostScript code actually involved, but the results are comparable.

It may be helpful to contrast the pros and cons of SuperPrint against those of the PostScript interpreter software covered in Chapter 20. In SuperPrint's plus column, check off speed. SuperPrint churns out pages considerably faster, since it attaches directly to Windows, eliminating the steps of translating graphics and text into PostScript commands and then reinterpreting these

Figure 17-8: *SuperPrint's SuperText module lets you create Windows screen fonts at any point size from Bitstream typeface outlines.*

commands to create a printed page. SuperPrint also consumes far less memory than the PostScript interpreters.

On the other hand, SuperPrint works only with Windows programs, while PostScript interpreter packages can perform their magic for any PostScript-compatible application. And at the present, at least. SuperPrint can't do anything with raw PostScript files—including the EPS type that often get embedded in PageMaker documents, for instance. An upgrade that will give SuperScript its own PostScript-interpreting ability will be ready sometime in 1990, according to the people at Zenographics.

In addition to the driver itself, the SuperPrint package includes SuperText, a module that creates Windows screen fonts from the same outline typefaces used for printing (see Figure 17-8); and SuperQueue, a print spooling program that lets you print several files successively while you get back to your work.

Publisher's Powerpak

Atech's Publisher's Powerpak is another route to freedom from the confines of the standard Windows driver. Like SuperPrint, Publisher's Powerpak lets you scale fonts to any size from within any Windows program. In this case, however, the master typeface outlines come from Atech and Monotype, a well-known typographic house, rather than Bitstream. When printed by the DeskJet, Powerpak fonts are slightly less sharp than the ones SuperPrint generates (see the discussion on Publisher's Powerpak for Ventura and the accompanying sample printout in Chapter 11). On the other hand, the variety of typefaces is wider, with more novelty faces than you'll find in the Bitstream library. There's even a musical symbol typeface in the Atech collection.

Special Topics

18

Printing Envelopes

When you go to the trouble of printing your letters with a typeset-quality font, you probably don't want to stuff them into hand-scrawled envelopes. With the DeskJet, you won't have to—unlike most computer printers, the DeskJet comes with a capable envelope-feeder built right in.

Once you know how to load envelopes and learn a few software tricks, you'll find it easy to make your envelopes look just as good as the letters inside. Before we get started with the how-to details, though, you should be aware of two limitations you'll face. The first is one of size. The built-in envelope feeder isn't adjustable, and only accepts regular business size (#10) envelopes. The second catch reflects the DeskJet's intended function as a low-volume personal printer: you have to feed in the envelopes one at a time.

Loading envelopes

The mechanics of feeding an envelope into your printer are simple:

1. Take off the output tray's dark translucent plastic cover.

2. If there's any paper in the output tray, remove it. You'll now be able to see the envelope guides, the two plastic wings attached to either wall of the output tray on the portion that fits into the printer. The guides nearly touch the the floor of the output tray, leaving a slit for the envelope.

3. Put the envelope into the guides with its top toward the pri and its address side down, or flap side up, if you prefer. You'll have to bend the envelope a bit to get it past the flippers and down on the floor of the output tray.

4. Keep the *right* side of the envelope flush with the wall of the output tray on that side as you gently push the envelope into the printer as far as you can, until it's stopped by the feeder rollers.

5. Your envelope is now in position, ready for the DeskJet to load it the rest of the way into the paper feed path. The printer will carry out its part of the envelope loading sequence when one of two things happen: either you press the envelope load keys on the keypad, or the DeskJet receives an envelope load software command from your computer.

The correct method for activating the DeskJet's envelope loader depends on the software you're using to print the envelope.

If your software doesn't send the envelope load command for you, you'll need to activate the envelope feeder using the DeskJet's keypad. Press the UP and DOWN keys on the keypad (the two leftmost keys in the back row) simultaneously.

⌒ **Caution:** *If your software sends the envelope command for you, you should not press the envelope keys—if you do, the software will try to load a second envelope, and the one you just fed in will come out unprinted.*

Printing the envelope

Loading an envelope into the DeskJet is simple—a more daunting challenge can be to print the addresses in the right places. Of course, if your word processor comes with its own envelope printing function, it should be able to do the job for you. WordPerfect 5.0, Nota Bene, PFS:Professional Write, and Q&A all have at least adequate envelope printing features. If your word processor lacks such features, or if you want to print envelopes without loading the word processor, read on.

The lowest-budget and least complicated envelope printing solution relies on an ordinary text file you create ahead of time with your word processor. The idea is to use this file as a template for envelope addressing. You place your return address and a dummy recipient address in the template file, positioning each address in the file so that they print in the right places. Then, when you need to print an envelope, you just load a copy of the file into your word processor and type the real recipient's address over the dummy. After you've loaded the envelope itself into the DeskJet (with the procedure outlined earlier in the chapter), you print.

This sounds simple enough, but the tricky part is positioning the text in your template file so that the addresses print where they're supposed to. Of course, the basic idea is to start near the top of the file close to left margin for the return address, skip down a few lines, and then space over so that the dummy recipient address is somewhere in the middle of the screen. But since the size of the characters, spaces, and lines that you print don't match the ones on your screen, you can't use a ruler to check the spacing on the monitor against a real envelope.

While a little trial and error will quickly produce the results you're after, I've found the following recipe to work well for the DeskJet's internal 12-point 10-pitch Courier font.

Creating an envelope template file

1. Load your word processor, then set the left margin to 0. The right margin can be anything over 75.

2. Start with the cursor at the very first position in the file (the top left corner).

3. Type in your return address, if any, pressing ⏎ at the end of each line. Align the left border of each line with the one above it.

4. If your return address is only 3 lines long, press ⏎ again. If you don't want a return address at all, press ⏎ 4 times.

5. Press ⏎ 6 more times.

6. Space or tab over to the 33rd column. Type the first line of your dummy recipient address. (By positioning the line with spaces or tabs, not by resetting your margins, you don't have to worry about having a DeskJet driver to get proper spacing.)

7. Type the remaining lines of the dummy address, aligning the left borders of all the lines.

8. Save your envelope template file—call it something like ENV.DOC.

Printing an envelope with the template file

When you want to print an envelope:

1. Place an envelope in the envelope guides as described above.

2. Press the envelope keys on the keypad at the same time to load the envelope (these are the two leftmost keys in the back keypad row).

3. If it's not already selected, select the DeskJet's internal 10-pitch point Courier font by pressing the Font button on the keypad until the adjacent indicator light is lit.

4. Create a new file in your word processor.

5. Without moving the cursor, import the ENV.DOC file into your new file (by importing the template into a new file, rather than opening ENV.DOC itself, you ensure that you won't accidentally change the copy of ENV.DOC on disk).

6. Type your recipient's address over the template's dummy address, without changing the placement of the lines.

7. Print the file. If the envelope doesn't emerge after printing stops, press the FF button on the keypad.

8. If you plan to print the same envelope again, you might want to save the new file under another name.

Adding DeskJet commands to your envelope template

If you'd prefer, you can include the DeskJet commands for loading the envelope and for switching to the correct font in your envelope template file so you don't have to press the keypad buttons. If your word processor has a good DeskJet driver, it may have its own commands for envelope loading and for switching to the right font. Otherwise, you'll need to type in a few escape sequences, so the word processor must allow you to embed printer commands with non-keyboard characters in your files.

If you take the escape sequence route, enter the sequences on the top line of the template file immediately in front of the first part of the return address. For example, to reset the printer, select load an envelope, then select the 10-pitch, 12-point Courier font, the top line of your file would look like this:

$^{E}s_{C}E^{E}s_{C}$&l3h$^{E}s_{C}$(1ØU$^{E}s_{C}$(spsb1Øh12v3T*Return address*

This line includes the several escape sequences just mentioned, plus the first line of the return address.

Using batch files to print envelopes

A slightly more elegant method of printing envelopes is to write a short DOS batch file to automate the process. With this approach, you print the envelope directly from DOS, not from within your word processor. (If you need a refresher course on the basics of creating batch files, see Chapter 9 or your DOS manual).

You'll need to create three files for your complete envelope printing set: a file to set up the printer properly and to print your return address; the batch file that lets you enter the recipient's address, or reads it from a file, and then prints it; and a file to eject the envelope from the printer.

Figure 18-1 on the opposite page shows the three files, set up to print the envelope in 12-point Courier. Create the files using a word processor that lets you enter non-keyboard characters, and store them as plain, unformatted ASCII text files. Create and save each of the files separately, naming them as indicated here. In the first file, the first escape sequence series resets the printer, feeds an envelope, sets the top and left margins to 0, then selects the font. You can enter additional return addresses as needed. The second escape sequence below the return address sets the left margin to 33.

Printing envelopes with ENVDJ.BAT

Once you've saved your three envelope printing files, you're ready to start printing envelopes. At some point in the process, of course, you have to enter the recipient's address. You can do this in one of two ways: by typing it in during the printing process, or by specifying a file that contains it.

To enter the address during the printing process:

1. Switch to the disk drive and directory where ENVDJ.BAT is stored. From the DOS command line, type

   envdj⏎

2. You'll see the following message on the screen:

   Type in the envelope's address,
   pressing [Enter] after each line.
   Press F6 when the address is complete.
   Press Ctrl-Break to quit without printing.

Type in the address, correcting any mistakes as you go with the backspace key. Once you press ⏎ to start a new line, you can't go back to the previous line. When the address is complete, press (F6). In a moment or two, the DeskJet will load your envelope and start printing.

File 1: Name: ENV1.DJ

ᴱsᴄEᴱsᴄ&l3hᴱsᴄ(1ØUᴱsᴄ(spsb1Øh12v3T*Return address name*
Street address
City, State, ZIP
ᴱsᴄ&a33Lᴱsᴄ&a11R

File 2: ENVDJ.BAT

```
echo off
cls
if "%1"=="" goto screen
rem If a file name was entered, will print envelope address from file
if not exist %1 goto exit
copy env1.dj+%1+env2.DJ lpt1
goto exit

echo The file you requested is not available.
echo Check the filename and try again. goto exit

:screen
rem If no file name was entered,  type in address on screen
echo
echo
echo Type in the envelope's address,
echo pressing [Enter] after each line.
echo Press F6 when the address is complete.
echo Press Ctrl-Break to quit without printing.
copy env1.dj+con+env2.dj lpt1

:exit
```

File 3: ENV2.DJ

♀

Figure 18-1: *Your three envelope printing files should contain the lines shown above. The* ♀ *in file 3, ENV2.DJ, represents the form feed control code, ASCII value 12 decimal.*

To print an address stored in a file

Although it's often handy to address envelopes on the fly, it would be nice not to have to retype an address every time you print it. That's why ENVDJ.BAT can print addresses stored in disk files. Even if you're never going to send another letter, Once you've typed an address into your word processor at the beginning of a letter, for example, it would be nice not to have to type it again. In most word processors, you can mark a block of text and export the block to a file of its own.

1. Switch to the disk drive and directory where ENVDJ.BAT is stored.

2. At the DOS prompt, type

   envdj bob.ltr (⏎)

Be sure to include the pathname for your address file, if it's different than the current path. For example, if you're in the DJ directory on drive C:, and the file bob.ltr is stored in the LETTERS directory on drive B:, you'd type

   envdj b:\letters\bob.ltr (⏎)

3. ENVDJ.BAT takes over at this point and prints the envelope, assuming it finds your file.

Envelope printing software

While templates and batch files work well, the easiest way to print envelopes is with a utility specifically designed for the task. This particular software category has gone from non-existent a few years ago to overcrowded today, and there are now a bewildering multitude of envelope printing programs to choose from. Fortunately, one inexpensive utility stands out from the pack.

Profile: GrabPlus

$49.95 (with LaserLabel)/**ZPAY Payroll Systems**
3516 Ruby St.
Franklin Park, IL 60131
312/671-3364

GrabPlus is an exceptionally powerful, exceptionally flexible envelope printing program, yet it's one of the least expensive.

As the name tried to suggest, GrabPlus runs as a memory resident program (TSR) that will "grab" addresses directly from the screen and print them on an envelope while you're running another program. (Like all TSR functions that read the screen, this feature only works with programs running in text mode; some word processors often (Microsoft Word) or always (Ami) use graphics mode instead.)

To use GrabPlus, you position the address you want to print somewhere on the screen and then pop up the utility. You'll see a highlighted block which you can move around with the cursor keys until it covers your address. Once you've got the highlight into position, another key press prints the envelope. Or you can edit the address first, and then print it.

Those are the basics, but GrabPlus does a lot more:

- You can adjust the size of the highlighted address block in both dimensions.

- The program will print either of two return addresses, or none at all, as you decide.

- It works with either of the two standard size envelopes automatically, and you can adjust the printing positions of the return and recipient addresses to accomodate oddball sizes as well, within limits.

- You don't have to grab addreses from the screen. Instead, you can simply type in the address you want in a little window, and print that.

- You can use any DeskJet font you like for your addresses—in fact, you can use a separate font for the top line

- You can run GrabPlus in a swap-to-disk mode that requires only 6K of system RAM when the program isn't active, or in a faster full-strength memory resident mode requiring about 60K, or as a non-memory resident ordinary DOS application for typed-in addresses. A separate configuration program lets you select defaults for all the above options and others.

In addition to the pop-up envelope printer itself, the GrabPlus package includes a separate database program for storing and retrieving your frequently-used your envelope addresses. You can enter addresses into the database either by typing them in on a simple screen, or by importing them from an outside file.

In the process, you can assign up to five "tags" to each address to help you track related addresses. Let's say you run a record store for collectors servicing several distinct interest groups. You might tag the addresses of your Rockabilly customers with an "R", the Do-wop customers with a "D", and the Old-timey customers with an "O." Then, when you want to send all the Do-wop customers a special mailing advertising a new shipment of obscure recordings by streetcorner groups, you just have GrabDB search your database for the D-tagged addresses.

GrabDB will also search the database file for individual names. Either way, when you find an address you want to print, GrabDB taps GrabPlus and out comes the envelope. But GrabDB has an automatic address formatting feature that goes GrabPlus one better. At the touch of a function key, you can choose any one of these three address formats. GrabDB can also export addresses to other programs such as mail-mergers or other databases. Again, you can use the tag system to export only the addresses that fall into a certain category.

Printing mailing labels

Like envelopes, mailing labels pose an everyday printing challenge. Though the DeskJet is too slow for volume label-printing chores, you can certainly rely on it for turning out smaller numbers of good-looking labels from time to time.

⌒ *Caution: Although the DeskJet does a creditable job of printing labels, the printer was not designed for this purpose. Specifically, Hewlett-Packard does not recommend the DeskJet for label printing.*

On the off chance you haven't seen them before, printable labels are made of heavy paper with an adhesive on one side applied to a peelable backing. The labels are available in several different precut sizes, and they come on both single sheets and continuous fanfolded sheets with pin-feed sprocket holes.

The most widely used kind of label stock is intended for photocopy machines. But this isn't the type to use with the DeskJet— get the kind for laser printers instead. Whereas copiers can print all the way out to the edges of the paper, the DeskJet, like laser printers, can't. Since copier labels have no margins, your alignment will be off if you print them with a DeskJet. Laser label stock has the necessary margins.

Another problem with copier labels is that the stock isn't flexible enough and tends to jam in the tight printer path of a laser printer or the DeskJet. By contrast, laser label stock is specifically designed for greater flexibility. (Laser labels also require a different adhesive to resist the high temperatures inside the laser printer—this isn't necessary for the cool-running DeskJet.)

Even with laser labels, there's one problem you can't overcome, at least at the moment. It has to do with the water-soluble ink the DeskJet uses. On the slick surface common to all label stock, the ink tends to spread out irregularly, blurring the normally razor-sharp characters. The text is still legible, but it's not as attractive as it should be.

The biggest name in printable labels is Avery. They offer several different sizes of mailing labels, as well as diskette labels for both 5¼" and 3½" floppies. They even have a technical support line you can call (see the tip below). By the way, Avery says that it's actively working to develop a label paper that will give good results with the DeskJet.

✻ *Tip: Avery is a good source of information about how to print mailing labels using your PC. When you buy a package of Avery laser printer labels, you get a small booklet with tips on printing labels from popular PC and Maintosh programs, including 1-2-3, Microsoft Word, WordPerfect, and dBase. For help over the telephone with label printing, call Avery's support line at* **818/792-8489***.*

Mailing label software

While few application programs sport envelope-printing functions, many tackle mailing labels. Any general-purpose database program worth its salt has a built-in routine for printing all the standard mailing label formats that should work well with the DeskJet, assuming you're happy with the internal Courier font.

Still, the label printing functions of database programs are hardly intuitive. If you really want to minimize the hassle of label printing, turn to a utility specifically designed for the job, such as LaserLabel. Avery sells an excellent label-printing software package called LabelPro. Though it's not currently compatible with the DeskJet, LabelPro should give you good results with the LaserTwin emulation utility described in Chapter 4.

LaserLabel

LaserLabel is another brainchild of Paul Mayer, the same developer who created the GrabPlus envelope printing utility. With its no-nonsense quality and low price, LaserLabel represents a great choice for basic mailing label printing.

As you'd expect, LaserLabel works hand-in-hand with the GrabPlus database, GrabDB. You choose the addresses you want to print from the database by specifying one of the tags you assigned when setting up your address collection (see the profile on GrabPlus a few pages back for details). LaserLabel culls the database file for the addresses marked with the matching tag, and sorts them at print time by last name or by ZIP code.

LaserLabel has a good selection of practical options for controlling the alignment and appearance of the printed labels. It's set up in advance for three popular Avery mailing label sizes, and you just pick the size you have from a simple menu. In a really classy touch, LaserLabel lets you print the first line of the label address in one font, and the rest of the label in another. It will even automatically send the DeskJet commands (escape sequences) that select the fonts you want in these two roles.

Compared to GrabPlus, LaserLabel supports fewer different printer models—but since one of them is the DeskJet, that shouldn't concern you. Interestingly, the LaserLabel manual says that the program isn't recommended for use with the DeskJet, because of the problem with ink spreading described earlier in this chapter. Nevertheless, the DeskJet is one of the choices on the printer menu, and the program even comes with a set of DeskJet soft fonts and a prefab batch file for downloading them.

19

Printing

Screenshots

∾

Over the course of any long-term love/hate relationship with a PC, there'll be times when you find it handy to print what you see on the screen.

For one thing, screen snapshots or "screenshots" make great quick-and-dirty reminders and crib sheets. Maybe you're due at a meeting and you want to make a fast copy of a single paragraph or a bar chart from a longer file. Maybe you've just received a short memo in your electronic mailbox, and you'd like to print it out without saving it on disk first.

But while the ability to print screenshots may save you a little time in situations like these, you could print the same information using a more conventional approach (such as the Print command in your word processor). What screenshots can do that other printing methods can't is give you an illustration of what the entire screen looks like, not just your file. When you need a way to document how a piece of software works and looks on the screen—its menus, dialog boxes, prompts, and so on—screenshots are far quicker and more accurate than freehand sketches and much cheaper than a professional typesetter or graphics artist.

It's easy to guess who needs this capability most: people who write or publish software manuals and software reviews. But even if you're in another line of work, there may well come a time when you'll want to print some software screens. You've probably experienced the frustration of trying to talk a computer novice through a maze of commands and menus. Print a few key screens that your apprentices can refer to as they work, and everything will seem much clearer to them. Among experienced users, a judiciously chosen screen shot can replace a long-winded technical explanation of how a spreadsheet macro works, or how you achieved a fancy desktop publishing layout.

Printing screens versus saving screen files

There are two routes to obtaining printed screenshots: printing the screen directly, while you're viewing it, and recording the screen image as a disk file to be printed later. The first approach has the advantage that you get your results immediately, you don't waste time and disk space saving and then printing a file. The primary drawback is that you can't incorporate the screen image into another document. If you save the screenshot as a file, you can merge it with text and other graphics in a word processor or desktop publishing program—perfect if you're illustrating a report, or writing a commercial software manual, or even putting together your own home-grown tutorial.

Text screens versus graphics screens

Just like the DeskJet, your PC has two main ways of displaying information. In text modes, you can only display a standard set of characters, and only in predetermined rows and columns on the screen. What's really going on is that each character has its own ASCII code, and special circuits in the PC automatically translate each code into a preset pattern of screen dots.

To print a screenshot of a text screen, all you have to to do is send the ASCII codes of the characters on the screen to the DeskJet. Likewise, if you're capturing the screenshot in a file, the file is mainly just a record of the screen ASCII codes. Fortunately for PC owners, the DeskJet's standard character set matches the character set you see on the screen. So, whether you print directly or from a stored file, you don't have to do anything special to set up the printer for screenshot printing. Because text mode screenshots consist of ASCII codes instead of the actual dots on the screen, you can print them in any font you like. In the case of stored files, you may even be able to edit them in your word processor.

When your display is in a graphics mode, by contrast, each and every dot you see—even a dot that's part of a text character—has to be placed independently on the screen by the PC's main microprocessor. In this case, without ASCII codes to fall back on, printing the screenshot entails sending every individual dot to the DeskJet. Similarly, graphics screenshot files consist of dot-by-dot bitmaps of the image.

Since you're not locked into the DeskJet's built-in preformed text characters, it's possible to squish, stretch, or otherwise manipulate the screen image before you print it. On the other hand, switching to another font doesn't do anything for text in the screenshot, since you're printing it in graphics mode.

Using DOS to print screenshots

The simplest way to get a printout of what you see on the screen is with the DOS "print screen" key. If your PC screen is in a text mode, just press Shift-Prt Sc, and your computer will immediately start sending all the ASCII characters on the screen to your DeskJet.

Though the print screen function works fairly well for ordinary text screens, it has many limitations. For one thing, the DeskJet can't print some PC screen characters. Yes, it's true that the little happy faces and musical notes you see on some screens are represented in the DeskJet's PC-8 character set. But unless the DeskJet receives a special command first—and DOS doesn't send it—the printer interprets these low-numbered ASCII codes as control codes instead of printable text.

Another problem is that there's no option for "printing" the screens to a disk file, so you can't incorporate the screen images into other documents. Worse yet, many programs disable the print screen function. And, on the DeskJet at least, you can't print graphics screens with DOS at all.

Using screen capture software

For printing all but the simplest text screens, you need a memory resident screen "capture" utility. A good capture utility will handle both text and graphics modes, and will reproduce either type of screen accurately on the DeskJet.

To use a screen capture program, you start the utility and then run your application software. When you see a screen that you want to capture, you press a special hotkey to activate the capture function. At this point, you can either print the screen directly, or store the screen image in a disk file. Depending on the utility, you may be able to edit your screenshot files before you print them, or translate them into other file formats.

Choosing a screen capture utility

As a look at the Access box will convince you, screen capture utilities have proliferated over the past few years. To get you started in your comparison shopping, here are some of the criteria you should consider when deciding on a capture program:

Video mode compatibility: A basic requirement is that your screen capture utility should work in the video modes you use to display your screens. If you want to record all the fine detail on your 1600 x 1200 ultra high-resolution monitor, a capture utility that tops out at VGA resolution (640 x 480) won't do. You can safely assume that every capture utility supports the Big Four graphics video modes: CGA, Hercules, EGA, and VGA. Obviously, if the program captures text screens, it will also work in the 25-line monochrome adapter (MDA) mode. On the other hand, support for the extended text modes of the EGA (43 lines) and VGA (50 lines) isn't universal. If you use one of these text modes or an uncommon graphics mode, make sure the utility you buy can capture its screens.

DeskJet compatibility: When choosing a screen capture utility, it may or may not matter whether the utility works directly with the DeskJet. Of course, if you want to use the utility itself to print the screenshots, it should have a DeskJet-specific driver, or at least a LaserJet driver that works well with the DeskJet. On the other hand, if you're planning to merge the screenshots into a larger document with a word processor or desktop publishing program, your want a utility that saves the screen files in a format understood by the destination program.

File format: If you're planning to merge screenshots into other documents, it's helpful if the capture program saves the screen files in a format your graphics program, word processor, or desktop publishing program can read directly. Otherwise, you'll have to run the non-standard screen files through a conversion process to produce a useable format.

Several utilities save screen files in PC Paintbrush .PCX format, the most widely used PC graphics format—the list includes GrafPlus, PCXGrab, and the Frieze utility that comes with PC Paintbrush itself. Obviously, this is ideal if you want to edit your screenshots with PC Paintbrush, but it's also good if you're using WordPerfect or any of the major desktop publishing programs, including Ventura and PageMaker can accept .PCX files.

Capture programs that generate non-standard screenshot files are always part of a larger software package that includes format conversion functions. Converting from one format to another consumes both time and disk space, but at least you end up with a screenshot file you can use. HiJaak is primarily marketed as a file-conversion program, with screen capture thrown in to boot. HotShot Graphics' format conversion options are a little less extensive, but the program also offers a full graphics editor and a graphics database, and has special features for working with text screens.

Memory requirements: Since these screen capture utilities are memory resident, they consume memory that your main application program may need. It won't do you much good to load your screen capture program and find that there's no room left to run the program whose screens you want to capture. GrafPlus and WordPerfect's Grab are the most frugal of the pack, weighing in at around 15K. They're followed by Hotshot Grab at 23K, pcxGrab and Pizazz Plus at around 35K. The most voracious capture program is Hijaak, which eats up more than 45K of your system RAM. (All of these figures are approximate, and depend on the type of display adapter in your computer.)

Editing capabilities: The simplest capture utilities just capture screens. Others let you modify the resulting images to one degree or another. GrafPlus, for example, lets you change the size of the image, crop it, change the aspect ratio, or reverse the screen colors (black to white and vice versa). Cropping lets you use only a particular portion of the screen image. Because screen dots (pixels) are rectangular while the dots the DeskJet prints are square, printed screenshots often look vertically squashed. By adjusting the aspect ratio (the ratio of height to width) you can correct for this proportion problem. And while many monitors display bright characters against a dark background, people expect to see dark characters on a white background in printed text—which is why the ability to reverse the colors or shades in the screenshot can come in handy.

More extensive editing capabilities are supplied in Hotshot Graphics and PC Paintbrush, the full-scale paint-style graphics packages of which Hotshot Grab and Frieze are respectively a part. Both Hotshot Graphics and PC Paintbrush treat your screenshots like any other graphic, allowing you to add new lines, shapes, colors, and text, and to copy or delete any portion of the image.

♪ **Note:** *Some word processors now come with their own screen capture utilities, so you don't have to buy a separate product or worry about file format compatibility. WordPerfect, for example, includes a utility called Grab which saves files in WordPerfect's .WPG graphics format, while the Total Word package has its Snapshot, which uses the .TWI format required by Total Word. However, these freebies don't have the range of options available with the capture packages sold separately.*

Creating screenshots in Windows

Taking snapshots of your Windows screens can be a little more tricky than with ordinary programs, partly because Windows takes such firm control over your computer. Some capture utilities don't work with Windows at all, while others will function in a limited way.

✂ *Tip: If you plan to print your Windows screenshots in black and white, use the Windows Control Panel to select black and white shades for your screen before you capture.*

The best software I've found for Windows screenshots is T/Maker's Scrapbook+, though it still has some drawbacks. Scrapbook+ is primarily designed as a filing system for your graphics images, so that you can more easily find the one file you need out of a large catalogue. One program function, however, lets you capture screens while other Windows programs are running. A nice thing about the Scrapbook+ capture function is that it works with any Windows screen, no matter what the resolution. In addition, it gives you several options as to which part of the screen you capture.

Scrapbook+ does have two disadvantages. First, it doesn't offer much in the way of file format translation. You can save images in Scrapbook+'s own format or in the format in which they were originally created or one closely related. For screen shots, this means you can export your files to Microsoft Paint or Windows Bitmap formats, but not to more useful formats such as PCX or IMG. You can get around this by using the Windows clipboard to transfer your screen images directly to another Windows program such as PC Paintbrush for Windows, and save them there. Scrapbook+'s second problem is price—$129 is a little too much to spend if all you want it for is screen capture.

Other options are HiJaak, which works very well when configured for the "active keyboard mode", the Windows capture utility that accompanies The Graphics Link Plus, and Wingrab, which is part of the HotShot Grab package. Wingrab performs pretty well, and I've used it to prepare illustrations for several magazine articles. However, when you're capturing color screens, it always reverses the screen colors—blue becomes red, light blue turns orange, and so on.

For Windows screen shots on a shoestring budget, turn to the shareware program TIFFANY. TIFFANY only captures in black and white, and it saves the screenshots in TIFF format. But TIFFANY works with any Windows-compatible monitor, the files are perfectly useable, and it will only set you back $10.

Merging screenshots in word processor documents

WordPerfect, Microsoft Word, WordStar, and Ami can all integrate graphics such as screenshots into text documents. If you favor another word processor without this capability, you can still place graphics into your text via the Inset utility, published by Inset Systems. In your word processor, you insert special Inset codes into your document where you want the graphic, along with the name of the graphics file. Then, at print time, Inset scans the file for its codes and inserts the graphic in the proper position on the page.

GrafPlus

GrafPlus is an inexpensive, few-frills package of utilities that's a good choice for screen capture if you don't need extensive editing capabilities. Requiring about 16K of RAM, GrafPlus is one of the smallest of the available screen capture programs, so you should have room to run all but the largest of your applications. Video versatility is another strong suit. GrafPlus works with a very long list of display systems, including the full page Genius monitor used by many desktop publishers. However, while GrafPlus requires less memory than most other capture utilities, it's decidedly slower in operation.

In the GrafPlus package, GrafLasr is the specific utility you use for DeskJet screenshots. As the name implies, GrafLasr was originally set up for LaserJet printers, but it works fine with the DeskJet as well. Anyway, once GrafLasr is loaded, it takes over the standard DOS print screen function. When you press Shift-Prt Sc, GrafPlus will run the show, not DOS, and you'll get accurate printouts of any text or graphics screen. Even better, you can choose from a number of options for your printouts when you install the program, including whether black and white portions of the screen are reversed. You can also select printer resolution, image size and proportions, and the location of the printed screenshot on the page.

If you wish you can have GrafPlus save the printer output as a file, with all the necessary DeskJet commands. You can print the image later simply by using the DOS COPY command to send the file to the DeskJet. Another option lets you store screenshot files in .PCX format for use in desktop publishing or word processing documents.

Hotshot Graphics

Hotshot Graphics started life as a screen capture utility, but it's grown into a complete screen image/graphics package. In addition to a pair of screen capture utilities, Hotshot Graphics capabilities include full-scale image editing, file format conversion, and a simple filing system for your image files. No DeskJet driver is provided, but the LaserJet driver substitutes adequately.

Hotshot Grab, the screen capture part of the package, takes only about 23K of RAM, supports a good variety of video display systems, and has worked very reliably for me. Unlike GrafPlus, Hotshot Grab doesn't let you print your screenshots directly. Instead, you type in a filename for the screenshot you want to store into a little window. A second little window then pops up where you can enter a detailed description of the image. When that's done, Grab stores the file.

Hotshot has two separate editing modes for your screenshots, one for text images, the other for graphics. In the graphics department, Hotshot's paint-type (bit-mapped) editing features rival those of PC Paintbrush. You can draw shapes and lines, paint colored swatches, inverse existing colors, and type graphics text. In fact, you're not limited to editing files you've captured with Grab—you can edit .PCX and .IMG files from other programs, or even paint new graphics from scratch. And you can interconvert captured screens and other graphics files between the .PCX, .IMG, TIFF, WordPerfect .WPG, MacPaint, and EPS formats, among others.

But Hotshot's most unique capabilities have to do with editing text-based screenshots. To emphasize particular portions of the screen image, you can highlight any area with colors or inverse video, or draw borders or boxes around it. You can type new characters or delete old ones, and you can insert special characters such as male and female symbols from a pop-up table.

You can even move or copy blocks of the text image from one location to another.

All the while, you're working with standard ASCII text, so the files remain printable in the DeskJet's text mode. Once your text screenshot edits are complete, you can print the images directly, or convert them into any of the graphics formats mentioned earlier. Whether you're printing text or graphics, you can optionally print a border around the image, print the description you saved when you captured the screen, or both. Graphics screenshots can be resized as well.

Though Hotshot offers an excellent collection of features, I have to mention some of its weak points. My biggest gripe is that Hotshot tends to print very slowly. I've found it more efficient to transfer images to a program such as Ventura Publisher and print them there. Another problem is that the keystrokes you have to use for some functions aren't very intuitive, and the menu system is a bit on the clunky side. In the graphics editor, the menus respond too slowly. Despite these weaknesses, I recommend that you consider Hotshot Graphics seriously if you're interested in a one-product solution to your basic PC screen image and graphics needs.

HiJaak

Currently, my favorite screen capture utility is the one that comes with Inset Systems' HiJaak. HiJaak is primarily a graphics conversion program, taking images stored in one format, say PCX and translating them into another, such as TIFF or IMG (the GEM format used by Ventura). Capture, the accomaning screenshot utility, works reliably in almost every type of graphics program I've tried. It even works when you're running Microsoft Windows, whereas other vendors typically supply a separate utility just for Windows. The only weak spot is that Capture consumes too much memory, around 45K. As a result, you won't be able to run some large programs after loading Capture.

Capture stores files in Inset's own PIX format, so you must translate them to another format unless you're printing directly from the Inset graphics utility discussed in Chapter 10. HiJaak performs its translations reliably. Another plus is that you can perform the translations from the DOS command line in a batch mode that lets you convert a group of files in one step.

PCX Toolkit

Primarily intended for programmers, the PCX Toolkit consists of a library of around 60 functions for manipulating PC Paintbrush PCX files within programs, along with a collection of several standalone utilities for fiddling around with PCX files. Among them is a good screen capture program—and of course, the capture utility saves its files in PCX format.

I guess it goes without saying—if you have any interest in graphics programming with PCX files, this is definitely the screen capture product for you. But even if you're not a programmer, you might still want to select the Toolkit as your screenshot software choice. The versatility of the standalone utilities, the fact that you probably won't need a time consuming conversion step to use your screenshots in another program, and the Toolkit's not-excessive price are all points to consider.

The capture utility, pcxGrab, can record text screens as well as the graphics kind, and it works in Windows as well as standard DOS programs. Other utilities in the package let you display PCX images in "slide show" fashion, combine them into efficient library files, and print your files. A particularly useful pair of programs lets you measure portions of your images via on-screen coordinates, and then precisely clip out and save the particular sections you really need.

Access: Screen Capture Utilities

HiJaak /$149
Inset Systems, Inc.
12 Mill Plain Rd.
Danbury, CT 06811
203/775-5866

pcxGrab (included in PCX Programmer's Toolkit)/$195
Genus Microprogramming
11315 Meadow Lake
Houston, TX 77077
800/227-0918; 713/870-0737

HotShot Graphics/$249
HotShot Grab/$99
Symsoft
444 First St.
Los Altos, CA 94022
415/941-1552

Scrapbook+/129.95
T/Maker Company
1973 Landings Dr.
Mountain View, CA 94043
415/962-0195

Tiffany/$10
Alan Anderson
3511 Camino del Rio South
Suite 408
San Diego, CA 92108

Frieze (included in PC Paintbrush)
ZSoft
450 Franklin Rd, Suite 100
Marietta, GA 30067
404/428-0008

GrafPlus $49.95
Jewell Technologies, Inc.
4740 44th Ave. SW #203
Seattle, WA 98116
206/937-1081

Pizazz Plus/$149
Application Techniques
10 Lomar Park Drive
Pepperell, MA 01463
800/433-5201; 508/433-5201

The Graphics Link Plus/$149
HSC Software
1661 Lincoln Blvd., Suite 101
Santa Monica, CA 90404
213/392-8441

20

Pretty in PostScript

∾

Chalk it up to the perverse human impulse that drives us to rise to impossible challenges just because they're there. Despite enormous technical obstacles, at least three companies have had tolerable success in creating PC software that turns your thousand-dollar DeskJet into a PostScript printer.

✂ ***Tip:*** *If you want to print Ventura files on your DeskJet, a PostScript interpreter or emulation program is one of the few ways to do it. To date, the folks at Xerox have yet to deliver a DeskJet driver, and none appears to be on the horizon. But all three PostScript interpreters covered in this chapter do an excellent job with Ventura printouts.*

The DeskJet already prints high quality text and graphics—why should you bother with PostScript? It depends entirely on how much you covet the sophisticated typographical control and amazing special effects that PostScript makes possible, and that the DeskJet can't hope to produce without help. Though the PostScript language has its critics and its challengers, it remains the only vehicle for advanced printing features that even begins to qualify as a standard in the personal computer industry. In fact, almost every high-quality graphics or desktop publishing program achieves its best output with a PostScript printer.

GoScript from LaserGo, Freedom of Press from CAI, and UltraScript from QMS all deftly manage the metamorphic feat of turning the DeskJet into a PostScript workalike. Before we l an examination of some basics relevant to all three is in order.

How does it work?

Inside every PC printer, including the DeskJet, lurks a specialized electronic intelligence. In the DeskJet's case, HP has provided a built-in computer with impressive smarts. The DeskJet's microprocessor can handle the complexities of translating incoming ASCII characters and graphics data into dots on the printed page, and of carrying out commands such as "set a 1" left margin," or "move to the middle of the page and then start printing." But in comparsion to a PostScript printer, the DeskJet is a relatively simple device.

That's because the PostScript language itself is so complex. A PostScript file consists of a long series of software commands specifying every aspect of the page to be printed in intricate detail. In PostScript, most printed shapes, including text characters, are represented as mathematically-described objects rather than as collections of dots (see Chapters 3 and 12 for more on the types of PC graphics). In addition to the descriptions of individual objects, many PostScript files also include complex instructions that tell the printer how to perform repeated tasks that are unique to that file. In other words, a PostScript file is truly a computer program, comparable to a program written in C or BASIC.

The PostScript printer must digest the objects and programming instructions it receives and translate them into a simple bitmap image of which dots are to be printed where. The printer constructs the bitmap for one entire page at a time, prints that page, and then moves on to the calculations for the next page.

To handle all this complexity, a PostScript printer needs a full-scale microprocessor of the same caliber, or better, as the one in a fast AT-compatible. The printer must also be permanently equipped with a highly sophisticated program of its own for interpreting the incoming PostScript files. And it must be endowed with large amounts of memory for storing the programs it receives, and for "composing" the final image of each page. These additional components explain why a PostScript machine costs so much more than an otherwise comparable laser printer such as the LaserJet. Although a LaserJet also composes and prints a page at a time, it does so by simply assembling the bitmap data it receives from the computer and its font files into a larger, page-sized bitmap.

On the other hand, once a PostScript printer has finished with its page description computations, all it does is print a pattern of dots, just like a standard LaserJet. Recognizing that the printer's only indispensable job is to place ink on the page, PostScript interpreter programs allow your PC to take back responsibility for PostScript-specific printing chores: interpreting the PostScript file, and converting the resulting commands into a final bitmap of the page to be printed. After all, the PC contains a sophisticated microprocessor, and it has the necessary memory; add a program that can interpret and execute the PostScript code, and your PC should theoretically be able to duplicate the PostScript printer's page composition abilities.

Working entirely with your system's own resources, the interpreter program interprets the PostScript code and performs the calculations, storing the final bitmap temporarily in RAM or on your hard disk. It then feeds the bitmap data to your printer a line at a time.

To the DeskJet, there's nothing to distinguish the incoming graphics data from the data it would receive from a non-PostScript program. The DeskJet knows how to print dots, and dots are all it is asked to print—all the printer sees are streams of numbers representing the dots it is to lay down, along with a few simple commands.

How well does it work?

While the idea of using a PC to duplicate a PostScript printer's computational functions is sound in concept, the complexities of PostScript make it an ambitious project. Nevertheless, several persistent programmers seem to have carried it off.

All three of the interpreter packages profiled below do an excellent job of producing PostScript printouts on the DeskJet. They can all reproduce the fancy special effects at which PostScript excels—greyscale shading, graduated fills of graphical shapes, scaled and rotated text—on the DeskJet. The opposite page shows three PostScript files printed by GoScript on the DeskJet (the musical example was created with Passport Designs' Score, a music printing program).

If you've ever used a PostScript laser printer, there is one major difference you'll notice when you print PostScript files on the DeskJet. To state it baldly, the DeskJet is a slow PostScript printer.

You can blame the DeskJet's leisurely performance partly on the fact that the printer just isn't as fast as a laser machine when it comes to actually putting dots on the page. Leaving PostScript out of the picture for a second, the DeskJet takes much longer to print a page of graphics that its older cousin the LaserJet requires.

Still, your PC and the interpreter packages have to take some of the blame for the slowdown. Your PC is just not as quick at turning PostScript code into bitmap images as a specialized PostScript printer is. After all, the computer inside a PostScript machine is optimized for the specific sorts of image-related calculations it must perform, so it has an innate advantage over any general-purpose PC. Installing a math coprocessor in your computer will improve the speed of any of the PostScript emulation products considerably.

One other stumbling block the interpreter packages face has to do with text. Fonts from Adobe Systems, which are stored in a special encrypted format, can't be used with any of the three packages. Eventually, this limitation should be overcome, since Adobe has announced that it plans to make public the technical specifications for its fonts. In the meantime, GoScript and Freedom of Press claim to work with non-encrypted PostScript fonts such as BitStream's; my limited tests verified these boasts.

W
hy is it no one ever sent me yet
One perfect limousine, do you suppose?
Ah no, it's always just my luck to get
One perfect rose.
—Dorothy Parker

These limitations are worth noting, but they hardly detract from the minor miracle the PostScript interpreters accomplish. For about $1000 at street prices, you can buy both a DeskJet and PostScript interpreter software. Assuming your PC already has enough memory to run the interpreter program, that's all you'll have to pay for a PostScript system that can equal the output quality of printers costing thousands of dollars more. That ought to make you feel pretty good about waiting that extra minute or three for your PostScript pages to pop out.

PostScript emulation roundup: GoScript, Freedom of Press, UltraScript

All three of the current crop of PostScript emulators achieve roughly equivalent quality on the DeskJet, and all three turn out finished pages at about the same speed. Still, there are important differences to note among them.

One concerns printing convenience. Printing with GoScript or Freedom of Press requires a two-step process. First, you must get your application program to save its PostScript printer output as a file on disk instead of sending it directly to the printer. Next, you exit the application program and start the PostScript emulator. This system works, but it's hardly ideal. If you find anything in your printout that needs correcting, you must restart your application software and go through the whole cycle again.

Using UltraScript is far simpler. To use the product, you just tell the application software that you want to print to a PostScript printer, just as if you'd actually attached a LaserWriter or other PostScript machine to your PC instead of the lowly DeskJet. Then, when you print a file, the UltraScript interpreter commandeers the PostScript code generated by your software before it ever gets to the printer port and translates it into DeskJet instructions. The one fly in UltraScript's ointment affects users of 80386-based PCs. The program is incompatible with memory management utilities such as the one built into Windows/386 and the Quarterdeck QEMMM.

Another important consideration in choosing a PostScript emulation package is how much memory it requires in your PC. Although all the products work best with plenty of additional memory (2 megabytes or more is ideal),

GoScript is the least demanding, and will perform acceptably in a 640K machine. Freedom of Press can get by with a minimum of 500K of expanded memory, while UltraScript needs 800K of extended memory (actually, UltraScript itself can run in a 640K by itself, but in this situation you can't print directly from your application software).

UltraScript includes the most typefaces, 47 in the Plus version compared to 35 in Freedom of Press and GoScript Plus. Currently, only Freedom of Press supports color printers such as HP's PaintJet, so it's a good choice if you own such a printer as well as the DeskJet. On the other hand, would be PostScript programmers should note that Freedom of Press lacks the interactive PostScript mode provided by both GoScript and UltraScript. In the interactive mode, you can send PostScript commands to the program and receive an immediate, informative response when you make a programming error.

Pricing is comparable for the top-of-the line versions of all three products. However, only GoScript and UltraScript offer less expensive versions with fewer fonts. On balance, given its sparing use of memory and the lowish cost of the entry-level version, GoScript has a slight edge for most price-conscious DeskJet users.

Access: PostScript Interpreter Software

GoScript $195
GoScript Plus $395
Lasergo, Inc.
9235 Trade Place, Suite A
San Diego, CA 92126
619/450-4600

Freedom of Press/$495
Custom Applications, Inc.
900 Technology Park Dr., Bldg B
Billerica, MA 01821
800/873-4367

UltraScript pc $195
UltraScript pc Plus $445
QMS, Inc.
One Magnum Pass
Mobile, AL 36618
205/633-4300

21

Printing with the Macintosh

～

While it's hardly a match made in heaven, the union of the DeskJet and an Apple Macintosh can gow into an amiable, productive relationship. The DeskJet certainly has some important limitations compared to printers designed specifically for the Mac, but with a little effort and the right software, you can get the the printer to produce both text and graphics from just about any Mac program, with good to excellent results.

The most likely reason you'd want to arrange this marriage is that you happen to wind up with both machines through some serendipitous combination of circumstances. In many companies, PCs and Macintoshs share the same offices, each computer valued for its own strengths. This being the case, the growing popularity of the DeskJet makes it increasingly likely that Mac users will find themselves in an office where the DeskJet is the only printer in the vicinity.

On the other hand, you shouldn't go out and intentionally buy a regular DeskJet just for use with a Mac. A far better choice would be HP's DeskWriter, a revamped DeskJet designed specifically for the Macintosh.

Hybrid capabilities

When your Mac-DeskJet hybrid system is properly configured, you'll be able to print both text and graphics from most application programs. But don't be surprised if you run into occasional problems or quirks with particular programs—there are too many variables for everything to work right every time.

Graphics: The simplest kind of Macintosh graphics files are based directly on the bitmapped images you see on the screen—MacPaint files are the classic example. The DeskJet can handle this type of graphic quite capably. The Macintosh screen displays 72 dots per inch, which is almost exactly one-fourth of the 300 dpi the DeskJet can print. To print a MacPaint graphic, the DeskJet lays down a four-by-four solid block of dots for each black dot in the original, thus rendering the image at 75 dpi. The slight discrepancy between the screen and printed resolutions means that the graphic comes out a bit reduced on paper, about 96% of the original's size (since there are slightly more dots per inch, each 16-dot block printed by the DeskJet is slightly smaller than the corresponding screen pixel).

Many other Macintosh graphics programs are designed to work with the 300-dpi Apple LaserWriter. Since the DeskJet prints at 300 dpi as well, it can reproduce these graphics flawlessly. The exception, of course, is PostScript graphics, which you just can't print on a DeskJet. PostScript-based programs such as Adobe Illustrator and Aldus Freehand are incompatible with the DeskJet.

Text: depending on the utility software you buy, you may have several options for printing Macintosh text on your DeskJet. The first method simply places the DeskJet in graphics mode and prints a dot-for-dot reproduction of the characters you see on your screen. At its best, this approach gives you reasonably readable text—at a resolution of 75 dots per inch, the outlines of the characters will be noticeably jagged. This is method is also much slower than printing in true text mode.

MacPrint, one of the best Mac-to-DeskJet utilities, uses a modified version of this approach to get far better resolution. By shrinking larger versions of the same fonts you see on the Mac's screen, MacPrint can use the DeskJet's graphics mode to print 150 or 300 dpi text. Results with this method look great, but it's even slower than printing the same-size screen fonts (see the profile on MacPrint for more details).

To get the best combination of quality and speed you need a way to access the DeskJet's own fonts from the Macintosh. It's not difficult for a DeskJet driver to put the DeskJet in text mode and simply send the sequence of characters in your file. Theoretically, the driver can select any DeskJet font you wish to use for the task.

The fly in the ointment is that your Mac's regular screen fonts don't correspond to the DeskJet's fonts. As a result, the spacing between the characters you print and those on the screen doesn't match. Justifying your text is out of the question, unless you're using a monospaced typeface like Courier. Again, MacPrint offers a solution, by supplying Macintosh screen versions of the common DeskJet fonts.

☙ *Caution:* *Macintosh PostScript fonts, of course, won't print on the DeskJet.*

How to mix Apples and DeskJets

As with any computer/printer pairing, you have both hardware and software considerations to worry about when you try to print on the DeskJet from the Macintosh.

Connecting the hardware

The hardware part of the equation is actually very straightforward, as long as you're trying to use the DeskJet with a single Macintosh, and not on a network. The Mac's printer port is of the serial variety, and the DeskJet has a built-in serial port, so all you need is a serial cable with the proper connectors on either end.

Before you actually connect the cable, though, you should first set the DeskJet to communicate at its fastest possible serial speed, 19,200 bits per second (baud). As you may know, the Mac can talk considerably faster, but the DeskJet sets the limits here. At any rate, making this change doubles the DeskJet's default speed, and will make printing much faster.

To set the DeskJet to the new speed, you need to change the position one of the little function (DIP) switches located on the lower front of the printer, a little to the right of center. Here's how:

1. Make sure the printer is off.

2. Scrounge up a small flatblade screwdriver, the tinier the better. In a pinch, a dinner knife, ball point pen, or similar instrument will suffice.

3. There are two banks of switches recessed behind cutouts in the DeskJet's plastic housing. Stand the printer on its rear end so you can see the switches and locate Bank B, the one on the right.

4. Assuming no one has changed the switch settings since your DeskJet left the factory, all of the switches will be pointing towards you (downward when the printer is sitting flat). Your job is to flip the fifth switch in Bank B so that it points away from you (or up with the printer in its normal position). Use the screwdriver to do the job, making sure you don't disturb any of the other switches.

Now go ahead and can connect the Mac to the DeskJet with the appropriate cable.

Network connections

The DeskJet can't be connected directly to an AppleTalk network, since it doesn't understand AppleTalk messages. However, you can buy special translating devices that convert AppleTalk into the DeskJet's lingo.

Using printer drivers

When it comes to the software part of the Mac-DeskJet connection, the major challenge is to find a good utility designed for the job. The core of any such utility is a DeskJet driver that you place in your Mac's system folder alongside the LaserWriter and/or ImageWriter drivers you already have there.

To print to the DeskJet, you must first select the utility's new DeskJet driver using the Chooser. Typically, you'll be asked at this point to choose a serial communications speed for the hookup—select 19200 by clicking on the corresponding button.

You make other printer setup choices from your application software menus. Depending on the driver you're using, you may be able to select paper size, choose between portrait and landscape orientation (remember, the DeskJet's landscape mode can only print in a few special fonts, and does not print graphics at all), and select which text printing method of those described earlier you want to use.

Speeding things up

Because of the Macintosh's heavy reliance on graphics, printing to the DeskJet can be painfully slow. I highly recommend a Mac print spooling utility such as SuperMac Software's SuperLaserSpool—it won't speed up the actual printing, but it will let you get back to your work in your application software in a fraction of the time that you'd otherwise have to wait (for more information about how print spoolers work, see Chapter 4).

Profile: MacPrint

$149/Insight Development Corp.
2200 Powell St., Suite 500
Emeryville, CA 94608
415/652-4115

If you're set on using your DeskJet with a Macintosh, do yourself a big favor and get a copy of Insight Development's MacPrint.

Like most DeskJet utilities, MacPrint works with any Hewlett-Packard PCL printer, which means all the models in the LaserJet family as well as the

DeskJet. The package consists of a driver for each of the printers it supports—to its credit, it provides separate drivers for the DeskJet and DeskJet Plus—along with a set of compressed fonts and a font generating utility.

MacPrint handles graphics from most Mac programs capably, the exception being any PostScript output. But it's in text printing that MacPrint really shines. The MacPrint driver lets you choose between printing text as graphics or with the DeskJet's own fonts, and it handles either option remarkably well.

With the graphics method, MacPrint can reproduce text characters dot-for-dot as they appear on the screen, and do so at a reasonable clip. But the program doesn't restrict you to the screen's low 72-dpi resolution. If you select Medium or High quality in the Print dialog box, MacPrint will search your system file for a larger version of the current screen font—double size for Medium quality, quadruple size for High quality. If the oversize font is available, MacPrint uses it for printing, and produces double or quadruple the resolution of the screen.

This is the same trick Apple uses to achieve high-quality output from its flagship dot matrix printer, the ImageWriter LQ. It works because each character in one of these larger fonts has many more dots than the corresponding character in the regular font. When you shrink the large character down to the size you want printed, all the extra dots are still there, just much tinier. As a result, any stair-step jaggedness in the curved outline of the character at its large size is far less apparent.

This system works well with any font for which you have the correct oversized version. Since most Mac screen fonts aren't provided in the large sizes required, however, MacPrint supplies complete screen font sets for four different typefaces, including renditions of Courier, Times, Helvetica, and Symbol. In each set you get 9, 10, 12, 14, 18, and 24 point fonts for use on the screen, and duplicates of each of these at four times the size for printing.

MacPrint's graphics method lets you print a wide variety of fonts and font sizes with excellent print quality, but it's terribly slow. Fortunately, MacPrint can also use a much faster technique, printing in text mode with the DeskJet's own fonts. The only drawback here is that the dimensions of ordinary Mac screen fonts don't match those of the DeskJet fonts. Since your program will space the characters in your text file based on whatever screen font you're using, not on the DeskJet font, spacing of the printed text will be incorrect. MacPrint overcomes this problem by supplying screen versions of all the DeskJet's internal and cartridge fonts. Actually, MacPrint doesn't come with the fonts themselves. Instead, you generate them with a program called Font Mapper—simply pick out the cartridges you own from a list, and Font Mapper generates the necessary screen fonts. Once you've installed the new screen fonts in your system file, your application programs will have the information they need to space the characters properly, and the letters themselves will look right on screen to boot.

Aside from the fact that it works so well, one of the nicest things about MacPrint is its manual. In addition to complete operating instructions, it features clear explanations of the obstacles that have to faced in connecting a Mac to a "foreign" printer, and frank discussions of the tradeoffs to be weighed when deciding among alternative solutions. The manual also offers tips about a large number of specific applications.

22

DeskJet Programming

∾

If you really want to make the DeskJet jump through hoops, you'll eventually have to learn to program it yourself. Given the complexities of escape sequences and control codes, the do-it-yourself approach may be more, well, challenging, than using a built-in DeskJet driver. But programming usually gives you better control of your printer, and sometimes it's the only way to get the results you want in your printouts.

Earlier chapters have introduced some of the most useful DeskJet commands, and some techniques for employing them with your application programs. In this chapter, though, we really roll up our sleeves and dive into DeskJet programming in depth. If you want the ultimate in DeskJet control from your application programs, or if you want to actually write your own DeskJet programs or drivers, this is your chapter.

We'll begin with an exploration of the PCL language in general: Then we'll look at each of the DeskJet commands in detail, in sections divided according to function: font selection, print positioning, graphics printing, and odds and ends. If you plan to use the PCL commands within application software, you'll find tips on how to do so in Section III. If you'll be incorporating the commands in programs you write yourself, you'll need to know how to send characters to the printer using your programming language.

PCL

Although versions of Hewlett-Packard's Printer Command Language, or PCL, were built into earlier printers, it was the release of the original LaserJet in 1984 that really established PCL as a major printer programming language. PCL was enlarged substantially with the LaserJet Plus, but it has been fairly stable in the subsequent members of the LaserJet family (the 500 Plus, the Series II, the 2000, the IID, and the IIP). However, with each new model, a few commands have been added that are specific to that particular printer. The two DeskJet models understand some, but not all, of the commands added to PCL with the LaserJet Plus, and have a set of ten or so commands that no other PCL printers recognize.

Thus, compatibility between PCL printers is good, but not perfect. While all printers in the extended family respond identically to a common core set of PCL commands, the original LaserJet can't carry out commands that have been added to PCL with the later models, and the DeskJet doesn't recognize some advanced commands. In addition, the commands that are unique to each printer model are ignored by all the other members of the family.

Understanding PCL levels

HP has separated PCL commands into categories called *levels,* with each level supposedly associated with a general type of function. Actually, each level includes such a hodgepodge of different kinds of commands that it's impossible to see any pattern in the groupings. There's certainly no point in memorizing which commands fit into which level, since the commands in all the levels work the same way. HP describes the DeskJet as a Level

III-compatible printer, but actually it responds to almost half of the Level IV commands as well.

Just in case you run across a reference to "Level such-and-such compatibility" in a discussion of a printer, here's a brief description of each of the levels, with its official HP designation:

PCL Level I: Print and Space PCL. Level I commands control underlining, basic graphics, and perforation skip mode, among other functions.

PCL Level II: EDP/Transaction PCL. Level II commands let you select margins, line spacing, symbols set, page length, and pitch, among other settings.

PCL Level III: Office Word Processing PCL. Some of the commands in Level III are for font selection, others for determining print position.

PCL Level IV: Page Formatting PCL. Includes commands to select font point size, page orientation, soft font ID number, and print position. In addition, there are commands that the DeskJet doesn't support, including primitive line-and rectangle-drawing commands, and macro commands.

The DeskJet and PCL

For the most part, PCL commands work the same on the DeskJet as they do on all PCL printers. However, there is one major exception, which results directly from a fundamental technological differerence between laser printers and the DeskJet.

Laser printers such as the LaserJet print an entire page at a time, after "composing" an image of the whole page as a bitmap in printer memory. For this reason, PCL lets you, the programmer, "paint" the page with the freedom that a painter would have. You can place text and graphics elements on the page in any order—if you want to, there's nothing wrong with filling in a bit-map graphic at the bottom right of the page, then jumping to the top left to start printing text.

This is a fundamentally different approach to printer control than the DeskJet demands. The DeskJet is a line printer, printing only one line of text or graphics at a time, then moving on to the next line. And, unlike many dot matrix line printers, the DeskJet can't move paper in the reverse direction because this would smear the ink of the previously printed parts of the page. Therefore, your DeskJet PCL programs must generally send each line to the printer in the order in which it will appear on the page (there is an exception to this rule, as noted in the section "Moving up on the page" later in this chapter). This is one of the most important differences between PCL for the DeskJet and PCL for the LaserJet.

In addition, a variety of special commands have been added to the DeskJet version of PCL. These control features of your printer not found on other PCL machines. For example, there are special commands for feeding envelopes, for switching back and forth between portrait and landscape orientation, for accessing the DeskJet's unique graphics compaction modes, and so forth.

Control codes and escape sequences

PCL consists of a large set of software commands, each of which consists of one or more consecutive ASCII codes. In ASCII, each code value occupies a single byte. Since an ASCII code corresponds to a printed character, the codes in a PCL command are also referred to as characters. In fact, you'll usually PCL commands are usually shown as the characters that correspond to their ASCII codes, even though these characters aren't printed when they're used in a command. For example, the command that sets the right margin to the 80th column requires these code bytes:

27 38 97 56 48 77

but would normally be written as

^{E}s$_c$&a8ØM

The first code, 27, is represented by the abbreviation ^{E}s$_c$ and is referred to as the *escape character*. It's one of a number of control codes, special codes that are the key to controlling the DeskJet.

Control codes

All PCL commands begin with a control code, a code value that the DeskJet recognizes as a printer command rather than printable data. The values of all the control codes are in the range of 0 to 32 (decimal notation), values which do not correspond to printable characters in the standard ASCII coding system. Nevertheless, control codes such as E_{s_c} or *Control-L* are commonly referred to as characters.

♪ ***Note:*** *Just to confuse the issue, in several DeskJet character sets, including the default PC-8 set, the control codes do correspond to printable characters. However, these characters are not part of the standard ASCII code, and you must send special commands to print them.*

DeskJet commands fall into two major categories, depending on their complexity and the control code they use: ordinary control codes and escape sequences.

- A few DeskJet commands consist solely of a single control code. When the DeskJet receives one of these one-character, single-byte commands, it takes an immediate action, and then returns directly to its regular printing mode. For example, the form feed control code, 12 decimal, ØC hexadecimal, causes the DeskJet to eject the page that is currently loaded.

- Escape sequences are commands that are two or more characters (or codes, or bytes) in length, always beginning with the control code for the escape character. Again, the escape character is code 27 in decimal notation (or 1B in hexadecimal). Escape sequences consist of at least one and usually several characters in addition to the escape character. Far more important and more numerous than the one-byte control code commands, escape sequences control DeskJet functions that have two or more possible settings. For example, escape sequences are used to select which font is active from all those available, and to fix the left margin at one of the many available columns.

Name	Abbreviation	Character	Value (dec)	Value (hex)	Screen char.	Function
Backspace	BS	Ctrl-H	008	008	▪	Moves the print position one character to the left
Tab	HT	Ctrl-I	009	009	○	Moves the print position to the next tab stop. Tab stops are preset at every eighth column, beginning from the left margin
Line Feed	LF	Ctrl-J	010	00A	◙	Advances the print position and the paper one line
Form Feed	FF	Ctrl-L	012	00B	♀	Ejects the current page, loads another page, and advances the print position to the top of the new page
Carriage Return	CR	Ctrl-M	013	00C	♪	Moves the print position to the left margin
Secondary Font (Shift Out)	SO	Ctrl-N	014	00D	♫	Selects the current secondary font
Primary Font (Shift In)	SI	Ctrl-O	015	00F	☼	Selects the current primary font
Escape	ESC	Ctrl-[	027	01B	←	Begins an escape sequence

Table 22-1: *DeskJet control codes. The list does not include the rarely-used codes for serial communications.*

Using control codes

Single-byte control codes are easy to understand and use: you send a single character or byte to the printer, the DeskJet reacts with a specific immediate response, and then it goes back to regular printing.

Table 22-1 lists the DeskJet's control codes and the printer functions they activate. For the most part, the control codes used by the DeskJet perform the same functions indicated by their names in the ASCII code—for example, the backspace code causes the printer to move back one character on the current line, and the tab control code makes the printer move ahead to the next tab stop, if any, on the current line. On the other hand, some control codes perform functions that are not obvious from their standard names. All the control codes are described in detail in the appropriate sections of this chapter.

Using escape sequences

Escape sequences can be considerably more complicated than control codes. A quick examination of a few representative escape sequences should give you some idea of their format:

E_{s_c}E	Resets printer
E_{s_c}&l0O	Selects portrait orientation
E_{s_c}(1U	Selects the legal character set
E_{s_c}*t75R	Sets graphics resolution to 75 dots per inch
E_{s_c})250X	Selects soft font 250 as secondary font

Hidden in the jumble of characters, there's a pattern here. Let's see if we can trace it.

The first character: E_{s_c}

Again, all escape sequences begin with the escape character, ASCII value 27 decimal, 1B hex. It's written out as E_{s_c}.

Two-character escape sequences

Six escape sequences, including the E_{s_c}E in the list above, consist of just two characters: escape followed by one other character, which may be a number or a letter. These two-byte escape sequences include commands to clear the current margins settings, advance the paper half a line, reset the printer, run a self-test, and turn display functions on and off.

Multiple-character escape sequences

In escape sequences with more than two characters, the characters following the escape character each have a different function.

The second character: &, (,), or *

After the escape character, the next character in all multiple-character escape sequences is known as the "parameterized" character, either **&**, **(**, **)**, or *****. When the DeskJet receives one of the four parameterized characters, it knows to expect several further characters in the escape sequence.

Of these four characters, the one that appears in the escape sequence gives you a general clue about the function of the sequence:

&: The ampersand character sees duty in the commands that set margins, determine print position and paper size, turn underlining off, and control other general functions.

(and **)**: Both parens are used in commands that determine font characteristics: typeface, character set, print quality, and so on. **(** is used in commands that alter the primary font, **)** in commands for the secondary font (primary and secondary fonts are discussed later in this chapter).

*: The asterisk is found in commands related to graphics and soft fonts, and in the command for obtaining the printer model number.

The third character: the group character

The third character, also called the "group" character, further narrows down the kind of function performed by the sequence. In most escape sequences, the group character is a letter. All escape sequences beginning with Es_c&d, for example, are related to underlining, while all those that start with Es_c*c have to do with soft fonts. As far as I can tell, the letters don't stand for anything in particular.

Escape sequences used to select character sets, such as the Es_c(1U command which activates the legal character set, do not contain a parameterized character. In these escape sequences, the third character begins the value field, the topic to which we now turn.

The value field

Beginning with the fourth character comes one or more numeric characters, the *value field.* The characters in the value field specify a particular value for the DeskJet function you're controlling. (Again, the value field in the escape sequences for selecting character sets begins with the third character, and the number you enter here helps determine which character set is activated.)

Sometimes there are only a few valid numbers to pick from, when there are just a few possible options for the command. For example, in the escape sequence for setting print quality, you only have two choices for the fourth character: ^{E}s$_C$(s2Q for high (letter) quality, and ^{E}s$_C$(s1Q for draft quality. Notice that the only difference between the two sequences is the number in the value field.

Other commands control a wider range of settings, and their escape sequences can contain a corresponding range of numeric values. In ^{E}s$_C$&a#L, the escape sequence used to set the left margin, for instance, you can specify any column the DeskJet can print in place of the "#" in the value field.

�ą *Tip:* *To enter a numeric value in a DeskJet escape sequence, you place the ASCII codes of the number's individual digits into the sequence. Do not send the actual number to the DeskJet. For example, if you're setting the left margin to the 30th column, you would place two bytes in the value field: a 3 (ASCII code 33 decimal), then a Ø (ASCII code 30 decimal). You would not send a single byte containing the number 30—the DeskJet would interpret that as a Ø, since the ASCII code for Ø is 30, and set the left margin accordingly.*

This system makes it easy to type escape sequences within an application program when you're embedding them in a document file. It works fine in programming languages as well, as long as you remember to specify that the numeric digits comprise a character string, just like the rest of the escape sequence. See the section "Using PCL commands in your programs" for practical tips on including escape sequences with various programming languages.

The terminator—"I won't be back"

The final character in any escape sequence longer than two bytes is a letter, the terminator. The terminator indicates that you've sent all the numbers in the value field, and completes the sequence.

In some cases, this letter has an obvious relationship to the function of the command—*Q* for the print quality commands, *T* for commands that choose a typeface, and "B" for commands that turn boldfacing on and off. But often, the terminator isn't mnemonic at all—*U* is the terminator for super- and subscripting commands, while underlining commands end in *D*.

Uppercase and lowercase letters

Here are the rules for using upper- and lowercase letters in escape sequences. If the escape sequence has a group character (remember, the character set commands do not), it is a letter, and must always be entered in lowercase. The final character or terminator is normally capitalized, and causes the DeskJet to return immediately to ordinary printing. If the terminator character is entered in lowercase form, however, the DeskJet interprets the characters that follow as another escape sequence in a combined escape sequence, a topic we'll cover next.

Combining escape sequences

If you're planning to send two or more escape sequences in succession, you may be able to combine them into a single sequence, reducing the number of characters you must type by cutting out those that repeat. In order to be combined, two or more succesive escape sequences must all begin with the same three characters (the escape character plus the two following characters). For example, you might combine

E_{S_C}(sØU$^E_{S_C}$(s1P$^E_{S_C}$(s12V

into the omnibus sequence

E_{S_C}(sØu1p12V

As you can see, all you do to combine escape sequences is:

1. Enter the first three characters shared by all of the escape sequences you're combining.

2. Enter the remaining characters from each escape sequence in succession.

3. The last character in each sequence you're combining will always be a letter. This letter should be capitalized when it falls at the very end of your combination escape sequence. Otherwise, you must enter it in lowercase form.

The capitalized letter functions as the terminator for the combined escape sequence. If you accidentally capitalize any another letter, the DeskJet will print the characters of the combined escape sequence, instead of carrying out the commands.

✄ *Tip:* *While combining escapes sequences might seem a good practice, don't assume it's always the best idea. Theoretically, you'll reduce the number of characters you have to enter, and thereby save little typing time and a few bytes of memory. In practice, you'll probably waste more time making sure that you combine the sequences properly. Besides, a combined sequence can be harder to read than a succession of individual sequences.*

Combined escape sequences will help you most when you're typing in a DeskJet program written by someone else. If the author has gone to the trouble of combining escape sequences when possible for you, you'll have fewer characters to type.

PCL COMMAND REFERENCE

This section describes each PCL command individually. They're grouped by general function: font and character commands (beginning on this page); print position commands (p. 349); and graphics commands (p. 363).

FONT AND OTHER CHARACTER COMMANDS

PCL offers a wide range of commands for selecting fonts and for specifying other aspects of the appearance of printed text.

Selecting fonts

Using PCL printer commands, there are three ways to select a specific font from among any of those currently resident in the DeskJet (including internal, cartridge, and soft fonts):

1. By defining each and every characteristic of the font you want to select through a long series of escape sequences.

2. By selecting a previously defined primary or secondary font through a single simple control code.

3. By selecting the font by its temporary identification number. This method only works with soft fonts.

Defining a font in every detail

The standard and usually most accurate method for choosing a particular font is what I call the "longhand" method. In the longhand method, you specify each of its characteristics, one at a time, with the necessary escape sequences. The font characteristics you can specify include: orientation (portrait or landscape); character set; character spacing (monospacing or proportional spacing); pitch (for monospaced fonts); size; type style (upright or italic); stroke weight (regular or bold); and typeface; placement (superscript, subscript, or normal); and print quality (letter or draft).

All the escape sequences for selecting font characteristics are described in detail individually later in this chapter. By the way, HP uses the vague term "print features" for what I've called font characteristics.

♪ ***Note:*** *Selecting a new font for immediate printing also selects the same font as the new primary or secondary font, depending on which is active at the time. If the secondary font is currently active, your escape sequences must be entered in a slightly different form than is shown here when you're selecting a new font for immediate use. See the section "Primary and secondary fonts" below for details.*

To switch to a new font, you simply send the required escape sequence for each of these characteristics in turn. If you want to select a portrait-oriented, legal-character set, proportionally spaced, 14-point, italicized, normal-stoke weight TmsRmn-typeface font, you'd send the following string of commands:

$^{E}s_{C}$&lØO$^{E}s_{C}$ (1U$^{E}s_{C}$(s1P$^{E}s_{C}$ (s14V $^{E}s_{C}$(sØS$^{E}s_{C}$(sØB $^{E}s_{C}$(s5T

Actually, you can cut down on the typing somewhat by combining related escape sequences, as you've learned earlier in this chapter. And you really only have to send commands for characteristics that will be different in the new font. If you're switching from a standard 10-point TmsRmn font to a 14-point TmsRmn that's otherwise identical, all you have to send the appropriate font size escape sequence.

But although font commands look similar to other PCL escape sequences, there's a subtle but important difference in how they work. The difference is based on the fact that every dot in every character in each font is predefined, so a font can't be changed by sending a new escape sequence. When you use an escape sequence to define, say, a new left margin, you're directly setting that new margin where you want it. In contrast, when you send a command to switch from a 10 point font to a 14 point font, you're not setting a new point size, you're asking the DeskJet to look for an entirely new font that matches your point size request.

Font characteristic priorities

What happens when it turns out that the font you've specified isn't currently available in the DeskJet? Instead of ignoring your request altogether, the printer does its best to give you what you asked for.

Whenever it receives a command that changes even a single font characteristic, the printer has to start a fresh search for a new font that best matches
the characterstics that are in effect. To conduct this search, the DeskJet starts
with what it considers as the most important characteristic of all, which
happens to be orientation. It picks out all the available fonts that match your
choice for the orientation setting, and eliminates all the other fonts. Working
with the fonts that remain, the DeskJet goes on to the next most important
characteristic, character set, culling out the fonts that aren't available with
the required set.

This process of elimination continues down the list of font characteristics, in
order of their priority. The search stops as soon as only a single font remains
in the group of eligibles. At this point, the remaining font is selected, even
if its characteristics don't match all those you've requested.

For better or worse, the system the DeskJet uses to decide which of your
commands has the highest priority is defined for you, and can't be changed.
Here's the priority list for font characteristics:

1. orientation (portrait or landscape)
2. character set
3. spacing (monospacing or proportional spacing)
4. pitch (for monospaced fonts)
5. size
6. type style (upright or italic)
7. stroke weight (regular or bold)
8. typeface

An example is clearly in order at this point. Let's say you have a DeskJet Plus
with built-in Courier landscape fonts, and you've installed the "TmsRmn
Collection" font cartridge, which doesn't include any landscape fonts. You
send the escape sequences for a landscape 12-point proportionally-spaced
TmsRmn font to the DeskJet. Examining your request, the DeskJet starts with
the landscape orientation command, and immediately rejects all your Tms-
Rmn cartridge fonts, and all the internal protrait-oriented Courier fonts. That
still leaves three fonts in contention, since the DeskJet Plus has 6, 12 and 24
point landscape fonts built in. All three of these fonts have the same character
sets available, and none of them will print in proportionally spaced mode.

The next eliminating point is size. Obviously, only the 12 point Courier makes the cut, and it becomes the selected font.

If you've been paying close attention, you may have noticed that two font characteristics mentioned at the beginning of this section aren't on the priority list above—even though they're included in the priority list that appears in your DeskJet *Owner's Manual*. The ones I've stricken from the list include placement (super- and subscript) and print quality.

The reason these characteristics don't belong on the priority list is that they're not actually a part of any font definition. When you give a command that alters one of these them, the DeskJet doesn't look for a matching font. Instead, the printer simply modifies the way it prints, so these commands can be used with *any* font. Since no font ever gets eliminated from the match based on the placement or print quality characteristics, they don't belong in the priority list.

Primary and secondary fonts

If you'll be switching between two fonts frequently during a given print job, you can define them in advance as *primary* and *secondary* fonts, and then switch between them as often as you like with a quick and easy control code.

Actually, the primary and secondary fonts are defined for you by default when you turn on the DeskJet—at this point, both are the same font, as determined by the printer's DIP switch settings. Of course, until you redefine at least one of the primary and secondary fonts for yourself, it won't do you much good to switch between identical fonts. But whether or not you redefine them, one of the two is always the active font (the font currently in use for printing). And unless you've explicitly switched to the secondary font, the active font is the primary font.

The primary/secondary approach to selecting fonts has two disadvantages. First, you can only set up two fonts for immediate access. Second, your primary and secondary font choices get erased and returned to the default font any time the printer is reset.

Defining a primary or secondary font

To set up a primary or secondary font of your own choice, you must use the longhand method outlined above, sending the complete set of escape sequences necessary to define all of the font's characteristics. Actually, each time you select a new font "on the fly" with the longhand method, you're really designating the new primary font or secondary font, whichever of these you're currently printing with.

If you wish, however, you can set up whichever of the two that's not currently active in advance, and then switch to it with a control code whenever necessary. When you define a primary or secondary font that isn't currently active, the DeskJet still goes through the regular process of searching for a matching font based on font characteristic priorities.

☝ *Caution: If you define a primary font while the secondary font is active, or vice versa, you must omit the orientation command, since you can't specify a primary or secondary font with this command, and it takes effect immediately.*

The escape sequences you use to define primary and secondary fonts are identical, except that you use a left parenthesis for primary font commands, a right parenthesis for secondary font commands. So, for example

$^E{s_c}$(1U selects the legal character set for the primary font,

while

$^E{s_c}$)1U selects the legal character set for the secondary font.

In the discussions of the individual font escape sequences in the rest of this section, only the escape sequences for defining the primary font are shown. If you're defining the secondary font, just replace the *(* in each escape sequence with a *)*.

Knowing this code, you can redefine the primary or secondary font at any time, whether or not the one you're redefining is currently in use for printing. If, for example, you're currently printing with the secondary font, and you want to redefine the primary font, just make sure the escape sequences you send contain the left parenthesis. When you switch to the primary font at a later time, the new font you've defined will become active.

You can also redefine the secondary font while you're printing with it, this time by sending escape sequences with the right parenthesis. In this case, the new font you choose will be selected for printing immediately. If you switch to the primary font and then back again to the secondary, this same font will again become active.

Selecting a primary or secondary font

CTRL-O   Select primary font
  (15d or ØFh)

CTRL-N   Select secondary font
  (14d or ØEh)

Once your primary and secondary fonts are defined, you can select either one with a single-byte commands. To select the secondary font, send the value **14** decimal (ØE hex, Control-N) to the DeskJet (send a single byte with the value 14, not the numerals *1* and *4* separately. To select the primary font, send the value **15** decimal (ØF hex, Control-O). Your *Owner's Manual* refers to these codes with their traditional but meaningless names, Shift-Out and Shift-In. If you're going to be remembering names, I recommend memorizing them as "secondary font" and "primary font" instead.

Setting the secondary font selection mode

^Es_c**&kØF**   Return to primary font automatically at the end of each line

^Es_c**&k1F**   Continue secondary font selection across lines until explicitly turned off

Default: Continuous secondary font

Notes: Not a PCL Level III feature.

The DeskJet provides two commands for controlling the way it manages your secondary font selections. In the default mode, once you select the secondary font, it continues to be the font used for printing until you explicitly reselect the primary font. In the line-by-line mode, the primary font is automatically reselected at the end of every line.

Restoring the default primary and secondary fonts

E_{S_C}(3@   Restore default font as primary font

E_{S_C})3@   Restore default font as secondary font

To restore the default font that was automatically selected when the DeskJet was turned on as either the primary or secondary font, just send the appropriate command from this pair.

Assigning a soft font as the default primary or secondary font

E_{S_C}(#@   Assign soft font # as default primary font

E_{S_C})#@   Assign soft font # as default secondary font

Valid values: Any soft font temporary ID number currently in use

Use one of these escape sequences to assign a soft font as the default primary or secondary font. When the printer receives a reset command, the current primary and secondary font assignments are cancelled, and the default primary and secondary fonts you've chosen with this command are automatically reestablished. The catch with this command is that the soft fonts chosen as the defaults will themselves be erased by the reset, unless you explicitly make them "permanent" when you download them. See the next section for more on soft fonts and ID numbers.

Selecting soft fonts by ID number

E_{S_C}(#X   Select ID number # soft font as primary font

E_{S_C})#X   Select ID number # soft font as secondary font

Valid values: Ø through 32767

The third and final method for selecting a font works only with soft fonts, the kind you download to the DeskJet from disk files. When you download a soft font, you must assign the entire font a temporary identification number. From then on, you can select the font with one simple escape sequence based on this ID number.

To use these commands, you need to know how primary and secondary fonts work, as detailed in the last section. With that background, let's examine the first of these commands, the one that lets you select a soft font as the primary font. Let's say you select soft font number 5 with this command. If you're already printing with the primary font when you give the command, the next text you print comes out in soft font 5. If you were printing with the secondary font, though, there's no immediate change in the appearance of your printed text. Soft font 5 still becomes the primary font, but you have to switch to the primary font with the control code **15** decimal before your text prints with the new font.

The second of the two commands works exactly the same way, except that it selects the chosen soft font as the secondary. If you're currently printing in the primary font, you have to switch to the secondary font to print with the new font you've just selected.

A soft reset command will erase the choices you've made for primary and secondary fonts, but not the ID numbers of your soft fonts. To restore your primary and secondary fonts, just resend the above escape sequences.

Selecting page orientation

⌒ *Caution:* *It's very easy to make mistakes in entering either of these two escape sequences. Check your work carefully!*

$^E\!s_C$&l1O	Select landscape orientation
$^E\!s_C$&lØO	Select portrait orientation
Default:	portrait orientation
Notes:	1. Both of these escape sequences contain characters that can be easily mistaken for others. In both commands, the first character after the & is a lower case "el." Then comes a numeral, either a "one" for landscape, or a "zero" for portrait. Both sequences end in the letter "oh."
	2. Both commands also cause a form feed, ejecting the current sheet of paper—this last effect is not a PCL Level III feature.
	3. Landscape orientation does not permit graphics printing, text scaling, or underlining via the underlining escape sequence.
	4. The DeskJet automatically switches to unidirectional printing when landscape orientation is selected. This can then be overriden by the bidirectional printing command.

We've gone over the difference between portrait orientation and landscape orientation before, but it won't hurt to repeat the definitions here. In portrait orientation, the ordinary mode, the long edge of the paper runs vertically, and you have lots of lines but not so many columns. In landscape mode, the long edge is oriented horizontally, so you can fit long lines, though not as many on a single page.

The DeskJet is capable of printing text in landscape orientation, but not graphics. Even in text mode, landscape printing only works with fonts specifically designed for that purpose. That's why the orientation escape sequence is functionally a font selection command, even though it's not listed as such in the PCL "dictionary." In fact, the orientation command has the highest priority in the DeskJet's heirarchy of font characteristics. In other words, if there's only a single font available for the orientation you've chosen, your printout will still be oriented properly—even if the font doesn't look anything like the one you've requested with your other font selection commands.

Of course, the easiest way to switch between landscape and portrait orientations is by pressing the FONT button on the keypad until the landscape light glows. Still, it's easy to imagine a situation where you'd want to change page orientation under software control.

Say you're planning to print a financial report, to use the standard hackneyed business-oriented scenario. Along with lots of explanatory text, the document includes a couple of tables, one of which is a month-by-month breakdown of sunflower seed sales over the past year. This means you have 12 columns to print, and the text has to be big and bold enough to make your bleary-eyed readership around the conference table take notice. With the necessary legends and margins, twelve ½" columns won't fit across an 8½" wide piece of paper, but they'll fit just fine if you turn the page sideways.

If you plan to insert the table as page 3 of your report, you need a command to switch out of portrait mode and into landscape mode after page 2, and to switch back to portrait again before page 4.

When you're switching between landscape and portrait modes, or vice versa, one thing you don't have to worry about is where the page breaks are going to fall. As soon as the printer receives the command to change orientation, it immediately spits out the page it was printing, even if the entire piece of paper hasn't been printed on.

Other points to note about the landscape mode

Valid *margin* settings change from those available in portrait mode because of the DeskJet's unprintable area. Remember that in portrait mode, the DeskJet cannot print on the bottom ½" of the page. In the "sideways" landscape orientation, the bottom of the page becomes the left margin, meaning you always have at least a ½" left margin from the edge of the paper. On the other hand, the maximum right margin is reduced from ¼" in portrait mode to ⅙" in landscape, corresponding to the unprintable ⅙" at the top of a portrait-oriented page. Anyway, you end up with a maximum line length (horizontal printing distance) of 10⅓" on letter paper, 13⅓" on legal.

Similarly, there are ¼" unprintable strips at the right and left of a portrait page and therefore at the top and bottom of a landscape page. On letter paper, that means that your landscape mode text can extend vertically over no more than 8" of the page. Disable the perforation skip mode if you want to automatically use these minimum ¼" top and bottom margins (see the discussion of the perforation skip function later in this chapter). If you want to set your own margins, set perforation skip on instead.

The *text scale* command, described later, has no effect in the landscape mode. Although the *underline* command doesn't work either, you can still create your own underlines by printing the text first, then moving the print position back on the same line and on print position commands).

When you switch the DeskJet to landscape orientation, the printer automatically configures itself for *unidirectional* (left to right) printing to ensure the best possible print quality. You can override this setup by sending the escape sequence E_{S_C}&k1W for bidirectional printing after you've switched to landscape mode.

Although the DeskJet doesn't print *graphics* in landscape mode, that shouldn't stop you from getting a landscape-oriented graphics printout. You just have to design your program so that it rotates the graphics data "sideways" first, and then sends it to the printer in ordinary portrait mode.

Choosing a character set

^Es_c(#x   Select character set

Values: # is a number and *x* is a letter which together represent the character set's designation

Notes: The default character sets are determined by the positions of DIP switches A-1 through A-4.

A character set is the specific collection of symbols, including letters, numerals, and punctuation marks, that is available for printing at any one time. In a given character set, each available symbol is assigned its own one-byte code number; to print a character, you just send its code to the DeskJet. If you change character sets, that same code number may correspond to an entirely different character, which will be printed instead.

Character sets are classified as 7-bit or 8-bit, depending on whether the printer recognizes or ignores the most significant bit in each character code byte. 7-bit character sets can contain up to 128 characters, while 8-bit character sets can have double that amount, for a total of 256 different symbols.

The DeskJet Plus has five built-in 8-bit character sets, adding the PC-850 set the ones in the original DeskJet. In all the built-in 8-bit character sets, the first 128 characters are the same, and follow the ASCII standard. Codes 0 to 32 are non-printing control codes (although the DeskJet doesn't respond to all of them). In the character sets intended for use with IBM-compatible PCs, this group of codes also represents a group of miscellaneous symbols such as arrows, musical notes, and happy faces, but you must send a special command to make the DeskJet interpret them as printable characters instead of control codes. Codes 33 to 127 are a standardized collection of letters, numbers, and punctuation marks. The additional 128 symbols in the 8-bit character sets vary from set to set.

In the 7-bit character sets, codes 0-32 are assigned to exactly the same control codes as in the 8-bit sets. The remaining characters, 33-128 vary from set to set. Most of the DeskJet's 14 built-in 7-bit character sets conform to definitions for various languages established by the International Standards Organization, and these are designated "ISO Germany," "ISO France," and so on.

When you turn on the DeskJet, the default character set is determined by the settings of DIP switches A-1 through A-4. As it's shipped from the factory, the US version of the DeskJet is set up with the PC-8 character set, which matches the standard IBM PC screen character set, as the default.

The character sets available in the DeskJet and on optional cartridges are listed in Table 22-2, each with the escape sequence needed to select it. Many of the character sets themselves are printed in Appendix B.

Assuming you're currently printing with the primary font, you can switch immediately to another set by sending the escape sequence for the primary font character set, $^Es_c(\#xD$. In this sequence, replace $\#x$ with the character set's identification number and letter. For example, to choose the ECMA-94 Latin 1 set (where do they get those names?), send the escape sequence $^Es_c(\text{Ø}N$.

To select a character set in advance for the secondary font, use a right parenthesis instead of a left one in the escape sequence. With the example just given, the sequence would be $^Es_c)\text{Ø}N$. Then, when you activate the secondary font with the appropriate command, the desired character set will already be in effect (see "Selecting primary and secondary fonts" above).

Character set	Escape sequence
Roman 8	E_{S_C}(8U
PC-8	E_{S_C}(1ØU
PC-8 Denmark/Norway	E_{S_C}(11U
PC-850	E_{S_C}(12U
ECMA-94 Latin 1	E_{S_C}(ØN
ISO United Kingdom (04)	E_{S_C}(1E
ISO Germany (21)	E_{S_C}(1G
ISO France (69)	E_{S_C}(1F
ISO Italy (15)	E_{S_C}(ØI
ISO Norway v. 1 (60)	E_{S_C}(ØD
ISO (Norway v. 2 (61)	E_{S_C}(1D
ISO Sweden: Names (11)	E_{S_C}(ØS
ISO Sweden (10)	E_{S_C}(3S
ISO Spain (17	E_{S_C}(2S
ASCIII	E_{S_C}(ØU
ISO IRV (02)	E_{S_C}(2U
ISO Portugal (16)	E_{S_C}(4S
JIS ASCII (14)	E_{S_C}(ØK
Legal	E_{S_C}(1U
Line Draw	E_{S_C}(ØL
Math7	E_{S_C}(ØM
Math8a	E_{S_C}(ØQ
Math8b	E_{S_C}(1Q
Math8	E_{S_C}(8M
Pi Font	E_{S_C}(15U
Pi Fonta	E_{S_C}(2Q

Table 22-2: *DeskJet Character Sets. Those above the heavy line are available with the internal fonts, those below on cartridges. See text regarding primary vs. secondary fonts.*

Selecting proportional or fixed spacing

$^{E}s_{C}$(s1P   Select proportional spacing

$^{E}s_{C}$(sØP   Select monospacing

Notes: All the DeskJet's internal fonts are monospaced, since all are based on the typewriter-like Courier typeface. Proportionally spaced fonts are only available on font cartridges and as soft fonts.

In monospaced spaced fonts, each character is alloted the same width—the same amount of space horizontally along a line of text—regardless of whether the character itself is wide (*m*) or skinny (*i*). Since all the characters are the same width, the number of them that will fit in one inch is always the same. This number is referred to as the font's pitch, and can be controlled by the next escape sequence we'll discuss below.

In proportionally spaced fonts, by contrast, the width alloted to each character is proportional to the character's actual width. Thus, a line of *ms* printed in a proportionally spaced font would be considerably longer than a line containing the same number of *is*.

Even though typefaces are designed as monospaced or proportionally spaced, you must still select monospacing or proportional spacing explicitly when you choose a font.

Selecting font pitch

$^{E}s_{C}$(s#H   Set pitch to # characters per inch (cpi)

Valid values: The pitch value may include up to two decimal place. 5, 10, 16.67, and 20 pitch fonts are available among the internal fonts on the DeskJet Plus. Fonts with other pitches are available in cartridge and soft font form.

Notes: Pitch is the reciprocal of horizontal motion index (HMI)—setting the pitch automatically resets the HMI and vice versa. Changing the pitch changes the position of the margins, but not the margin setting. The pitch setting is not relevant to proportionally spaced fonts.

Example: $^{E}s_{C}$(s12H sets the pitch to 12 cpi

Pitch refers to the number of characters of a monospaced font that are printed per inch along a line of text, and is given in characters per inch or cpi. You can also think of cpi as standing for columns per inch, since there's one character in a text column. By extension, pitch determines the width of each individual character or column.

In addition to helping specify the font you want to print with, the pitch setting also determines the horizontal motion index (HMI), and in turn the distance the print position moves when you set it in columns. Since the DeskJet measures margins in terms of column numbers, and not by absolute measurements, the pitch setting also affects your margins. If you change the pitch from 10 cpi to 12 cpi, a right margin set to 80 columns will change from 8" to 6½".

To select the font with the desired pitch, send the escape sequence $^{E}s_{C}$(s#H, substituting the value of the desired pitch for #. If you choose a pitch value that doesn't exist among the fonts currently available in the DeskJet, the printer will select the font with the next largest pitch. Since the pitch will then be larger than what you wanted, there'll be more characters per inch, and the individual characters will be skinnier.

Because the width of each character varies in proportionally spaced fonts, the number of characters per inch depends on which characters you're talking about. For this reason, the pitch setting has no effect on proportionally spaced fonts.

Selecting font size (character height)

$^{E}s_{C}$(s#V   Set font size to # points

Valid values: For the internal fonts, 6 and 12 points are the only valid values. Other sizes are available in cartridge and soft fonts, with the maximum size generally considered to be 18 points for the original DeskJet and 30 points for the DeskJet Plus. The font value may include up to two decimal places.

Example: Es$_C$(s14.25V sets the font size to 14.25 points

Notes: The DeskJet *Owner's Manual* is incorrect when it defines character height as the height of an uppercase character.

As you can guess, the *font size* or character height command lets you select the height of your font based on the distance from the bottom of the descenders to the top of the ascenders (see Chapter 5 for further details on the measurement of font size). Font size is given in points, which are each equal to about 1/72".

You can only select a given font size if it's available among the fonts that are currently resident in your DeskJet. There's one exception to this rule that works only with the DeskJet, not other PCL printers: you can request a font that's half the size of any installed font, and the DeskJet will automatically scale the existing font down to match your request.

Only 12 point (and thus half-sized 6 point) fonts are built in as internal fonts, so to use other font sizes you'll have to install cartridge or soft fonts first. If no font is available that matches the size you've requested, the DeskJet will substitute the font with the next closest size.

Printing in italics (selecting type style)

^{E}s$_C$(s1S	Begin italics printing
^{E}s$_C$(sØS	Stop italics printing, return to normal upright printing
Notes:	To print in italics in landscape orientation on either DeskJet model, you need the 22706L landscape fonts cartridge.

Italics are usually used to emphasize a word or phrase within ordinary upright text. HP uses the term *type style* to refer to the font attributes of italic versus upright text. To print a passage in italics, send the escape sequence to begin italics printing, then the text you want italicized, then the escape sequence to stop italics and return to the normal upright type style.

If it's going to honor your request to print in italics, the DeskJet must have a specific italics font to work with. In other words, the printer can't take an upright font and italicize it for you. The DeskJet Plus comes with italics versions of its Courier fonts built in internally. However, the internal italics fonts are not available in landscape orientation, and you'll need the 22706L landscape cartridge if you want to print italics in landscape.

Of course, italics fonts are available in cartridge and soft font products. If the typeface on which a font package is based is intended for use in the body of a document, the font package will probably include both upright and italics fonts from the same typeface family. On the other hand, if the typeface is a display face meant for headlines and other attention-getting short stretches of text, the package usually won't include the italics version.

Printing boldface text (selecting stroke weight)

E_s_c(s3B   Begin boldface printing

E_s_c(sØB   Stop boldface printing, return to normal stroke weight

Text printed in boldface looks darker than ordinary text, another way to add emphasis. Actually, the difference is that the strokes of the bold characters are very slightly wider than those of ordinary characters, though the shapes of the characters remain almost the same. The general term *stroke weight* refers to how heavy the characters in a font look.

In the DeskJet, any font can be made bold, with an occasional exception (see the discussion on this point in Chapter 6). Thus, this command doesn't really belong in the list of font selection priorities. However, in other PCL printers, a separate bold font must be installed to select it with this command.

To print a bold passage, send the escape sequence to begin bold printing, then the text you want printed in bold, then the escape sequence to stop bold printing and return to normal stroke weight.

Choosing a typeface

E_s_c(s#T   Select typeface number #

Valid values: The typeface identification number is assigned by the font supplier. HP typefaces are numbered as follows: Courier—3; Helv—4; TmsRmn—5; Letter Gothic—6; Prestige—8; Presentations—11; Univers Condensed—87

Typeface is the very last font characteristic on the list of print feature priorities. In other words, the DeskJet will make sure that your selections for orientation, character set, pitch, font size, style (italics or upright), and weight (bold or normal) have been met before it even looks to see whether the typeface you request is available. That way, even if the characters aren't shaped the way you hoped, your overall page format will be printed as close as possible to the way you planned it.

To request a typeface change, send the escape sequence $^{E}s_C$(s#T, substituting the typeface's identification number for the # in the sequence. ID numbers for the typefaces sold by HP are shown in the table above. If you're using a font package supplied by another manufacturer, you'll need to get the typeface ID numbers from the vendor.

Underlining text

$^{E}s_C$&dØD	Select single fixed underline (default)
$^{E}s_C$&d1D	Select single fixed underline
$^{E}s_C$&d2D	Select double fixed underline
$^{E}s_C$&d3D	Select single floating underline
$^{E}s_C$&d4D	Select double floating underline
$^{E}s_C$&d@	Turn underlining off
Notes:	Underlining does not work in landscape mode.

All of the underlining commands print continuous underlines below the affected text, the underline extending across the spaces between words. Two underline positioning techniques are available, and either can be used with single or double underlining, bringing the total of available underlining options to four. With the "fixed" underline position option, the vertical position of all underlines on a given line of text stays constant at five dot positions below the baseline, even if you change fonts on the line. With the "floating" option, the underline position is set to where it looks best with the current font.

In general, you should choose floating underlining if you're only using one font on a line, fixed if you're mixing fonts within the same line. Note that you cannot adjust the distance from the text baseline to the underline(s).

Selecting the underlining mode

$^{E}s_C$&kØE   Cancel underlining automatically at the end of each line

$^{E}s_C$&k1E   Continue underlining across lines until explicitly turned off

Default: continuous underlining

Notes: Not a PCL Level III feature.

Underlining can work in one of two ways, depending on which of these commands is in effect. In the default underlining mode, once you start underlining it continues until you turn it off. In the line-by-line mode, underlining is automatically cancelled at the end of every line. That helps prevent runaway underlines, but it means you have to resend an underlining command at the beginning of every line in a block of underlined text. For some reason, HP refers to these options as the "Print Enhancement Control."

Printing subscripts and superscripts

$^{E}s_C$(s1U   Begin superscript printing
  or $^{E}s_C$(s+1U

$^{E}s_C$(s-1U   Begin subcript printing

$^{E}s_C$(s0U   Discontinue super- or subscripting, resume normal print position

Example: To print $x_n + y^2 = z$
         x$^{E}s_C$(s-1Un $^{E}s_C$(sØU + y$^{E}s_C$(s+1U2 $^{E}s_C$(sØU = z

Notes: You can use either $^{E}s_C$(s1U or $^{E}s_C$(s+1U to initiate superscript print positioning. Not a PCL Level III feature.

Superscripting simply shifts the text baseline half a line or so above the normal position, while subscripting shifts it half a line below. Since this shift of position doesn't require a change in the appearance or spacing of the super- or subscripted characters, these two commands can be used with any font—you don't need a separate font file as you would to change from upright to italics, for example.

For this reason, you can ignore super- and subscripting in the heirarchy of print feature priorities, even though HP has them the third highest on the priority list in your *Owner's Manual* (see the discussion of print feature priorities at the beginning of this section).

To use the super- or subscript escape sequence, send the one you've chosen to the DeskJet immediately before the characters whose placement you want to change. Immediately after the characters, send the escape sequence that stops super- and subscripting and returns the text baseline to its normal position.

If you want smaller characters than normal for your super- and subscripts, send the escape sequence for the size change after the one for super- or subscripting. Then, when the super- or subscripted characters have been sent, send the command to shut off super- or subscripting, then the command to return to the original point size.

Changing print quality

E_{s_C}(s1Q	Select draft quality text printing
E_{s_C}(s2Q	Select letter quality text printing
Default:	Letter quality
Notes:	Not a PCL Level III feature

The *print quality* command lets you choose the best compromise between appearance and speed for the work you're doing. In letter quality mode, the DeskJet prints approximately 120 razor-sharp characters per second; in draft mode it spits out 240 slightly rougher characters per second, and uses less ink in the process. (Those numbers are according to HP, and they'll serve for comparison, though your real-world results will usually be considerably slower in either mode.)

Generally, it's a good idea to set the printer to a lower quality mode while you're printing draft copies. Once the printout looks perfect, you can then select letter quality for your final copies. Since you want to be able to switch from one quality mode to another quickly, as circumstances dictate, don't set the print quality permanently from a program. Instead, give yourself (and the users of your program) control at print time. Of course, you can always select the print quality setting from the keypad MODE button. If you want the convenience of software selection, though, you can build a print quality option into your program.

Selecting unidirectional or bidirectional printing

^{E}s$_c$&kØW	Select left-to-right unidirectional printing
^{E}s$_c$&k1W	Select bidirectional printing
^{E}s$_c$&k2W	Select right-to-left unidirectional printing
Default:	Bidirectional printing
Notes:	Not a PCL Level III feature.

Bidirectional printing is faster than unidirectional, but print quality is slightly lower because alignment of the printhead is not as accurate. In text printing, this problem is most likely to be noticeable when you print characters larger than 50 dots (12 points) high—the top and bottom portions of the characters may be slightly offset from one another.

Using text scale mode

^{E}s$_c$&k6W	Enable text scale mode
^{E}s$_c$&k5W	Disable text scale mode
Default:	As shipped from the factory, the DeskJet has text scale mode disabled. Moving DIP switch B1 to the UP position changes the default to text scale mode enabled.
Notes:	Text scale mode is ignored with perforation skip enabled, which is the default; and when printing in the landscape orientation. Not a PCL Level III feature.

Text scale mode squeezes more lines of text onto a page, allowing you to use the same page length settings typically used for other printers, despite the DeskJet's inability to print on the bottom ½" of the paper.

The fact that the DeskJet can't print on this strip has the effect of decreasing the usable page length by ½". If you're using letter size paper, it's just as if the paper was 10½" instead of 11" long. As a result, the page length settings commonly used for printers that actually do print on the entire piece of paper won't work on the DeskJet, at least not in its ordinary printing mode.

Page length settings are defined as the number of lines that can be printed on a page. Of course, the actual number of lines that will fit depends on how far apart the lines are, as well as how long the paper is.

At any rate, there are two ways to get around the mismatch between the physical length of the paper and its effective length for DeskJet printing. The simplest alternative is to reset the page length to the value that corresponds to the effective page length you're working with. For example, if you're printing 6 lines per inch on letter paper, the correct page length setting would be 63 lines.

On the other hand, there may be situations where you want to jury-rig things so you can use a standard page length value. That's where the text scale command comes in. When you give this command, the DeskJet reduces the space between lines just enough to fit the standard number of lines on a page.

Printing control codes as characters

In some character sets, printable characters have been assigned to the lowest-numbered ASCII code values, which were previously reserved for non-printing control codes. Character sets with these extra printable characters typically duplicate the screen character sets used by IBM PCs and compatibles.

Normally, the DeskJet interprets the first 32 or 33 ASCII codes as control codes (the exact number depends on whether you view code 32 which leaves a space between characters as a control code or a "space character"). To print these codes as characters instead, you must first enable one of two special modes, the display functions mode or the transparent print mode.

Using display functions mode

^{E}s$_C$Y	Enable display functions mode
^{E}s$_C$Z	Disable display functions mode
Default:	Display functions mode disabled

In display functions mode, the DeskJet prints all control codes and escape sequences as characters, and ignores all but two of them as printer commands. The two software commands to which it continues respond are the carriage return control code (13 decimal) and the "disable display functions mode" escape sequence, ^{E}s$_C$Z. Upon receiving either of these two commands, the DeskJet prints the characters represented by the code or codes in the command, but then executes the command itself. In the case of a carriage return, the printer prints the associated character, and then executes both a carriage return and a line feed, regardless of the line terminator setting in effect. When it receives the "disable display functions mode" command, the DeskJet prints the command as characters, then switches back to its ordinary printing mode.

Using transparent print mode

^{E}s$_C$**&p#X<data>** Print # bytes of data in transparent print mode

Valid values: # may be any integer value between 0 and 32,767 inclusive. The notation "<data>" refers to the actual data bytes you wish to print. The bracket characters "<" and ">" should not be included in the data you actually send.

In transparent print mode, the DeskJet prints all control codes as characters, and completely ignores them as control codes. There are two differences between transparent print mode and display functions mode. First, transparent print mode requires you to specify exactly how many bytes of data to print "transparently," while display functions mode continues in effect until you turn it off. Second, no control codes whatsoever are executed in transparent print mode, while two are executed in display functions mode.

Resetting the printer

^{E}s$_C$**E**   Reset the printer

The *soft reset* command restores all the DeskJet's settings to their status as determined by the most recent choices made on the keypad. If no keypad buttons have been pressed, the settings are restored to their defaults, just as they were when the printer was first powered up. The soft reset command also ejects any paper in the printer, moving the print position to the top left margin of the next sheet. It does not erase the data in the print buffer, nor does it erase "permanent" soft fonts (see Chapter 7 for more information on permanent versus temporary soft fonts).

Performing a self test

^{E}s$_C$**z**   Perform self test

Notes: Unlike most escape sequences, the self test command terminates in a lowercase letter.

During the self test procedure, the DeskJet goes through a built-in diagnostics routine, checking that its microprocessor and ROM firmware are in good order. As part of the self test, it also prints two pages of sample text, one in portrait mode, the other in landscape, as shown in your *Owner's Manual.* At the conclusion of the test, the DeskJet executes a soft reset command as described above. If a problem is discovered during the test, the printer goes off line and flashes all the lights on the keypad. If this occurs, or if the test pages don't look anything like the ones shown in your manual, your printer may need service. Before you call the repairshop, consult the troubleshooting section in Chapter 23 for advice.

Moving the print position and paper feeding

PCL provides many commands with which you can set the location of the *print position,* the point on the page where the next printed characters or graphics will be placed. You're free to reset the print position at any time, as long as you follow this one set-in-stone rule: you can't move the print position upward on the page. Even though PCL permits you to send commands that would move the print position up, the DeskJet cannot move the paper backwards, and it will ignore these commands.

By the way, the DeskJet automatically advances the print position automatically advances every time it prints a character or graphic dot to the next available space to the right if there's room on the same line, or to the left margin on the following line if there isn't.

Basic print position commands

Several PCL commands move the print position to a predetermined loc without giving you any further say in the matter. Most of these basic commands are control codes held over from the ASCII system: the carriage return command moves the print position to the left margin, the tab command moves the print position to the next tab stop, and so on.

While most of these basic print position commands can be vital to the programmer in certain circumstances, they don't let you move the print position freely, wherever you want it on the page— that's what the advanced print position commands are for. Note, though, that two of the basic commands, the tab and backspace control codes, have little value for programmers. Several PCL commands for ejecting and loading paper are included as print position commands, since they do establish the print position at the top of the next page.

Starting a new line: the line terminator characters

In standard ASCII files, the end of a line of text is indicated by a pair of special characters, the carriage return and line feed characters. Ordinarily, this pair of control codes combine to cause the DeskJet to start a new line at the left margin. As a programmer, you can use either of these codes separately if you wish. A third control code, the form feed character, ejects the current page and loads the next. It's also considered a line terminator, since the DeskJet stops printing the current line when it receives the form feed code.

A special PCL escape sequence lets you change how the DeskJet responds to the three line terminator characters, as described later in this chapter.

Moving down a line: the line feed control code

CTRL-J   Line feed
(1Ød or ØAh)

Normally, the DeskJet responds to the line feed control code by executing a line feed: it moves the print position to the next line on the page, but stays in the same column (horizontal position). Just how far the print position advances is determined by the current line spacing, which you can select with the line spacing escape sequence as described on below.

If the line terminator function is changed to a value of 2 or 3, sending the line feed character produces the same results that you'd normally get by sending both a carriage return and a line feed together: the print position moves down a line and over to the left margin. See the section "Changing the line terminator function" for information on the escape sequence used to change the line terminator.

Moving down a half line: the half line feed command

^{E}s$_C$=   Half line feed

PCL also provides an escape sequence to advance the vertical print position half of the space of a line, as defined by the current line spacing setting. Otherwise, the ^{E}s$_C$= sequence works exactly like the regular line feed control code, moving the print position down the page without changing its horizontal location. Changing the setting of the line terminator function has no effect on the half line feed command.

Moving to the left margin: the carriage return control code

CTRL-M   Carriage Return
(13d or Øh)

Normally, the carriage return control code causes the DeskJet to execute a carriage return—it moves the print position horizontally to the left margin, without changing the vertical position (the print position stays on the same line).

If you change the line terminator function to a value of 3, however, a carriage return causes the same effect that you'd ordinarily get with the combination of both a line feed and carriage return: the print position advances one line, and moves over to the left margin.

Selecting a paper path

CTRL-L   Form Feed
(12d or ØCh)

^{E}s$_C$&lØH   Eject current page

^{E}s$_C$&l1H   Feed from tray

^{E}s$_C$&l2H   Feed envelope

In many situations, the DeskJet handles paper loading and ejecting automatically. If a a page is not already in the paper path when you send print data to the DeskJet, the printer loads a new sheet of paper or a new envelope, depending on which paper path is currently active. If the document being printed is longer than one page, the DeskJet automatically ejects each finished page as soon it receives print data for the next page, and then loads another one.

Still, PCL provides several explicit commands for ejecting the current page and loading the next one, and there are several reasons you might want to use them. For one thing, you may want to move on to a new page before the current page has been printed all the way down to the bottom margin—perhaps you want to start a new section or chapter on the next page, for example. Another function performed by two of these commands is to select a paper path, so that paper feeds either from the paper tray or the envelope path.

Finally, it is essential that one of the page-ejecting commands gets sent at the end of a print job. Until the DeskJet receives the command, the printer doesn't eject the last page of the file, even after you've finished sending data to the printer.

Here are the details on each of the page ejecting/loading commands:

When the DeskJet executes a *form feed*, it ejects the page that's currently being printed, if any, loads the next sheet of paper, and moves the print position to the top printing line of the new page. You can get the DeskJet to execute a form feed by pressing the FF button on the keypad, or you can send the form feed control code instead.

As alternatives to the form feed character, the DeskJet's version of PCL provides three escape sequences that also eject the current page:

E_{s_c}&lØH ejects the page but does not load a new one.

E_{s_c}&l1H ejects the page, if any, and immediately loads a new sheet of paper from the paper tray. This command also establishes the paper tray as the active paper path, so that when the DeskJet loads subsequent pages automatically during a multi-page print job, it loads them from the papery tray.

^Es_c&l2H ejects the current page and loads an envelope from the envelope path (you have to stuff the envelope into the path first, as detailed in chapter 19). This command also sets the envelope path as the active paper path, so that from then on the DeskJet loads envelopes when it loads "pages" automatically during multiple-page print jobs.

The difference between the form feed command and the second of these escape sequences is as follows: the DeskJet does not load the next sheet of paper immediately after receiving a form feed command, but rather waits until it begins to receive print data for the new page. This way, the paper won't get permanently curled up by sitting inside the paper path waiting to print. The ^Es_c&l1H sequence, by contrast, does load the next page immediately.

Whether you need to send the eject page command yourself depends on a couple of factors. If you're programming the DeskJet by way of commands embedded in your document, but you're having your application program actually print the file, you probably won't need to embed a form feed character in the file, since many application software programs send will send it for you. If you're printing text files from DOS or writing your own DeskJet program, you must send an eject page command yourself, or plan on pressing the FF button a lot.

Normally, the form feed character causes the DeskJet to simply spit out the current page, without changing the horizontal print position. However, if the line terminator function is set to 2 or 3, a form feed ejects the page and moves the horizontal position over to the left margin, as if you'd sent a carriage return as well. See the following section for information on the escape sequence used to change the line terminator.

Changing the line terminator function

$^E s_c$&k#G   Set line terminator function to #

Valid values: 0—CR=CR; LF=LF; FF=FF
1—CR=CR-LF; LF=LF; FF=FF
2—CR=CR; LF=CR-LF; FF=CR-FF
3—CR=CR-LF; LF=CR-LF; FF=CR-FF

By default, the DeskJet is set to respond to the three line terminator characters, line feed, carriage return, and form feed, as follows: line feed advances the print position by one line without changing the print column, carriage return moves the print position to the left margin but doesn't change the current line, and form feed ejects the current page and loads a new sheet. If necessary, however, you can change how DeskJet responds to the line terminator control codes via an escape sequence.

The reason for changing the line terminator function is to print files that don't use the line terminator characters according to DOS conventions. In DOS's ASCII text files, each line ends in a carriage return/line feed pair. In other types of files, however, the end of a line may be marked only by a line feed character, or rarely, only by a carriage return. If you leave the DeskJet's line terminator function on its default setting, and try to print a file whose lines end with line feeds but no carriage returns, you'd get something like this on your printout:

These lines end
        in line feed characters
                but not carriage returns.

Likewise, printing a file whose lines end only in carriage returns would produce something like this:

bieakspstlhetatehittleedtionriael. feiedscthatadtents exeriprilintee taed otharacTeis

The escape sequence for changing the line terminator function is $^E s_c$&k#G. You can substitute one of four different values for the #:

0 (default): causes the DeskJet to execute all three line terminator characters as they are normally intended: the line feed character results in a line feed

only, a carriage return character produces a carriage return only, and a form feed character executes a form feed, pushing out the current page.

1: In this setting, a carriage return causes the DeskJet to execute both a carriage return and a form feed, moving the print position to the left margin of the next line. Line feed and form feed characters retain their normal functions.

2: Carriage return characters retain their normal function, but line feed characters casue the DeskJet to execute both a carriage return and a line feed, and form feed characters result in both a form feed and a carriage return.

3: Carriage return and line feed characters each cause the DeskJet to execute both a carriage return and a line feed. At this setting, sending both a carriage return and a line feed moves the print position to the left margin *two* lines down. This setting also makes the DeskJet execute both a carriage return and a form feed when you send a form feed character.

Selecting or disabling end-of-line wraparound

$^{E}s_{c}$&sØC	Enable end-of-line wraparound
$^{E}s_{c}$&s1C	Disable end-of-line wraparound
Default:	end-of-line wraparound disabled
Notes:	Not a PCL Level III feature.

The end-of-line wraparound setting determines how the DeskJet will respond if it is sent text to print beyond the permissible right border, which is the right margin or right paper edge, depending on the situation. This can happen either because the current line of text is too long to print within the right margin, or because you've sent a command to move the print position past the right margin, but the print position is now beyond the right edge of the paper.

Either way, if end-of-line wraparound is disabled, the text that falls beyond the right boundary will simply be ignored, and the DeskJet will go on to print the next line. If end-of-line wraparound is enabled, the extra text will be placed on the next line starting at the left margin. As a result, you'll have more lines in your printout than you did in your file, but all the text will be printed.

Moving left one column

CTRL-H   Backspace
(Ø8d or Ø8h)

The backspace command is an essentially useless control code that moves the print position one column to the left. Interestingly, column size does not depend on the current font, but is determined by the pitch setting or the equivalent horizontal motion index, settings you can alter via escape sequence. Because column size is independent of the current font selection, sending the backspace command may not place the print position directly on top of the last character you printed. This is especially true if you're using a proportionally spaced font, since the horizontal space alloted to each letter, numeral, or punctuation mark varies from character to character. The backspace command has no effect when the cursor is at the left margin.

Moving right to the next tab stop

CTRL-I   Tab
(Ø9d or Ø9h)

The tab command is a control code that works much like the tab key in your word processor, advancing the print position to the next tab stop. Unfortunately, the DeskJet's tab stops are fixed at every eighth character position, starting at the left margin, and you can't change them. For this reason, the tab command is too inflexible for most purposes, and you'll probably want to use other position control commands in your programs. The main benefit of the DeskJet's tab command is that it lets you print ASCII files that already contain tab codes—in the printout, columns of text will be aligned properly, even if their exact position on the page isn't right.

Advanced print position commands

PCL's advanced commands for moving the print position let you specify any printable location on the page, down to the level of the individual dot, as the spot where printing should begin. In PCL, you can specify a new print position with the advanced commands using three different units: rows and columns, decipoints, and dots. Whichever unit system you're working with, you set horizontal and vertical print positions via separate commands—changing one doesn't affect the other. For example, let's say the current print position is at row 4, column 16. If you send a command to change the vertical print position to the 13th row, you'll still be in column 16.

In all three unit systems, and both vertically and horizontally, the first print position is 0. In the vertical direction, the 0 position corresponds to the top margin, while in the horizontal position it corresponds to the left edge of the maximum area on which the DeskJet can print, and not the left margin.

The highest number for print position depends on the unit system you're using. Vertically, it corresponds to the bottom of the physical sheet of paper. Horizontally, it corresponds to the right edge of the printable area, not to the right edge of the paper.

Caution: Remember that the DeskJet cannot print within a strip around all four edges of the paper. You cannot move the print position to this unprintable area horizontally, but you can do so in the vertical direction. If you send print data to the DeskJet with the vertical position outside the printable area, the DeskJet simply ignores the data.

Moving up on the page

PCL lets you move the print position with complete freedom on any one page—if you like, you can give a command to print a page number at the bottom right of the page first, then one that prints a letterhead at the top left. Unfortunately, the DeskJet isn't equally free to follow these commands. While it can move its printhead from side to side, it can only move the paper forward in the paper path, and thus you can't freely move the print position to higher locations on the page.

In general, sending the DeskJet a command to move the print position higher on the page causes problems. The new text or graphics may print on top of previously printed lines, or may print on the next page. However, you *can* back up successfully over a very short distance, one or two lines up on the page. This works because the DeskJet reads through the data in its buffer before printing, looking for such commands. If it finds them, it then prints the lines in the order indicated by the commands rather than the order in which it received the data. However, this built-in function scans only a few lines worth of data before deciding to print. Otherwise, the DeskJet would have to wait until it received all the data for an entire page before beginning to print, as it must in landscape mode.

Default print position

Whenever the DeskJet loads a new page, whether in response to a paper load command or automatically during a print job, the print position is set to the top margin vertically (the 0th position) and the left margin horizontally (which may not be the 0th position).

For each direction (horizontal and vertical) and for each set of units, you're given three escape seqeunces for specifying the new print position: a command to move to an absolute position on the page, and commands to move a specified number of units in either direction relative to the current position.

Positioning by rows and columns

Vertical movement:

^{E}s$_C$&a#R	Move to specified row
^{E}s$_C$&a+#R	Move # rows down from current position
^{E}s$_C$&a-#R	Move # rows up from current position

Horizontal movement:

^{E}s$_C$&a#C	Move to specified column
^{E}s$_C$&a+#C	Move # columns to the right from current position
^{E}s$_C$&a-#C	Move # columns to the left from current position

Setting the print position via rows and columns is easier than doing it with the other units, since rows and columns are larger and there are fewer of them to keep track of. On the other hand, you can't be nearly as precise, for the same reasons. Of course, moving by rows and columns makes a lot of sense when you're working with text, since rows are equivalent to lines, and columns correspond to the size of a character when you're using a monospaced font such as Courier (in proportionally spaced fonts, a column is equivalent to the width of a space character, the kind you enter by pressing the spacebar).

In the vertical direction, the first available row is numbered 0, and is located at the first line of text below the top margin of the page. This is slightly different in concept than the way the way the decipoint and dot coordinate systems work. With those units, the 0th vertical position is actually flush with the top margin itself.

By contrast, setting the print position to the 0th row locates the baseline of the first text line at a distance below the top margin equal to a line, as determined by the line spacing command or the vertical motion index. Characters extend upward from the baseline toward the top margin, but depending on the font size you're using and which characters you print, they may not actually reach the margin.

The distance from one row to the next is also equal to the height of a line, again as set by the line spacing or vertical motion index commands. The greatest row position is the one at the bottom of the physical page, or as close to it as your line spacing setting will take you. The maximum number of rows on a page depend both on your line spacing setting and the size of your paper.

Horizontally, the first column is number 0, and is located at the left boundary of the area on which the DeskJet can print, which is ¼" from the paper edge (the first or 0th column is not at the left margin). The size of a column, and thus both the distance between columns and the total number of columns on a page, is determined by the print pitch or the horizontal motion index currently in effect, if you're using a monospaced font.

With text, often your main concern is just to keep columns properly aligned, rather than to print at a specific measured distance along a line. If that's your situation, all you need to to keep track of in your program is the column number where you want to be.

On the other hand, it's easy to keep track of where you are in terms of inches if you need to for any reason. Remember that pitch is expressed as the number of characters (or columns) per inch. To move to a position that's a particular distance from the left paper edge, subtract ¼" from the desired distance, and then multiply that number by the pitch (that ¼" is for the unprintable strip at the paper edge). You can also figure out the size of a column by dividing 1" by the pitch value—if the pitch is 10, for example, each column is ⅒" wide.

Proportionally spaced fonts have no pitch setting, since the width of each character is different. In these fonts, a column is equal in size to a space character. But since there's no way to tell how wide the space character is in any given font, you'll have to make do with relative positioning if you want to use the column commands. If you need to move the print position a measured horizontal distance, you'll have to use the decipoint or dot commands instead.

Positioning by dot

Vertical movement:

$^{E}s_C$&a#Y	Move to specified vertical dot position
$^{E}s_C$&a+#Y	Move # dots down from current position
$^{E}s_C$&a-#Y	Move # dots up from current position
Notes:	When printing text, the baseline moves to the dot position specified by the command. In graphics mode, the first raster row prints at the specified position only if you print using the escape sequence $^{E}s_C$*r1A.

Horizontal movement:

$^{E}s_C$&a#X	move to specified horizontal dot position
$^{E}s_C$&a+#X	move # dots to the right from current position
$^{E}s_C$&a-#X	move # dots to the left from current position
Example:	Es_C&a35ØY moves the print position to the 350th dot position.

Although the DeskJet can print 300 dots per linear inch, it can only print those dots at fixed locations along the page. Therefore, the most precise way to control the DeskJet's print position is to specify the actual dot location you want. There's a drawback to measuring distances on your page in dot positions, however: the units don't match up too well with any common system of measurement. Sure, there are exactly 300 dots in an inch, and 75 in a quarter inch, but ⅛" inch contains 37.5 dots. Of course, one-half dot's worth of imprecision shouldn't hurt the appearance of your document. It's just that it's a little harder to make the necessary calculations than with decipoints, which fit neatly with the typographer's point-based measuring system.

The dot coordinate system begins with position 0, 0. This corresponds to the top margin vertically and the left edge of the DeskJet's printable area horizontally. When printing text, the text baseline moves to the dot position specified by the command. In graphics mode, the first row of dots prints at the dot position selected by this command.

On a standard 8½x11" piece of paper with a top margin set to 0, the greatest possible dot position in the vertical direction is 3100, corresponding to the bottom edge of the DeskJet's printable area. Horizontally, the maximum dot position is 2400, corresponding to the furthest right position that the DeskJet can print.

Positioning by decipoint

Vertical movement:

E_{s_C}&a#V	Move to specified vertical decipoint
E_{s_C}&a+#V	Move # decipoints down from current position
E_{s_C}&a-#V	Move # decipoints up down from current position

Horizontal movement:

E_{s_C}&a#H	Move to specified horizontal decipoint
E_{s_C}&a+#H	Move # decipoints right from current position
E_{s_C}&a-#H	Move # decipoints left from current position

A decipoint is ¹⁄₁₀th of a typographer's point, and is therefore equal to ¹⁄₇₂₀". This is the most precise positioning system available for the DeskJet. Since the printer can only print at 600 different dot positions per horizontal inch, and 300 in a vertical inch, it's obvious that you can't actually print at every decipoint location. Nevertheless, this system works well for typographic purposes, because typographers measure so many distances in points and fractions of points. Decipoint positions align exactly with the dot positions at which the DeskJet can print every ¹⁄₁₀" vertically and ¹⁄₂₀" vertically—when you specify a decipoint position that does not align exactly with a dot position, the DeskJet rounds off your request to the closest dot.

The 0,0 position in the decipoint coordinate system corresponds to the top margin in the vertical direction and the first dot the DeskJet can print, ¼" from the left edge of the paper, in the horizontal direction. On a standard 8½x11" piece of paper, the highest possible decipoint locations are 7440 vertically, corresponding to the bottom edge of the DeskJet's printable area, and 5760 horizontally, corresponding to the right margin of the printable area.

You can readily convert inches into decipoint measurements and vice versa. To go from inches to decipoints, just multiply the number of inches by 720; two inches equal 1440 decipoints, 5½" is 3960 decipoints, and so on. To convert a measurement in decipoints into inches, divide by 720.

Decipoint-to-inches translations work a little more smoothly than do dots-to-inches conversions. Because 720 can be divided evenly by more factors, the decipoint system lets you work with smaller distances—even multiples of ⅟16" or ⅟20"—without mucking around with fractional decipoints. For this reason, it may make sense to use decipoint print position commands, even if you're not already familiar with the typographic point system. Remember, though, that because the DeskJet doesn't print 720 dots per inch, the actual print position you get will usually be a tiny bit off from the one you specify.

Specifying the print area

A number of PCL commands allow you to determine the area of the page where text will actually be printed. You can set the right, left, and top margins directly. Other commands determine how tall the print area is and thus the bottom margin.

Setting right and left margins

E_{S_C}&a#L	Set left margin to column #
E_{S_C}&a#M	Set right margin to column #
E_{S_C}9	Clear both left and right margins, reset both to their defaults. Does not affect top or bottom margin.
Units:	Columns. The size of a column is based on the current pitch setting.
Default:	Left margin 0, right margin 79 (based on pitch 10)
Valid values:	0 is the minimum value possible. The maximum allowable column number is determined by the pitch setting and is located at the rightmost boundary of the printable area.

Margin settings work just as they do on a typewriter or in your word processor: as soon as it finishes printing one character or graphics dot, the DeskJet automatically advances the print position to the right until the right margin is reached, whereupon it stops printing on that line. When you send the command to start a new line (ordinarily a carriage return/line feed pair) the DeskJet begins printing the new line at the left margin.

The left and right margins are defined in terms of column numbers, so it helps to know how the DeskJet counts its columns. The 0th (first) column is located flush with the leftmost position that the DeskJet can print. On a standard 8½x11" sheet of paper, the leftmost printable position is located ¼" from the paper edge (see Chapter 2 for more on the printable area).

When a monospaced font is selected, the pitch setting, expressed in characters or columns per inch, determines the width of a column—if the pitch is 12, for example, there are 12 columns per inch, and each column is ¹⁄₁₂" wide. Since column width varies with the pitch setting, the same margin settings will give you different margins if you change pitch. For example, a left margin setting of 10 places the left margin 1¼" from the left edge of the paper if the pitch is 10 cps (the extra ¼" represents the strip at the paper edge that the DeskJet can't print). If you change the pitch to 12, that same left margin setting of 10 puts the left margin a little more than 1¹⁄₁₆" from the paper edge.

Unless you set them otherwise, the DeskJet's margins are set to column 0 on the left, and column 79 on the right by default. Because the DeskJet counts columns starting with 0, that gives you a total of 80 columns in which you can print characters. The default columns are ¹⁄₁₀" wide, as if the pitch was set to 10. That puts the right margin eight inches from the left, at the boundary of the printable area on the right side, ¼" from the right edge of the paper.

Left and right margin settings do not affect the way the print position commands work—regardless of the margin settings, you can still select any column position within the printable area.

Vertical spacing commands

Together, a set of several interrelated commands determine the vertical spacing characteristics of your printouts, including the spacing between lines, the number of lines per page, and the top and bottom margins. The values of all but one of the vertical spacing settings are calculated partly from the values of other settings. For instance, since page length is measured in lines, the correct page length depends on the line spacing currently in effect. For this reason, you must give these commands commands in the following order:

1. Set line spacing
2. Set paper size or page length

If you want to define top and bottom margins:

3. Set perforation skip to ON
4. Set the top margin
5. Set the text length

Setting line spacing

$^E\text{s}_\text{c}$&l#D	Set lines per inch to #
Units:	Lines per inch.
Default:	6
Valid values:	1 - 48
Notes:	Reciprocal of verical motion index (VMI). Setting line spacing automatically resets VMI and vice versa.

The line spacing setting determines the distance the DeskJet skips down the page when starting a new line of text, from the baseline of the previous line to the new baseline. Line spacing is measured in lines per inch, so you can figure the distance between the baselines of two consecutive lines by dividing 1 by the line spacing setting.

Line spacing, or leading, Changing the line spacing setting can be useful in two common situations: when you switch to a smaller or larger font, and you need to adjust the line spacing to match; and when you want to increase the space between lines for easier reading or to make room for penciled comments on the printout.

The line spacing setting also determines the size of rows when you move the vertical print position using the vertical motion by rows command. An alternative command for setting the size of a line or row is the vertical motion index, discussed next.

Setting the vertical motion index

$^E{}_{S_C}$&l#C	Set vertical motion index to #/48"
Units:	$\frac{1}{48}$"
Notes:	Reciprocal of line spacing. Setting line spacing automatically resets VMI and vice versa.

The vertical motion index (VMI) is an alternative to the line spacing command for setting the size of a line or row (see the previous section). It determines how far the paper moves every time the DeskJet goes to the next line while printing text. It also determines the size of rows when you move the vertical print position using the vertical motion by rows command.

Whereas the line spacing determines the number of lines the DeskJet will print in a vertical inch, the VMI sets the line size directly, in $\frac{1}{48}$" increments. Setting either of these commands automatically resets the other to a corresponding value. For example, if you set the VMI to 6/48", line spacing becomes 8 lines per inch.

You may find the lines-per-inch units of the line spacing command more familiar than the VMI's $\frac{1}{48}$"s, since lines per inch are also used to determine line size in many older printers and typewriters. Each of the two commands can give you line sizes the other command can't. A VMI of 5 (5/48"), for instance, translates into an invalid fractional line spacing of 9-3/5 lines per inch. By the same token, a line spacing setting of 10 lines per inch would be equivalent to a VMI of 4.8, also invalid because it's fractional.

There's a comparable command for setting the horizontal motion index, discussed in the next section.

Setting the horizontal motion index

^{E}s$_c$&l#H	Set horizontal motion index to #/120"
Units:	$\frac{1}{120}$"
Notes:	Reciprocal of pitch. Setting pitch automatically resets HMI and vice versa.

The horizontal motion index (HMI) is an alternative to the pitch command (see the previous section) when you want to specify how much space each text character or column consumes in the horizontal direction. It also determines the size of columns when you move the horizontal print position using the horizontal motion by columns command described earlier. HMI is just the reciprocal of the pitch setting—inches per character (in $\frac{1}{120}$" increments) instead of characters per inch. Setting either of these commands automatically resets the other to a corresponding value. For example, if you set the HMI to 10 (10/120"), the pitch becomes 12 characters per inch.

Pitch is a familiar term to those who've used typewriters, so you may prefer the pitch command to setting the HMI. Each of these commands can give you character sizes the other command can't. An HMI of 16 (16/120" per character), for instance, is perfectly acceptable, but it translates into an invalid fractional pitch of 7.5 characters per inch. Likewise, a pitch of 13 is equivalent to a VMI of 9.2, also invalid because it's fractional.

There's a comparable command for setting the vertical motion index, discussed above.

Selecting paper size

Es_C&l#A	Select paper size corresponding to #
Units:	Arbitrary (each available paper size has a unique code number)
Default:	The default paper size depends on the positions of DIP switches A5 and A6. Entering a 0 in the paper size escape sequence restores the default paper size setting.
Valid values:	See table
Notes:	Not a PCL Level III feature

Paper size	Escape sequence	Dip switch settings	
		A5	**A6**
Letter (8½" x 11")	Es_C&l2A	Down	Down
Legal (8½" x 11")	Es_C&l3A	Up	Down
Envelopes (9½" x 4⅛")	Es_C&l81A	Up	Up
A4 (210 x 297 mm)	Es_C&l26A	Down	Up
(Reselect default)	Es_C&l∅A	—	—

As you can probably figure out yourself, the *paper size* setting tells the DeskJet what size paper you're going to be feeding it. The printer uses the paper size information along with other settings to calculate where the margins are and when the current page ends.

The default *paper size* setting is determined by the positions of the A5 and A6 DIP switches. Of course, the DeskJet comes from the factory set to print on 8½x11" paper as the default. If you usually print on some other size paper, change the switch positions according to the table.

Sending a *paper size* command to the DeskJet automatically clears any margin settings you've made, restoring them to their default values.

Setting page length

$^E s_c$&l#P	Set page length to # lines
Units:	Lines
Notes:	The height of a line is set by the line spacing command. To determine the proper value to enter in this escape sequence, divide the desired height of the printed page in inches by the current line spacing. Sets top margin and text length to default values.
Default:	The maximum number of lines that will fit on the paper size set by functions switches A5 and A6. The default page length does not reflect changes made to the paper size setting with escape sequences.
Valid values:	0 to the maximum number of lines that will fit on the current paper size.

The *page length* command sets the number of lines the DeskJet prints before ejecting the current page and loading the another. In turn, it determines the length or vertical distance of the page, based on the current line spacing setting.

✄ *Tip: It's easier to set page length automatically with the page size command discussed previously.*

Why do you need a *page length* command when you already have a command to select page size? The answer is simple—usually, you don't. Whenever you set the page size, the page length gets automatically set for you, based on the number of lines that would fit on the size of paper you've selected.

There are two situations where it might make sense to set page length explicitly. Obviously, if the paper you're feeding is of non-standard length, none of the page size commands. For another thing, the original LaserJet and the LaserJet Plus don't recognize the *page size* command. If you want to write programs that will work on all PCL printers, you'll have to use the page length command instead.

Setting the page length is a little tricky, since it refers to the number of lines the DeskJet could theoretically print on the paper you're feeding, not the lines the DeskJet can actually print. In other words, you have to ignore the fact that the DeskJet is incapable of printing on the top ⅙" or the bottom ½" of a portrait-oriented page. You also have to remember that the page length includes the areas above the top margin and below the bottom margin that you normally don't print on.

If you're printing on 11" paper and your line spacing is set to 6 lines per inch, you should set the page length to 66 lines. At a line spacing of 8, the page length should be 88 lines.

Setting the top margin

^{E}s$_C$&l#E	Set top margin to # lines
Units:	Lines
Notes:	The height of a line is set by the line spacing command. To determine the proper value to enter in this escape sequence, divide the desired height of the top margin in inches by the current line spacing.
Default:	½", regardless of line spacing setting
Valid values:	Ø to the value of the current page length setting
Example:	^{E}s$_C$&l9E sets top margin to 1½", assuming current line spacing is 6 lines per inch (9 lines/6 lines per inch = 1½").
Notes:	The top margin setting is ignored if perforation skip mode is ON. Sets text length to default value. Not a PCL Level III feature.

Setting the top margin determines where the DeskJet starts printing on each new page. The top margin is measured from the top edge of the paper to the line specified by the top margin setting. This command has no effect if perforation skip mode is ON.

Change the top margin before you change the text length setting, covered in the next section. Whenever you set the top margin, the text length gets reset to its default value.

Setting text length

$^E{s_C}$&l#F	Set text length to # lines
Units:	Lines
Valid values:	1 to page length minus the top margin
Default:	Maximum number of lines that will fit on current page size at current line spacing and with current top margin
Notes:	The text length value determines the bottom margin. The height of a line is set by the line spacing command; to determine the proper value to enter in this escape sequence, divide the desired text length in inches by the current line spacing. Has no effect when perforation skip mode is ON. Use this formula: text length = page length - (top margin+desired bottom margin)
Examples:	$^E{s_C}$&l54F sets text length to 9", when line spacing is 6 lines per inch (9 lines * 6 lines per inch = 54 lines). $^E{s_C}$&l64F sets bottom margin to 1½", when line spacing is 8 lines per inch, page length is 88 lines (11"), and top margin is 12 lines (1½") (88-(12+12)=64)

The *text length* command determines how many lines of text the DeskJet actually prints on a page, beginning with the line at the top margin. In turn, since it specifies where the DeskJet stops printing, the text length determines the bottom margin as well. In other words, you don't explicitly set a bottom margin—you just set the text length, and whatever's left over at the end of the page is the bottom margin. Since the bottom margin depends on the line spacing, page length, and top margin settings, be sure to set text length *after* you set line spacing, page length, and top margin.

Setting the perforation skip mode

E_{S_C}&l1L	Set perforation skip mode to ON
E_{S_C}&lØL	Set perforation skip mode to OFF
Default:	determined by position of DIP switch A8 (up = OFF, down = ON). Factory setting is ON, switch A8 in down position.
Notes:	With perforation skip OFF, the top margin and text length settings are ignored, and the DeskJet prints on the entire printable length of the page. Changing perforation skip setting resets top margin and text length to their defaults.

The perforation skip mode determines whether or not the DeskJet pays any attention to the top margin and text length settings. When perforation skip is ON, it does pay attention, and the printer advances to the next page as soon as it moves past the area specified by the text length. When perforation skip is OFF, the top margin and text length settings are ignored, and the DeskJet prints on as much of the page as it is physically can.

Since neither the DeskJet nor any member of the LaserJet family feeds the kind of paper with perforations between each sheet (the fan-folded, continuous feeding type of computer paper), this command seems out of place, or at least misnamed. But if you can imagine the DeskJet printing on perforated paper, you should be able to get an idea of what this command does. If perforation skip is ON, the imaginary DeskJet moves past the perforation separating the pages to the top margin of the next page before starting to print.

Switching the perforation skip mode to OFF is a quick way of squeezing the maximum amount of text on each page. The OFF setting might come in handy when you're printing draft copies of your text for editing. Otherwise, it's of no use. Remember that the top margin and text length settings are returned to their default values every time you change the perforation skip mode, so you'll have to reset them when you switch perforation skip back ON again.

When the DeskJet comes from the factory, perforation skip is set via the A8 DIP switch to ON, and you should leave that switch alone.

Graphics commands

Programming the DeskJet to print graphics images is straightforward in concept but laborious in practice.

Your most fundamental task, of course, is to form the image you want to see on the page. As you'll recall, the DeskJet only prints bit-mapped graphics, meaning that you must tell it explicitly where to print each dot. Fortunately, the encoding scheme you must use in sending this bit-mapped data is as simple as you could imagine.

Each *pixel* (picture element) on the printed page corresponds to one data bit. If the value of the bit is 1, the pixel is printed; if the bit is 0, the pixel is left unprinted. At the DeskJet's top resolution of 300 dots per inch, a pixel is a single dot, and each data bit represents a dot. At lower resolutions, the DeskJet prints more than one dot per pixel, but each pixel is still controlled by just one bit (see the section "Setting graphics resolution" later in this chapter for details on graphics resolution).

When you send a byte of graphics data, the DeskJet reads the byte's 8 binary bits just as you would—the bit at the left (in computerese, the most significant bit or bit 7) represents the pixel at the beginning print position, the next bit to the right, bit six, represents the next pixel to the right, and so on.

For instance, if you send the byte 10110011 (binary notation), the DeskJet will print the following pattern of pixels:

X O X X O O X X

In actual printing, of course, adjacent pixels touch each other. A given sequence of data bytes codes for one row of pixels at a time in an unbroken series—each successive byte in the data stream picks up where the last one left off.

There are other things to attend to besides just sending the actual data to be printed. At a minimum, you have to switch the DeskJet out of text mode and into graphics mode before you , and you must signal the DeskJet to expect more data at the beginning of each row of pixels. Then, when you're through printing graphics, you must send a command to turn graphics printing off and switch back to text mode.

If you want to get fancier, you can also set margins for your graphic, change resolution, or invoke a graphics compaction mode to cut the amount of data you have to transfer.

Graphics command order

Whenever you send graphics to the DeskJet, your commands must follow a specific sequence.

1. Set graphics resolution (optional)
2. Set graphics width (optional)
3. Set graphics compaction mode (optional)
4. Start graphics
5. Set temporary horizontal offset (optional)
6. Transfer graphics
7. End graphics

As you can see from the list, several of the commands are optional—if you're not changing the current settings for resolution, width, or mode, and if you don't want a temporary horizontal offset, you don't need to send these commands. If you do send one or more of them, though, you must send them in the order shown.

Setting graphics resolution

$^E{s_c}$*t#R	Set resolution to # dots per inch
Units:	Dots per inch
Valid values:	300, 150, 100, 75
Default:	Determined by position of DIP switch B2 (up = 300 dpi, down = 75 dpi).
Notes:	If this command is used it should be sent before the start graphics command (ignored after start graphics command). Not reset to default by end graphics command. Not a PCL Level III feature.
Example:	$^E{s_c}$*t15ØR sets graphics resolution to 150 dots per inch.

Use the *graphics resolution* command to select from the DeskJet's four available graphics resolutions: 75, 100, 150, and 300 dots per inch. Depending on the selected resolution, the DeskJet prints a different number of dots for each bit of graphic data it receives. At a resolution of 300 dpi, it prints one dot for each graphic bit. At 150 dpi, it prints a square two dots wide by two dots high for each bit; at 100 dpi, a 3 x 3 dot square; and at 75 dpi, a 4 x 4 dot square.

Following HP's lead, I use the term *pixel* to refer to the entire square printed for each data bit, no matter what the resolution. Since pixel size varies with resolution, it follows that the size of the printed image will change when you print the same graphics data at different a resolution. A square block that is 1" on all sides at 300 dpi will be 3" x 3" at 100 dpi, or 9 times larger in area. But both squares will contain the same number of pixels.

Lower resolution graphics look just as nice as the high-res kind for objects with perfectly vertical and horizontal edges, such as the bars in bar graphs. With curved objects, though, the lower the resolution, the more jagged the edges. You need less data to cover the same area of the page at lower resolutions than at higher, so low res printing takes less time to transfer the data and less time for the DeskJet to interpret it (printing the dots themselves takes just as long, however).

You don't need to reset the resolution each time you print graphics. If you do wish to change the setting, though, be sure you send the command before you send the *start graphics* command—the *resolution* command will be ignored if you send it after start graphics.

Setting graphics width

^{E}s$_C$*r#S	Set graphics width to # dots
Units:	Dots
Valid values:	0 to maximum dot position for full width of the current paper, excluding unprintable strip at each edge (2400 on legal or letter paper)
Default:	Maximum value for current paper width
Notes:	Reset to default by end graphics command. Must be send before start graphics command.
Example:	^{E}s$_C$*r1200S sets width of area to be printed to 4" (1200dots/300 dots per inch)

The graphics width is the maximum number of graphics dots that the DeskJet will print horizontally across each line, and thus limits the width of your graphics images. This command can speed graphics printing somewhat, because the DeskJet can make more efficient use of its memory when it knows how much data to expect per line.

If you wish to take advantage of this speedup, set the graphics width to the value equal to the maximum width of your graphic before you send the *start graphics* command. Assuming you don't mistakenly set the width smaller than the graphic you're printing, the image won't look any different than if you'd left the width setting alone.

The graphics width setting is automatically reset to its default value, the maximum value permitted by the current page size, as soon as the DeskJet receives the *stop graphics* command.

Starting graphics printing

$^E\!s_c$*r∅A	Start graphics at leftmost position
$^E\!s_c$*r1A	Start graphics at current position
Notes:	This is not the standard PCL Level III function for the $^E\!s_c$*r1A escape sequence. In other PCL printers, this sequence sets left margin for graphics at position 1.

Obviously, the *start graphics printing* command tells the DeskJet that it's time to begin printing graphics. But the command also sets the left margin for the graphic to be printed.

If you send the *start graphics* command with a value of 0, the left margin of your graphic will be the leftmost printable position on the paper, which is ¼" from the paper edge on legal and letter paper. Sending the command with a value of 1 sets the left margin of the graphic to the current horizontal print position.

Of course, if you use the latter option (value = 1), you should first set the horizontal print position you want using any of the commands for moving the horizontal print position. Either way, printing will begin at the current vertical print position, so you should set the desired vertical position before sending the command. After you've sent the *start graphics* command, you can't change the graphics resolution, graphics width, or left margin until you send the *stop graphics* command.

Transferring graphics data

^{E}s$_C$*b#W<data> Transfer # bytes of graphic data.The notation <data> refers to the actual data to be sent immediately following the escape sequence.

Units: Bytes

Valid values: For # (number of bytes): 0-maximum number of data bytes that will fit within the current graphics margins. Calculate the number of bytes needed to fill between the two margins by this formula:

- at 300 dpi resolution: graphics width-graphics left margin/8 (where the graphics width and graphics left margin are specified in dots);
- at 150 dpi, divide the calculated result above by 2;
- at 100 dpi, divide the result by 3;
- at 75 dpi, divide the result by 4

For data bytes: Ø-FF hexadecimal (Ø-255 decimal)

Notes: Graphics printer data must follow this command immediately, in the format described below. Send a separate transfer graphics command for each line (dot row) of the graphic.

Example: ^{E}s$_C$*b8W<255><255> prints a horizontal line 16 dots long at 300 dpi:

Use the *transfer graphics* command immediately before you send the graphics data for the current line. The command specifies how many bytes you want the DeskJet to print. To print the next line, move the print position to the left side of the image, send the transfer graphics command again, followed by the data for that line. When you're finished with the entire graphic, send the stop graphics command, which we'll cover in the next section.

⌒ **Caution:** *You must send the transfer graphics command at the beginning of each graphics line (row of dots) in the image you're printing.*

Each byte of the data itself must be sent as a single number— don't translate the decimal digits of the number into ASCII codes. Thus you'd send the data byte 126 as a single byte, not as separate ASCII code bytes for "1", "2", and

"6". (By contrast, you do break down the values you send *within* escape sequences into their component digits.)

To determine the correct value for each data byte, remember that each pixel in the printed image is specified by one bit of data. In a data byte, the most significant bit (bit number 7) codes for the pixel at the current print position. The next bit (bit 6) codes for the pixel at the next position to the right, and so on.

So, to send the data byte for this pattern of dots

> **X O X O X O X O**

you'd send a byte containing the bits 10101010. If you don't think in this binary notation, you can translate the byte to decimal (170) or hexadecimal (AA), depending on which system you're comfortable with, and which system is best supported by the programming language you're using.

⌒ *Caution:* *This discussion assumes you're in the default graphics mode. See "Setting graphics compaction modes" later in this chapter for tips on how to send compacted graphics data.*

Here's a table you can use to make the necessary translations. Just add the values of the bits you want to print to give you the correct data byte.

	Bit							
	7	6	5	4	3	2	1	0
Decimal	128	64	32	16	8	4	2	1
Hex	80	40	20	10	8	4	2	1

For example, to calculate the value for the dot pattern **X X O O X X O O**, you'd add 128 + 64 + 8 + 4. You'd then send the result, 204, to the DeskJet as a byte of data.

Ending graphics printing

^{E}s$_C$*rB

Notes: Returns DeskJet to text mode. Resets the left graphics margin, graphics width, and graphics mode to defaults.

When you're finished printing an entire graphics image, send the *end graphics printing* command. The DeskJet returns to text mode. In the process, the graphics width, left graphics margin, and graphics mode settings are reset to their default values. The graphics resolution setting is not reset.

Selecting graphics compaction modes

^{E}s$_C$*bØM Select normal graphics mode, mode 0 (no compaction)

^{E}s$_C$*b1M Select graphics compaction mode 1

^{E}s$_C$*b2M Select graphics compaction mode 2

Default: Mode 0

Notes: Reset to mode 0 by end graphics command. Not a PCL Level III feature.

You can use these escape sequences to choose between the DeskJet's three available modes for interpreting graphics data sent with the *transfer graphics* command. Modes 1 and 2 allow you to compact or compress the printer data, so that you can send fewer bytes to the printer and speed up printing to some extent.

Mode 0, called *full graphics mode*, is the default. In this mode, every pixel in the printed image is specified by a corresponding bit of data.

When you have stretches of repeating data bytes to send, you can use *compacted graphics mode 1* to reduce the amount of data you send, sometimes considerably.

In mode 1, the very first data byte you send after the transfer graphics command functions as a repeat value. This first byte specifies how many times the DeskJet prints the bytes that follow. For example, if you transfer graphics data in mode 1 with the escape sequence ^{E}s$_C$*b2W<1Ø><255>

the DeskJet will print the data byte 255 eleven times (once to begin with, then ten repetitions). Since the data byte 255 is the code for printing a pixel at every possible location, the result will be an unbroken line 88 pixels long (11 bytes x 8 bits/byte x 1 bit/pixel). To print the same line in mode 0, you would have had to send 11 bytes of data, not two. Note that the value for the number of data bytes in the *transfer graphics* escape sequence includes the repeat value as well as the actual graphics data.

Compacted graphics mode 2 lets you combine repeated graphics data bytes and "blocks" of individual bytes. This way you don't have to switch back and forth between modes 0 and 1 all the time if you have frequent runs of repeated data bytes in your image.

Just as in mode 1, the first byte of data after the *transfer graphics* escape sequence is a special value that tells the DeskJet about the graphics data to follow. In this case, though, this first byte can be either a repeat count or a block length. After sending the data associated with this special value, you can then send another value to set up the next repeated byte or block of data.

To specify a repeat count in mode 2, you must convert the repeat count you want into a negative number using the bytewise two's complement system (all you do is subtract the repeat count from 256.) To print the following data byte four times, for instance, the first byte should be 253, which is equal to -3, and which the DeskJet will interpret as a repeat value of 3. Again, the DeskJet prints the graphics data byte once and then repeats it the number of times specified by the repeat value.

To print a block of individual bytes in mode 2, you first send a byte value one less than the length of the block. This time you use a positive rather than a negative number—that's how the DeskJet knows you're calling for a block instead of a repeated byte. Just as with the repeat count, the DeskJet automatically expects to print at least one byte in a block. To print a four-byte block, you'd send a block length value of three, which is how many more bytes the block contains.

In mode 2, the largest permitted value for either the repeat count or the block length can be is 127. If you're setting a repeat count of 127, you'd send the value 81 hexadecimal, which is actually -127 in the two's complement system.

Once you've sent a repeat count and the byte to be repeated, you can follow that with another repeat count and another byte to be repeated, or a block length value followed by the block data. Likewise, you can send a repeat count and its data byte after the last byte in a block. Just remember as you mix and match that you must place the number of total bytes, including all the bytes that set repeat counts and block length, in your initial *transfer graphics* escape sequence.

Here's an example. Using mode 2, you could compress the 17 data bytes 128 124 54 54 54 54 255 255 255 255 255 255 255 255 94 12 147 to 11 bytes with this escape sequence:

E_{S_C}*b11W<1><128><124><253><54><249><255><2><94><12><147>

The first data byte, 1, is a positive number and therefore sets up a block. In this case, the value of 1 means the block will be two bytes long. This takes care of the bytes 128 and 124.

The fourth data byte starts another special sequence. It's a negative number (-3) in the two's complement system, so it sets a repeat count of 3, causing the DeskJet to print the next byte, 54, a total of 4 times. Then comes another negative number, this time -7. Again, it's a repeat count, so the DeskJet prints the following byte, 255, a total of 8 times. Finally, the positive number 2 sets up a three byte block with the values 94, 12, and 147.

Setting a temporary horizontal offset for graphics

E_{S_C}*b#X	Set temporary horizontal offset to # dots
Units:	Dots
Valid values:	Multiples of 8
Default:	Ø
Notes:	Added to left graphics margin for the current line only. Reset to 0 after the current line is printed.

If portions of the graphic you're printing have lots of white space on the left side, use the *temporary offset* command. With this command, you can move the beginning printing position for the current line to the location where you want your first black dots. That way, you don't have to send long strings of 0 bytes to the DeskJet just to get past the white space.

The value you send for the temporary offset is added to the left graphics margin previously set by the *start graphics* command. The temporary offset is indeed temporary—it's only in effect for the next printed line, and you have to reset it before you send the next *transfer graphics* command. The value you enter in the escape sequence must be an even multiple of 8.

Setting graphics quality and speeding graphics printing

$^E{}_{S_C}$*rØQ	Select highest graphics quality
$^E{}_{S_C}$*r1Q	Select draft quality
$^E{}_{S_C}$*r2Q	Select letter quality
Default:	Highest quality
Notes:	Not a PCL Level III feature.

The *graphics quality* setting determines how much ink the DeskJet applies when printing in graphics mode, and thus how dark the blacks are. In the high quality mode, it applies the optimal amount of ink, but this takes longer than in the lower quality mode. This command lets you choose the most appropriate compromise between printed quality and speed for the work you're doing. Generally, it's a good idea to set the printer to a lower quality mode while you're printing draft copies. Once the printout looks perfect, you can then select highest quality for your final copies.

Since you want to be able to switch quickly from one quality mode to another, don't set the graphics quality permanently from your program. Instead, give yourself or your program's users control at print time. Of course, you can always select the print quality setting from the keypad blank button. If you want the convenience of software, though, you can build a print quality option into your program.

23

Troubleshooting

❦

This chapter is devoted entirely to troubleshooting—what to do if your DeskJet acts up, cuts out, or collapses in ruins. The material presented here is expanded over what you'll find in the *Owner's Manual*, and it is organized by major categories of malfunction. These are indicated by the larger-type section headings.

NOTHING AT ALL HAPPENS WHEN YOU TRY TO PRINT

1. The printer is plugged in and turned on, of course.

2. Check to make sure the ON LINE light is glowing. If not, the DeskJet is off-line and can't print. Press the ON LINE button on the keypad so that the light comes on, and try again.

3. Check the cable connection. Your cable should be securely seated into the correct port at both the printer and the computer.

4. Check to see that your computer is properly configured for the type of connection you've made. If your printer is connected to LPT1:, for example, make sure your software is set to print to LPT1:, not LPT2:, COM1:, or any other port. If you're using a serial connection, check to be sure that you've successfully executed the necessary MODE commands, as described in your *Owner's Manual* (in this book, I've assumed you have used a parallel rather than a serial connection, for the reasons laid out in Chapter 2).

5. If you're using a switching box that lets you send data from more than one computer to your DeskJet, or that lets you send data to more than one printer, make sure the switch is set properly to direct data from the active computer to the DeskJet.

6. Does the print cartridge have ink? If not, replace it.

7. Is there paper in the paper tray, and is it properly loaded?

8. Check to see if the print cartridge is seated correctly. The green arrow on the top of the cartridge should be aligned with the green dot on the cartridge cradle. The cartridge should be fully seated, so that it clicks into place.

9. Make sure that the packing tape has been removed from the "nose" of the cartridge.

LIGHTS BLINKING

All the lights on the keypad are blinking at the same time

Either you've installed the wrong font cartridge—22707K and 22707E won't work in the DeskJet Plus—or the printer may require service. Before you take your printer to the shop, though, see if you can clear the problem by turning the printer off for a few seconds, then back on.

All the lights on the keypad are blinking one at a time

1. The print cartridge may have stalled. Try turning the DeskJet off for a few seconds, then back on.

2. Open the printer's top cover and check to be sure that the packaging tape that ties down the cartridge cradle has been removed. If you've previously printed successfully, and haven't shipped the printer since, you can skip this step.

3. See if the print carriage moves properly. With the DeskJet turned off, try moving the print carriage from side to side by hand. If it doesn't move, and there's nothing obvious blocking its path, the printer needs service.

4. This pattern of blinking lights also is used to indicate a RAM or ROM failure discovered by the automatic self-testing procedure the DeskJet completes every time you turn it on. If this is the cause, the printer needs to be serviced.

BUSY and ON LINE lights are blinking

This indicates a paper jam. Instructions for clearing it are found below.

ON LINE light is blinking

This indicates that the paper isn't properly loaded.

1. Check to make sure that there's paper in the printer bin, and that it's stacked squarely and pushed all the way forward.

2. Be sure you're using the right weight of paper. Use 16 to 24 pound paper for best results.

BUSY light is blinking, with the printer in landscape orientation

This indicates that the DeskJet has received data to print, but less than a full page worth. The printer won't start printing until you press the FF key, or send a form feed control code.

PAPER FEEDING PROBLEMS

How to clear a paper jam

Paper jams are rare in the DeskJet, but when they occur you'll probably lose the data that's already been sent to the printer. Follow these steps:

1. Take out the paper tray cover and the out tray, and lift the printer's top cover.

2. Locate the jammed piece of paper. Press the UP and DOWN buttons on the keypad to move the paper out of the printer by the path of least resistance.

3. If the paper is really stuck, help it along by pulling on it with one hand while you continue to fiddle with the UP and DOWN keys with the other hand.

4. Should you tear the paper, just go after each piece separately until they're all free.

5. Press the RESET button to bring the DeskJet back on line.

Paper jams repeatedly, or

The paper comes out at an angle, or printing is slanted on the page, or

Paper doesn't load at all, or

More than one sheet gets loaded at a time

1. Be sure you've loaded the paper into the paper tray squarely, with the right edge of the paper stack flush with the right side of the tray.

2. Don't load the tray with more than ½" of paper at a time. That works out to about 100 sheets.

If you're not getting paper to load at all, you should check to make sure you've put some paper in the tray to begin with, of course, and also that the paper tray extender is positioned properly so that it pushes the paper firmly against the printer.

If more than one sheet loads at a time, the paper itself may be sticky.

Envelopes don't load

1. Make sure you're inserting the envelope under the envelope guides on the out tray. See Chapter 18 for details on envelope loading and printing.

2. The envelope should be inserted top first, flap up, with its right edge square against the right side of the out tray. The top edge of the envelope should be placed under the paper feed rollers.

3. If you're loading envelopes by hand, be sure you're pressing both the UP and DOWN buttons on the keypad at the same time.

4. If you're letting your software load the envelopes, go over the proper steps for envelope feeding in your software manual.

Last page of your document doesn't appear

This is a common event, caused when the printer doesn't receive a final form feed control code. The page has actually been printed already, and will emerge as soon as the form feed command gets there. Take matters into your own hands by pressing the FF button on the keypad.

PRINT QUALITY PROBLEMS

Print is fuzzy but dark

1. Try reactivating the print cartridge by pressing the PRIME key.

2. Some kinds of paper don't hold the DeskJet ink very well. Try a recommended type of paper.

Incomplete characters or graphics—dots or lines are missing

1. Reactivate the print cartridge by pressing the PRIME key.

2. To be sure that the print cartridge is seated properly, remove it and reinstall it. The green arrow on the top of the cartridge should be aligned with the green dot on the cartridge cradle. The cartridge should be fully seated, so that it clicks into place.

Intensity of the print varies

Reactivate the print cartridge by pressing the PRIME key.

Print appears faded

Try reactivating the print cartridge by pressing the PRIME key. If this doesn't work, the cartrdige is running out of ink and needs to be replaced.

Paper comes out wrinkled

You've probably just printed a large, very dark graphic. In quantity, the DeskJet's water-based ink causes the same effect as pouring a glass of water on the paper would. Try to use lighter and/or smaller graphics.

PRINT POSITIONING AND SPACING PROBLEMS

Graphics or text are in the wrong position on the page:

1. If you're attempting to tell the DeskJet where to position some text or graphics via escape sequences, without the aid of an applications program, you've probably miscalculated the coordinates. Remember that the 0 point of the DeskJet's coordinate system is at the top left corner of the area the DeskJet can print, not the top left of the actual paper. The printable area begins ⅙" from the top edge and ¼" from the left edge.

2. If this happens in an application program, be sure the paper size you've selected in the program matches the size of the paper you're actually using.

Too much space between lines

Assuming you've set the line spacing command properly, the problem may be that your margins are just a little too wide for the font size you're using. If the DeskJet can't fit a line of your file on a single line of paper, it may automatically wrap the remaining characters down to the next line or simply ignore them, depending on the End-of-Line Wraparound setting. If the line you're trying to print are only slightly too long, this may result only in extra space between lines, not in bad line breaks.

Only a few lines print on each page

Check the page length setting. An occasional mistake is to leave off one of the digits when you type in the page length setting—you might have accidentally entered a page length of six lines instead of 60, for instance.

UNEXPECTED RESULTS

Text prints in a font other than the one you selected (internal and cartridge fonts)

1. Be sure you've actually selected the font you want by pressing the FONT key repeatedly until the light beside the font's name glows.

2. If it's a cartridge font, be sure the cartridge is fully seated in its slot.

3. Application software often overrides the choices you make from the keypad. If this is the case, you'll have to select the desired font from within your software—consult the software manual for instructions.

Text doesn't switch to bold from italics

To switch from bold to italics, you must first send the command to switch from italics to upright type style, ESC(s0s, then the command to switch from normal stroke weight to bold, ESC(s3B. That's because style has a higher priority in the heirarchy of font attributes than does stroke weight.

Unexpected characters or wierd symbols appear on the printout

Check to make sure you're using the character set that matches the one you want to print. If you select a different character set, your software may be sending out the correct character codes to the printer, but those codes represent match up with characters you don't want.

The DeskJet ignores a software command

Before you blame your printer, make sure you're sending the correct control code or escape sequence. In particular, take care that you haven't mixed up the lowercase letter *l* with the numeral 1 or the uppercase I. Likewise, check to see that you haven't substitued uppercase O for the numeral 0, or vice versa. Check too that you've entered all the uppercase letters in uppercase and the lowercase ones

The DeskJet ignores all your software commands

The problem: You're sending a series of escape sequences to the printer from DOS or with a setup utility, but the DeskJet switches back to its default settings when you then try to print with your application program.

The explanation: your application program is automatically sending a soft reset command to the DeskJet every time it starts to print. This command returns all printer settings to their defaults.

Solution: embed the escape sequences directly within your document as described in Chapter 8 or with BackLoader, covered in Chapter 7.

SELF TEST PROBLEMS

Self test doesn't print

1. For the self test to work, the printer must be plugged in, it must have paper in the paper tray, and there must not be a paper jam. If there's a jam, clear it following the instructions in the "Paper feed problems" section above.

2. Try the self test again—maybe you made a mistake in executing the procedure.

3. If it still doesn't work, the printer needs service.

Self test prints unexpected results

Not to worry if the character patterns look a little different from those on the sample self test pages shown in your *Owner's Manual,* but basically similar and legible. The pattern changes depending on whether you have a font cartridge installed, and which one it is. If you get strange patterns of dots or lines, or completely disorganized characters, your printer needs service.

© Steve Holt
'88

Appendices

Appendix A

DeskJet
Specifications
¢

Dimensions:

17.3" wide x 8" high x 14.8" deep
(440mm wide x 202mm high x 377 mm
deep)

Weight:

14.3 lbs (6.5 kg)

Noise:

46 dB(A) at front bystander position;
44 dB(A) at four bystander
positions

Communications ports:

Centronics parallel
RS-232C serial

Buffer:

16 kilobytes RAM

Paper handling:

Built-in single sheet feeder (100 sheet
capacity)
Manual envelope feeder

Paper type:

Ordinary bond or xerographic 16 to
24 pound (60-90 g/m2)

Paper size:

U.S. letter (8½ x 11")
U.S. legal (8½ x 14")
European A4 (210 x 297 mm)
#10 Envelope (4⅛ x 9½")

Unprintable area of 8½x11" page:

¼" left and right margin
⅙" top margin
½" bottom margin

Ink:

Water-based proprietary formula

Character cell structure:

Letter quality mode: 30 dots horizontal
x 50 dots vertical
Draft mode: 15 dots horizontal x 50
dots vertical

Built-in Fonts:

For both original DeskJet/DeskJet Plus:
Typeface: Courier
Pitch 5, 10, 16.67, 20
Point size: 6, 12
Stroke weight: regular or bold
Style: upright
Orientation: portrait
DeskJet Plus only:
Portrait fonts also include italics
Landscape fonts:
Typeface: Courier
Pitch 10, 16.67, 20
Point size: 6, 12, 24
Stroke weight: regular or bold
Style: upright

Graphics resolutions:

75, 100, 150, or 300 dots per inch

Operating conditions:

Recommended temperature range:
59° F / 15°C to 95°F / 35°C
Minimum operating temperature:
41°F / 5°C
Maximum operating temperature:
104°F/40°C
Storage temperature range:
- 40°F / - 40°C to 140°F / 60°C
Humidity: 10-80%

Maximum power consumption:

25 watts during printing, operating at
120 volts AC, 60 Hz

Reliability rating:

60,000 lifetime pages. Mean time
between failures (MTBF) 20,000
hours. Rated for 50 pages per day,
12,000 pages and 2000 hours of
power on per year.

Appendix B

DeskJet
Character Sets
¢

This appendix contains character set tables for 11 of the DeskJet Plus's 19 character sets (the original DeskJet has only 18 sets; the PC-850 set is new with the Plus). In each table, the grey boxes show characters that aren't available in that set. The tiny number in each in box is the ASCII code value for that character. The charts were printed with MoreFonts, a font generating utility discussed in Chapter 7.

Symbol set code: US Full name: ASCII   95 characters.
Font name: Geneva Roman

0	**16**	**32**	0 48	@ 64	P 80	' 96	p 112	128	144	160	176	192	208	224	240
1	**17**	! 33	1 49	A 65	Q 81	a 97	q 113	129	145	161	177	193	209	225	241
2	**18**	" 34	2 50	B 66	R 82	b 98	r 114	130	146	162	178	194	210	226	242
3	**19**	# 35	3 51	C 67	S 83	c 99	s 115	131	147	163	179	195	211	227	243
4	**20**	$ 36	4 52	D 68	T 84	d 100	t 116	132	148	164	180	196	212	228	244
5	**21**	% 37	5 53	E 69	U 85	e 101	u 117	133	149	165	181	197	213	229	245
6	**22**	& 38	6 54	F 70	V 86	f 102	v 118	134	150	166	182	198	214	230	246
7	**23**	' 39	7 55	G 71	W 87	g 103	w 119	135	151	167	183	199	215	231	247
8	**24**	(40	8 56	H 72	X 88	h 104	x 120	136	152	168	184	200	216	232	248
9	**25**	) 41	9 57	I 73	Y 89	i 105	y 121	137	153	169	185	201	217	233	249
10	**26**	* 42	: 58	J 74	Z 90	j 106	z 122	138	154	170	186	202	218	234	250
11	**27**	+ 43	; 59	K 75	[91	k 107	{ 123	139	155	171	187	303	219	235	251
12	**28**	, 44	< 60	L 76	\ 92	l 108	| 124	140	156	172	188	204	220	236	252
13	**29**	- 45	= 61	M 77	] 93	m 109	} 125	141	157	173	189	205	221	237	253
14	**30**	. 46	> 62	N 78	^ 94	n 110	~ 126	142	158	174	190	206	222	238	254
15	**31**	/ 47	? 63	O 79	_ 95	o 111	▩ 127	143	159	175	191	207	223	239	255

0	16	32	48	64	80	96	112	128	144	160	176	192	208	224	240
			0	@	P	'	p				‾ 176	â 192	Å 208	Á 224	Þ 240
0	16	32	48	64	80	96	112	128	144	160					
		!	1	A	Q	a	q			À 161	Ý 177	ê 193	î 209	Ã 225	þ 241
1	17	33	49	65	81	97	113	129	145						
		"	2	B	R	b	r			Â 162	ý 178	ô 194	Ø 210	ã 226	· 242
2	18	34	50	66	82	98	114	130	146						
		#	3	C	S	c	s			È 163	° 179	û 195	Æ 211	Ð 227	µ 243
3	19	35	51	67	83	99	115	131	147						
		$	4	D	T	d	t			Ê 164	Ç 180	á 196	å 212	ð 228	¶ 244
4	20	36	52	68	84	100	116	132	148						
		%	5	E	U	e	u			Ë 165	ç 181	é 197	í 213	Í 229	¾ 245
5	21	37	53	69	85	101	117	133	149						
		&	6	F	V	f	v			Î 166	Ñ 182	ó 198	ø 214	Ì 230	— 246
6	22	38	54	70	86	102	118	134	150						
		'	7	G	W	g	w			Ï 167	ñ 183	ú 199	æ 215	Ó 231	¼ 247
7	23	39	55	71	87	103	119	135	151						
		(	8	H	X	h	x			´ 168	¡ 184	à 200	Ä 216	Ò 232	½ 248
8	24	40	56	72	88	104	120	136	152						
		)	9	I	Y	i	y			` 169	¿ 185	è 201	ì 217	Õ 233	ª 249
9	25	41	57	73	89	105	121	137	153						
		*	:	J	Z	j	z			^ 170	¤ 186	ò 202	Ö 218	õ 234	º 250
10	26	42	58	74	90	106	122	138	154						
		+	;	K	[	k	{			¨ 171	£ 187	ù 203	Ü 219	Š 235	« 251
11	27	43	59	75	91	107	123	139	155						
		,	<	L	\	l	|			~ 172	¥ 188	ä 204	É 220	š 236	■ 252
12	28	44	60	76	92	108	124	140	156						
		-	=	M	]	m	}			Ù 173	§ 189	ë 205	ï 221	Ú 237	» 253
13	29	45	61	77	93	109	125	141	157						
		.	>	N	^	n	~			Û 174	ƒ 190	ö 206	ß 222	Ÿ 238	± 254
14	30	46	62	78	94	110	126	142	158						
		/	?	O	_	o	▓			£ 175	¢ 191	ü 207	Ô 223	ÿ 239	255
15	31	47	63	79	95	111	127	143	159						

0	16	32	**0** 48	**@** 64	**P** 80	**°** 96	**p** 112	128	144	160	176	192	208	224	240
1	17	**!** 33	**1** 49	**A** 65	**Q** 81	**a** 97	**q** 113	129	145	161	177	193	209	225	241
2	18	**'** 34	**2** 50	**B** 66	**R** 82	**b** 98	**r** 114	130	146	162	178	194	210	226	242
3	19	**#** 35	**3** 51	**C** 67	**S** 83	**c** 99	**s** 115	131	147	163	179	195	211	227	243
4	20	**$** 36	**4** 52	**D** 68	**T** 84	**d** 100	**t** 116	132	148	164	180	196	212	228	244
5	21	**%** 37	**5** 53	**E** 69	**U** 85	**e** 101	**u** 117	133	149	165	181	197	213	229	245
6	22	**&** 38	**6** 54	**F** 70	**V** 86	**f** 102	**v** 118	134	150	166	182	198	214	230	246
7	23	**"** 39	**7** 55	**G** 71	**W** 87	**g** 103	**w** 119	135	151	167	183	199	215	231	247
8	24	**(** 40	**8** 56	**H** 72	**X** 88	**h** 104	**x** 120	136	152	168	184	200	216	232	248
9	25	**)** 41	**9** 57	**I** 73	**Y** 89	**i** 105	**y** 121	137	153	169	185	201	217	233	249
10	26	***** 42	**:** 58	**J** 74	**Z** 90	**j** 106	**z** 122	138	154	170	186	202	218	234	250
11	27	**+** 43	**;** 59	**K** 75	**[** 91	**k** 107	**§** 123	139	155	171	187	203	219	235	251
12	28	**,** 44	**=** 60	**L** 76	**®** 92	**l** 108	**¶** 124	140	156	172	188	204	220	236	252
13	29	**-** 45	**=** 61	**M** 77	**]** 93	**m** 109	**†** 125	141	157	173	189	205	221	237	253
14	30	**.** 46	**¢** 62	**N** 78	**©** 94	**n** 110	**TM** 126	142	158	174	190	206	222	238	254
15	31	**/** 47	**?** 63	**O** 79	**_** 95	**o** 111	**▦** 127	143	159	175	191	207	223	239	255

Symbol set code: PM   Full name: PC-850 Multilingual   253 characters.
Font name: Geneva Roman

▨ 0	► 16	▨ 32	0 48	@ 64	P 80	` 96	p 112	Ç 128	É 144	á 160	▦ 176	└ 192	ð 208	Ó 224	- 240
☺ 1	◄ 17	! 33	1 49	A 65	Q 81	a 97	q 113	ü 129	æ 145	í 161	▩ 177	⊥ 193	Đ 209	ß 225	± 241
☻ 2	↕ 18	" 34	2 50	B 66	R 82	b 98	r 114	é 130	Æ 146	ó 162	▦ 178	┬ 194	Ê 210	Ô 226	= 242
♥ 3	‼ 19	# 35	3 51	C 67	S 83	c 99	s 115	â 131	ô 147	ú 163	│ 179	├ 195	Ë 211	Ó 227	¾ 243
♦ 4	¶ 20	$ 36	4 52	D 68	T 84	d 100	t 116	ä 132	ö 148	ñ 164	┤ 180	─ 196	È 212	ō 228	¶ 244
♣ 5	§ 21	% 37	5 53	E 69	U 85	e 101	u 117	à 133	ò 149	Ñ 165	Á 181	┼ 197	ı 213	Õ 229	§ 245
♠ 6	▬ 22	& 38	6 54	F 70	V 86	f 102	v 118	å 134	û 150	ª 166	Â 182	ã 198	Í 214	µ 230	÷ 246
• 7	↕ 23	' 39	7 55	G 71	W 87	g 103	w 119	ç 135	ù 151	º 167	À 183	Ã 199	Î 215	þ 231	¸ 247
◘ 8	↑ 24	(40	8 56	H 72	X 88	h 104	x 120	ê 136	ÿ 152	¿ 168	© 184	╚ 200	Ï 216	Þ 232	° 248
○ 9	↓ 25	) 41	9 57	I 73	Y 89	i 105	y 121	ë 137	Ö 153	® 169	╣ 185	╔ 201	┘ 217	Ú 233	¨ 249
◙ 10	→ 26	* 42	: 58	J 74	Z 90	j 106	z 122	è 138	Ü 154	¬ 170	║ 186	╩ 202	┌ 218	Û 234	· 250
♂ 11	← 27	+ 43	; 59	K 75	[91	k 107	{ 123	ï 139	ø 155	½ 171	╗ 187	╦ 203	█ 219	Ù 235	¹ 251
♀ 12	└ 28	, 44	< 60	L 76	\ 92	l 108		124	î 140	£ 156	¼ 172	╝ 188	╠ 204	▄ 220	ý 236	³ 252
♪ 13	↔ 29	- 45	= 61	M 77	] 93	m 109	} 125	ì 141	Ø 157	¡ 173	╜ 189	═ 205	¦ 221	Ý 237	² 253
♫ 14	▲ 30	. 46	> 62	N 78	^ 94	n 110	~ 126	Ä 142	× 158	« 174	¥ 190	╬ 206	Ì 222	¯ 238	■ 254
☼ 15	▼ 31	/ 47	? 63	O 79	_ 95	o 111	⌂ 127	Å 143	ƒ 159	» 175	┐ 191	¤ 207	▀ 223	´ 239	▨ 255

▓ 0	► 16	▓ 32	0 48	@ 64	P 80	‘ 96	p 112	Ç 128	É 144	á 160	▦ 176	└ 192	┴ 208	α 224	≡ 240
☺ 1	◄ 17	! 33	1 49	A 65	Q 81	a 97	q 113	ü 129	æ 145	í 161	▤ 177	┴ 193	╤ 209	ß 225	± 241
● 2	↕ 18	" 34	2 50	B 66	R 82	b 98	r 114	é 130	Æ 146	ó 162	▦ 178	┬ 194	╥ 210	Γ 226	≥ 242
♥ 3	‼ 19	# 35	3 51	C 67	S 83	c 99	s 115	â 131	ô 147	ú 163	│ 179	├ 195	╙ 211	π 227	≤ 243
♦ 4	¶ 20	$ 36	4 52	D 68	T 84	d 100	t 116	ä 132	ö 148	ñ 164	┤ 180	─ 196	╘ 212	Σ 228	⌠ 244
♣ 5	§ 21	% 37	5 53	E 69	U 85	e 101	u 117	à 133	ò 149	Ñ 165	╡ 181	┼ 197	╒ 213	σ 229	⌡ 245
♠ 6	▬ 22	& 38	6 54	F 70	V 86	f 102	v 118	å 134	û 150	ª 166	╢ 182	╞ 198	╓ 214	µ 230	÷ 246
● 7	↨ 23	' 39	7 55	G 71	W 87	g 103	w 119	ç 135	ù 151	º 167	╖ 183	╟ 199	╫ 215	τ 231	≈ 247
◙ 8	↑ 24	(40	8 56	H 72	X 88	h 104	x 120	ê 136	ÿ 152	¿ 168	╕ 184	╚ 200	╪ 216	Φ 232	° 248
○ 9	↓ 25	) 41	9 57	I 73	Y 89	i 105	y 121	ë 137	Ö 153	⌐ 169	╣ 185	╔ 201	┘ 217	Θ 233	· 249
◎ 10	→ 26	* 42	: 58	J 74	Z 90	j 106	z 122	è 138	Ü 154	¬ 170	║ 186	╩ 202	┌ 218	Ω 234	· 250
♂ 11	← 27	+ 43	; 59	K 75	[91	k 107	{ 123	ï 139	¢ 155	½ 171	╗ 187	╦ 203	█ 219	δ 235	√ 251
♀ 12	└ 28	, 44	< 60	L 76	\ 92	l 108		124	î 140	£ 156	¼ 172	╝ 188	╠ 204	▄ 220	∞ 236	ⁿ 252
♪ 13	↔ 29	- 45	= 61	M 77	] 93	m 109	} 125	ì 141	¥ 157	¡ 173	╜ 189	═ 205	▌ 221	φ 237	² 253
♫ 14	▲ 30	. 46	> 62	N 78	^ 94	n 110	~ 126	Ä 142	Pt 158	« 174	╛ 190	╬ 206	▐ 222	∈ 238	■ 254
☼ 15	▼ 31	/ 47	? 63	O 79	_ 95	o 111	⌂ 127	Å 143	ƒ 159	» 175	┐ 191	┴ 207	▀ 223	∩ 239	▓ 255

Symbol set code: PD   Full name: PC-8 Danish/Norwegian 253 characters.
Font name: Geneva Roman

▓ 0	► 16	▓ 32	0 48	@ 64	P 80	` 96	p 112	Ç 128	É 144	á 160	⠿ 176	└ 192	╨ 208	α 224	≡ 240
☺ 1	◄ 17	! 33	1 49	A 65	Q 81	a 97	q 113	ü 129	æ 145	í 161	▓ 177	┴ 193	╤ 209	β 225	± 241
☻ 2	↕ 18	" 34	2 50	B 66	R 82	b 98	r 114	é 130	Æ 146	ó 162	▓ 178	┬ 194	╥ 210	Γ 226	≥ 242
♥ 3	‼ 19	# 35	3 51	C 67	S 83	c 99	s 115	â 131	ô 147	ú 163	│ 179	├ 195	╙ 211	π 227	≤ 243
♦ 4	¶ 20	$ 36	4 52	D 68	T 84	d 100	t 116	ä 132	ö 148	ñ 164	┤ 180	─ 196	╘ 212	Σ 228	⌠ 244
♣ 5	§ 21	% 37	5 53	E 69	U 85	e 101	u 117	à 133	ò 149	Ñ 165	╡ 181	┼ 197	╒ 213	σ 229	⌡ 245
♠ 6	▬ 22	& 38	6 54	F 70	V 86	f 102	v 118	å 134	û 150	õ 166	╢ 182	╟ 198	╓ 214	µ 230	÷ 246
• 7	↨ 23	' 39	7 55	G 71	W 87	g 103	w 119	ç 135	ù 151	Õ 167	╖ 183	╠ 199	╫ 215	τ 231	≈ 247
◘ 8	↑ 24	(40	8 56	H 72	X 88	h 104	x 120	ê 136	ÿ 152	¿ 168	╕ 184	╚ 200	╪ 216	Φ 232	° 248
○ 9	↓ 25	) 41	9 57	I 73	Y 89	i 105	y 121	ë 137	Ö 153	ã 169	╣ 185	╔ 201	┘ 217	Θ 233	∙ 249
◙ 10	→ 26	* 42	: 58	J 74	Z 90	j 106	z 122	è 138	Ü 154	Ã 170	║ 186	╩ 202	┌ 218	Ω 234	· 250
♂ 11	← 27	+ 43	; 59	K 75	[91	k 107	{ 123	ï 139	ø 155	ℓ 171	╗ 187	╦ 203	█ 219	δ 235	√ 251
♀ 12	∟ 28	, 44	< 60	L 76	\ 92	l 108		124	î 140	£ 156	'n 172	╝ 188	╠ 204	▄ 220	∞ 236	ⁿ 252
♪ 13	↔ 29	- 45	= 61	M 77	] 93	m 109	} 125	ì 141	Ø 157	¡ 173	╜ 189	═ 205	▌ 221	φ 237	² 253
♫ 14	▲ 30	. 46	> 62	N 78	^ 94	n 110	~ 126	Ä 142	L· 158	³ 174	╛ 190	╬ 206	▐ 222	∈ 238	■ 254
☼ 15	▼ 31	/ 47	? 63	O 79	_ 95	o 111	⌂ 127	Å 143	·| 159	¤ 175	┐ 191	╧ 207	▀ 223	∩ 239	▓ 255

Symbol set code: EC Full name: ECMA-94 Latin 1   190 characters.
Font name: Geneva Roman

0	16	32	48	64	80	96	112	128	144	160	176	192	208	224	240
			0	@	P	`	p				°	À	Ð	à	ð
		!	1	A	Q	a	q			¡	±	Á	Ñ	á	ñ
		"	2	B	R	b	r			¢	²	Â	Ò	â	ò
		#	3	C	S	c	s			£	³	Ã	Ó	ã	ó
		$	4	D	T	d	t			¤	´	Ä	Ô	ä	ô
		%	5	E	U	e	u			¥	µ	Å	Õ	å	õ
		&	6	F	V	f	v			¦	¶	Æ	Ö	æ	ö
		'	7	G	W	g	w			§	·	Ç	×	ç	÷
		(	8	H	X	h	x			¨	¸	È	Ø	è	ø
		)	9	I	Y	i	y			©	¹	É	Ù	é	ù
		*	:	J	Z	j	z			ª	º	Ê	Ú	ê	ú
		+	;	K	[	k	{			«	»	Ë	Û	ë	û
		,	<	L	\	l					¬	¼	Ì	Ü	ì	ü
		-	=	M	]	m	}				½	Í	Ý	í	ý
		.	>	N	^	n	~			®	¾	Î	Þ	î	þ
		/	?	O	_	o	▓			¯	¿	Ï	ß	ï	ÿ

Symbol set code: U2 Full name: ISO 2: IRV   95 characters.
Font name: Geneva Roman

0	16	32	48	64	80	96	112	128	144	160	176	192	208	224	240
			0 (48)	@ (64)	P (80)	` (96)	p (112)	128	144	160	176	192	208	224	240
		! (33)	1 (49)	A (65)	Q (81)	a (97)	q (113)	129	145	161	177	193	209	225	241
		" (34)	2 (50)	B (66)	R (82)	b (98)	r (114)	130	146	162	178	194	210	226	242
		# (35)	3 (51)	C (67)	S (83)	c (99)	s (115)	131	147	163	179	195	211	227	243
		¤ (36)	4 (52)	D (68)	T (84)	d (100)	t (116)	132	148	164	180	196	212	228	244
		% (37)	5 (53)	E (69)	U (85)	e (101)	u (117)	133	149	165	181	197	213	229	245
		& (38)	6 (54)	F (70)	V (86)	f (102)	v (118)	134	150	166	182	198	214	230	246
		' (39)	7 (55)	G (71)	W (87)	g (103)	w (119)	135	151	167	183	199	215	231	247
		((40)	8 (56)	H (72)	X (88)	h (104)	x (120)	136	152	168	184	200	216	232	248
		) (41)	9 (57)	I (73)	Y (89)	i (105)	y (121)	137	153	169	185	201	217	233	249
		∗ (42)	: (58)	J (74)	Z (90)	j (106)	z (122)	138	154	170	186	202	218	234	250
		+ (43)	; (59)	K (75)	[(91)	k (107)	{ (123)	139	155	171	187	203	219	235	251
		, (44)	< (60)	L (76)	\ (92)	l (108)	| (124)	140	156	172	188	204	220	236	252
		- (45)	= (61)	M (77)	] (93)	m (109)	} (125)	141	157	173	189	205	221	237	253
		. (46)	> (62)	N (78)	^ (94)	n (110)	‾ (126)	142	158	174	190	206	222	238	254
		/ (47)	? (63)	O (79)	‾ (95)	o (111)	▓ (127)	143	159	175	191	207	223	239	255

Symbol set code: S3 Full name: ISO 10: Swedish   95 characters.
Font name: Geneva Roman

0	16	32	0 48	@ 64	P 80	` 96	p 112	128	144	160	176	192	208	224	240
1	17	33	! 49	1 49	A 65	Q 81	a 97	q 113	129	145	161	177	193	209	225	241
2	18	34	" 34	2 50	B 66	R 82	b 98	r 114	130	146	162	178	194	210	226	242
3	19	35	# 35	3 51	C 67	S 83	c 99	s 115	131	147	163	179	195	211	227	243
4	20	36	¤ 36	4 52	D 68	T 84	d 100	t 116	132	148	164	180	196	212	228	244
5	21	37	% 37	5 53	E 69	U 85	e 101	u 117	133	149	165	181	197	213	229	245
6	22	38	& 38	6 54	F 70	V 86	f 102	v 118	134	150	166	182	198	214	230	246
7	23	39	' 39	7 55	G 71	W 87	g 103	w 119	135	151	167	183	199	215	231	247
8	24	40	(40	8 56	H 72	X 88	h 104	x 120	136	152	168	184	200	216	232	248
9	25	41	) 41	9 57	I 73	Y 89	i 105	y 121	137	153	169	185	201	217	233	249
10	26	42	* 42	: 58	J 74	Z 90	j 106	z 122	138	154	170	186	202	218	234	250
11	27	43	+ 43	; 59	K 75	Ä 91	k 107	ä 123	139	155	171	187	203	219	235	251
12	28	44	, 44	< 60	L 76	Ö 92	l 108	ö 124	140	156	172	188	204	220	236	252
13	29	45	- 45	= 61	M 77	Å 93	m 109	å 125	141	157	173	189	205	221	237	253
14	30	46	. 46	> 62	N 78	^ 94	n 110	‾ 126	142	158	174	190	206	222	238	254
15	31	47	/ 47	? 63	O 79	_ 95	o 111	▓ 127	143	159	175	191	207	223	239	255

Symbol set code: JS Full name: ISO 14: JIS ASCII   95 characters.
Font name: Geneva Roman

0	16	32	48	64	80	96	112	128	144	160	176	192	208	224	240
			0 48	**@** 64	**P** 80	**`** 96	**p** 112	128	144	160	176	192	208	224	240
1	17	**!** 33	**1** 49	**A** 65	**Q** 81	**a** 97	**q** 113	129	145	161	177	193	209	225	241
2	18	**"** 34	**2** 50	**B** 66	**R** 82	**b** 98	**r** 114	130	146	162	178	194	210	226	242
3	19	**#** 35	**3** 51	**C** 67	**S** 83	**c** 99	**s** 115	131	147	163	179	195	211	227	243
4	20	**$** 36	**4** 52	**D** 68	**T** 84	**d** 100	**t** 116	132	148	164	180	196	212	228	244
5	21	**%** 37	**5** 53	**E** 69	**U** 85	**e** 101	**u** 117	133	149	165	181	197	213	229	245
6	22	**&** 38	**6** 54	**F** 70	**V** 86	**f** 102	**v** 118	134	150	166	182	198	214	230	246
7	23	**'** 39	**7** 55	**G** 71	**W** 87	**g** 103	**w** 119	135	151	167	183	199	215	231	247
8	24	**(** 40	**8** 56	**H** 72	**X** 88	**h** 104	**x** 120	136	152	168	184	200	216	232	248
9	25	**)** 41	**9** 57	**I** 73	**Y** 89	**i** 105	**y** 121	137	153	169	185	201	217	233	249
10	26	***** 42	**:** 58	**J** 74	**Z** 90	**j** 106	**z** 122	138	154	170	186	202	218	234	250
11	27	**+** 43	**;** 59	**K** 75	**[** 91	**k** 107	**{** 123	139	155	171	187	203	219	235	251
12	28	**,** 44	**<** 60	**L** 76	**¥** 92	**l** 108	**|** 124	140	156	172	188	204	220	236	252
13	29	**-** 45	**=** 61	**M** 77	**]** 93	**m** 109	**}** 125	141	157	173	189	205	221	237	253
14	30	**.** 46	**>** 62	**N** 78	**^** 94	**n** 110	**―** 126	142	158	174	190	206	222	238	254
15	31	**/** 47	**?** 63	**O** 79	**_** 95	**o** 111	**▓** 127	143	159	175	191	207	223	239	255

Symbol set code: S4   Full name: ISO 16: Portugese   95 characters.
Font name: Geneva Roman

			0	§	P	`	p							
0	16	32	48	64	80	96	112	128	144	160	176	192	208	224	240
		!	1	A	Q	a	q							
1	17	33	49	65	81	97	113	129	145	161	177	193	209	225	241
		"	2	B	R	b	r							
2	18	34	50	66	82	98	114	130	146	162	178	194	210	226	242
		#	3	C	S	c	s							
3	19	35	51	67	83	99	115	131	147	163	179	195	211	227	243
		$	4	D	T	d	t							
4	20	36	52	68	84	100	116	132	148	164	180	196	212	228	244
		%	5	E	U	e	u							
5	21	37	53	69	85	101	117	133	149	165	181	197	213	229	245
		&	6	F	V	f	v							
6	22	38	54	70	86	102	118	134	150	166	182	198	214	230	246
		'	7	G	W	g	w							
7	23	39	55	71	87	103	119	135	151	167	183	199	215	231	247
		(	8	H	X	h	x							
8	24	40	56	72	88	104	120	136	152	168	184	200	216	232	248
		)	9	I	Y	i	y							
9	25	41	57	73	89	105	121	137	153	169	185	201	217	233	249
		*	:	J	Z	j	z							
10	26	42	58	74	90	106	122	138	154	170	186	202	218	234	250
		+	;	K	Ã	k	ã							
11	27	43	59	75	91	107	123	139	155	171	187	203	219	235	251
		,	<	L	Ç	l	ç							
12	28	44	60	76	92	108	124	140	156	172	188	204	220	236	252
		-	=	M	Õ	m	õ							
13	29	45	61	77	93	109	125	141	157	173	189	205	221	237	253
		.	>	N	^	n	°							
14	30	46	62	78	94	110	126	142	158	174	190	206	222	238	254
		/	?	O	_	o	▨							
15	31	47	63	79	95	111	127	143	159	175	191	207	223	239	255

Appendix C

Product Directory

¢

**1-2-3/Release 2.2 $495;
  Release 3.0, $595**
Lotus Development Corp.
55 Cambridge Parkway
Cambridge, MA 02142
617/577-8500
Description: Spreadsheet (Chapter 14)

A

**Adobe Illustrator, Windows version
  $695**
Adobe Systems, Inc.
1585 Charleston Rd.
Mountain View, CA 94039
800/344-8335; 415/961-4400
Description: Illustration software
    (Chapter 12)

Allways $149.95
Funk Software
222 Third St.
Cambridge MA 02142
800/822-3865
Description: Spreadsheet formatting
    utility (Chapter 14)

**Ami $199
Ami Professional/$495**
Samna Corp
5600 Glenridge Dr.
Atlanta, GA 30342
404/851-0007
Description: Windows word processor
    with desktop publishing
    capabilities (Chapters 10, 11)

GEM Artline/$495
Digital Research, Inc.
Box DRI
Monterey, CA 93942
800/443-4200; 408/649-3896
Description: Illustration software
    (Chapter 12)

Arts & Letters Graphics Editor/$695
Computer support Corporation
15926 Midway road
Dallas, TX 75244
214/661-8960
Price: $695
Description: Illustration software
    (Chapter 12)

B

BackLoader 2/$89
Roxxolid Corporation
3345 Vincent Road
Pleasant Hill, CA 94523
800/336-7699
415/256-0105
Description: Font management utility
(Chapter 7)

BarCODE Composer/$79.95
Delrina Technology, Inc.
4454 Genesee St.
Buffalo, NY 14225
716/835-0405
Description: Utility for generating bar
codes for use in Ventura and
Windows applications (Chapter 16)

C

Corel Draw/$495
Corel Systems Corp.
1600 Carling Ave.
Ottowa, Ontario
K1Z 8R7 Canada
613/728-8200
Description: Illustration software
(Chapter 12)

D

dBase IV/$895
Ashton-Tate
20101 Hamilton Ave.
Torrance, CA 90502
213/329-8000
Description: Database management
system (Chapter 15)

Designer/$695
Micrografx, Inc.
1303 Arapaho Rd.
Richardson, TX 75081
800/272-3729; 214/234-1769
Description: Illustration software
(Chapter 12)

GEM Desktop Publisher/$299
Digital Research, Inc.
P.O. Box DRI
Monterey, CA 93942
800/443-4200; 408/649-3896
Description: Simple desktop
publishing software (Chapter 11)

GEM Draw Plus/$299
Digital Research, Inc.
Box DRI
Monterey, CA 93942
800/443-4200; 408/649-3896
Description: Draw-type graphics
software (Chapter 12)

DwLaser/$195
Koch Software Industries
11 W. College Dr., Bldg G
Arlington Heights, IL 60004
Description: Setup utility for
DisplayWrite (Chatper 10)

E

Exact/$495
Technical Support Software
72 Kent St. #110
Brookline, MA 02146
617/734-4130
Description: Adds equations to word
processor documents (Chapter 10)

Excel for Windows 2.1/$495
Microsoft Corp.
16011 NE 36th Way
Redmond, WA 97017
206/882-8080
Description: Spreadsheet (Chapter 14)

F

Font Effects/$95
SoftCraft, Inc.
16 N. Carroll St. #500
Madison, WI 53703
608/257-3300
Description: Utility for generating
fonts with special effects. Works
only on LaserJet fonts (Chapter 7)

Fontastic/$120
Koch Software
11 W College Dr. Bldg G
Arlington Heights, IL 60004
312/398-5440
Description: Setup utility (Chapter 4)

Freedom of Press/$495
Custom Applications, Inc.
900 Technology Park Dr., Bldg B
Billerica, MA 01821
800/873-4367
Description: PostScript interpreter
(Chapter 20)

Freelance Plus/$495
Lotus Development Corp.
55 Cambridge Parkway
Cambridge, MA 02142
617/577-8500
Description: Charting software
(Chapter 13)

G

GEM Software
(Artline, Desktop Publisher, Draw
Plus, Presentation Team)
Digital Research, Inc.
P.O. Box DRI
Monterey, CA 93942
800/443-4200; 408/649-3896

Glyphix/$99.95
SWFTE International
P.O. Box 219
Rockland, DE 19732
800/237-9383; 302/658-1123
Description: Font generator (Chapter 7)

Grab Plus with LaserLabel/$49.95
ZPAY Payroll Systems
3516 Ruby St.
Franklin Park, IL 60131
312/671-3364
Description: Envelope and mailing
　　label printing utility (Chapter 18)

GrafPlus/$49.95
Jewell Technologies, Inc.
4740 44th Ave. SW #203
Seattle, WA 98116
206/937-1081
Description: Screen capture utility
　　(Chapter 19)

Graph Plus/$495
Micrografx, Inc.
1303 E. Arapaho Rd.
Richardson, TX 75082
800/272-3729
214/234-1769
Description: Charting software
　　(Chapter 13)

The Graphics Link Plus/$149
HSC Software
1661 Lincoln Blvd., Suite 101
Santa Monica, CA 90404
213/392-8441
Description: Graphics file format
　　conversion utility with screen
　　capture programs (Chapter 19)

GoScript/$195
GoScript Plus/$395
Lasergo, Inc.
9235 Trade Place, Suite A
San Diego, CA 92126
619/450-4600
Description: PostScript interpreter
　　(Chapter 20)

H

Harvard Graphics/$495
Software Publishing Corp.
1901 Landings Dr.
Mountain View, CA 94309
415/962-8910
Description: Charting software
　　(Chapter 13)

HiJaak 1.1C/$149
Inset Systems, Inc.
12 Mill Plain Rd.
Danbury, CT 06811
203/775-5866
Description: Graphics file format
　　conversion utility with screen
　　capture program (Chapter 19)

HotShot Graphics/$249
HotShot Grab/$99
Symsoft
444 First St.
Los Altos, CA 94022
415/941-1552
Description: Grab is a screen capture
  utility included in Graphics, a
  paint-type graphics software
  package (Chapter 19)

I

Impress/$139.95
PC Publishing
1801 Avenue of the Stars, #815
Los Angeles, CA 90067
800/634-4555
Description: Spreadsheet formatting
  utility (Chapter 14)

Inset 2.2B/$149
Inset Systems
12 Mill Plain Road
Danbury, CT 06811
203/794-0396
Price: $149
Description: Utility that permits
  graphics to be integrated into word
  processor documents. Also
  includes paint-type graphics
  editing functions (Chapter 10)

J

JETDESK
Koch Software Industries, Inc.
11 West College Drive, Bldg G
Arlington Heights, IL 60004
312/398-5440
Price: $19.95
Description: Converts LaserJet soft
  fonts into DeskJet format
  (Chapter 7)

JetForm Design/$495
Indigo Software
400-560 Rochester St.
Ottawa, Canada
K1S 5K2
800/267-9976
Description: Forms software (Chapter 16)

L

Laser Control/$149
Insight Development Corp.
2200 Powell St., Suite 500
Emeryville, CA 94608
415/652-4115
Description: Setup utility (Chapter 4)

LaserTorq/$99
LaserTools Corp.
3025 Buena Vista Way
Berkeley, CA 94708
415/843-2234
Description: Print spooling utility
(Chapter 4)

LaserTwin/$179
Metro Software, Inc.
2509 N. Campbell Ave., Suite 214
Tucson, AZ 85719
800/621-1137
Description: Utility that allows the
DeskJet to emulate a LaserJet
Series II (Chapter 4)

LJ2DESK/$42
S.H. Moody & Associates
1810 Fair Oaks Ave.
South Pasadena, CA 91030
Description: Converts LaserJet soft
fonts into DeskJet format (Chapter 7)

M

MacPrint/$149
Insight Development Corp.
2200 Powell St., Suite 500
Emeryville, CA 94608
415/652-4115
Description: Macintosh printer driver
for the DeskJet (Chapter 21)

Manuscript/$495
Lotus Development Corp.
55 Cambridge Parkway.
Cambridge, MA 02142
617/577-8500
Description: Word processor (Chapter 10)

Microsoft Word/$450
Microsoft Corp.
16011 N.E. 36th Way
Redmond, WA 98073
206/882-8080
Description: Word processor (Chapter 10)

MoreFonts/$99.95
MicroLogic Software, Inc.
6400 Hollis St., Suite 9
Emeryville, CA 94608
800/888-9078
Description: Font generator (Chapter 7)

Multimate PFTs
Hewlett-Packard
DeskJet Cusomter Support
Mail Stop 516
11311 Chinden Blvd.
Boise, ID 83714
Description: DeskJet printer drivers for
Multimate (Chapter 10)

P

Paradox 3.0/$725
Borland International
1800 Green Hills Rd.
Scotts Valley, CA 95066
408/438-4800
Description: Database management
software (Chapter 15)

PC Paintbrush IV /$99.95
PC Paintbrush Plus
   for Windows/$149
ZSoft
450 Franklin Rd, Suite 100
Marietta, GA 30067
404/428-0008
Description: Paint-type graphics
software (Chapter 12)

PC-Write/$99
Quicksoft
219 First Ave. N. #224
Seattle, WA 98109
206/282-0452
Description: Shareware word
processor (Chapter 10)

PerFORM2.0/$495
Delrina Technology, Inc.
4454 Genesee St.
Buffalo, NY 14225
716/835-0405
Description: Forms software (Chapter 16)

PFS: First Graphics/$149
Software Publishing Corp.
1901 Landings Dr.
Mountain View, CA 94309
415/962-8910
Description: Simple charting software
   (Chapter 13)

Pixie/$195
Zenographics
Zenographics
19752 MacArthur Blvd.
Irvine, CA 92715
714/851-6352
Description: Easy-to-use Windows
   charting software (Chapter 13)

GEM Presentation Team/$495
Digital Research, Inc.
P.O. Box DRI
Monterey, CA 93942
Description: Trio of programs (Draw
   Plus, Word Chart, and Chart) for
   chart design (Chapter 13)
800/443-4200; 408/649-3896

Printer Genius/$89.00
Nor Software, Inc.
P.O. Box 1747
New York, NY 10156
212/213-9118
Description: Setup utility (Chapter 4)

Publisher's Powerpak/$199.95
Atech Software
5962 La Place Court #245
Carlsbad, CA 92008
619/438-6883
Description: DeskJet drivers with
 scalable fonts for Ventura Publisher
 and Windows applications
 (Chapters 11 and 17)

Q

Q&A/$349
Symantec Software
10201 Toree Ave.
Cupertino, CA 95014
408/253-9600
Description: File management system
 with word processing (Chapter 15)

Quattro Pro/$495
Borland International
1800 Green Hills Rd.
Scotts Valley, CA 95066
408/438-8400
Description: Spreadsheet with
 advanced graphics capabilities
 (Chapter 14)

S

Scrapbook+/$129.95
T/Maker Company
1973 Landings Dr.
Mountain View, CA 94043
415/962-0195
Description: Windows scrapbook
 utility with screen capture function
 (Chapter 19)

Sprint/$199.95
Borland International
1800 Green Hills Rd.
Scotts Valley, CA 95066
408/438-4800
Description: Word processor
 (Chapter 10)

SuperCalc 5.0/$495
Computer Associates
1240 McKay Drive
San Jose, CA 95131
408/432-1727
Description: Spreadsheet (Chapter 14)

SuperPrint/$195
Zenographics
19752 MacArthur Blvd.
Irvine, CA 92715
714/851-6352
Description: DeskJet driver with
 scalable screen and printer fonts
 for Microsoft Windows (Chapter 17)

T

Tiffany/$10
Alan Anderson
3511 Camino del Rio South Suite 408
San Diego, CA 92108
Description: Shareware Windows
    screen capture utility (Chapter 19)

Total Word/$495
Volkswriter, Inc.
411 Pacific St.
Monterey, CA 93940
408/373-4718
Description: Word processor with
    equations and chemical formulas

TSR Download/$35
Elfring Soft Fonts
P.O. Box 61
Wasco, IL 60183
312/377-3520
Description: Font management utility
    (Chapter 7)

U

UltraScript pc/$195
UltraScript pc Plus/$445
QMS, Inc.
One Magnum Pass
Mobile, AL 36618
205/633-4300
Description: PostScript interpreter
    (Chapter 20)

W

WordPerfect 5.0/$495
WordPerfect Corp.
288 West Center
Orem, UT 84057
800/321-5906
Description: Word processor
    (Chapter 10)

WordStar 5.5/$495
WordStar International, Inc.
33 San Pablo Ave.
San Rafael, CA 94903
800/227-5609; 415/499-1200
Description: Word processor
    (Chapter 10)

Xerox Formbase/$495
Xerox Corp.
101 Continental Blvd.
El Segundo, CA 90245
800/822-8221
Description: Forms software
    (Chapter 16)

Z

Zing/$199.95
Enabling Technologies, Inc.
6005 Dearborn St, #1304
Chicago, IL 60605
312/427-0408
Description: 3-D graphics software
    (Chapter 12)

Appendix D

Resources

¢

Hewlett-Packard Telephone Numbers

- Technical support and repairs 208-323-2551

- Supplies and accessories 800/538-8787

- Information, local dealer location 800/752-0900

DeskNews

Elfring Soft Fonts publishes a DeskJet newsletter called DeskNews containing news, tips, and miscellany. For information, call 708/377-3520, or write Elfring Soft Fonts, P.O. Box 61, Wasco, IL 60183.

Free fonts

A vast collection of public domain and shareware LaserJet fonts are available on electronic bulletin board services. You can convert these to DeskJet format with the font conversion utilities described in Chapter 7. By now, some of these bulletin boards are also beginning to list DeskJet fonts as well, though the number and variety don't compare to what's available for the LaserJet.

The following list of bulletin boards which offer LaserJet fonts was supplied by Skene Moody, author of the LJ2DESK font conversion utility:

- The Other Woman BBS (North. CA) 707/938-3508

- Canadian Publisher's Info (Toronto) 416/791-9801

- Computer Connections (Wash. D.C.) 202/547-2008

- East Coast Pub Net (Maryland) 301/277-5990

- Eastern Publisher's Exchange (Florida) . . . 813/989-3375

- Exec-PC (Wisconsin) 414/964-5160

- Form Feed BBS (New Jersey 201/869-1327

- Houston Publisher's Exchange (Texas) . . . 713/781-2432

- The Lunacy Board (So. Calif.) 818/894-1248

- Rogers & Blake (Mass.) 617/373-2204

- Ruppel Set II BBS (Kentucky) 606/781-4478

- Super Systems (Florida) 813/796-5627

- The Phoenix TBBS (Colorado) 303/841-9570

- The Tardis BBS (New Jersey) 609/448-1361

- Ventura Professional! Forum (Calif.) 408/227-4818

- Western Publisher's Exchange (So. CA) . . . 714/739-5150

Index

D

E

F

G